Oil and Gas Risk Assessment and Management:

Emerging Research and Opportunities

Vojo Bubevski
Vojo Bubevski Consulting, UK

IGI Global
Scientific Publishing
Publishing Tomorrow's Research Today

Vice President of Editorial — Melissa Wagner
Director of Acquisitions — Mikaela Felty
Director of Book Development — Jocelynn Hessler
Production Manager — Mike Brehm
Cover Design — Phillip Shickler

Published in the United States of America by
IGI Global Scientific Publishing
701 East Chocolate Avenue
Hershey, PA, 17033, USA
Tel: 717-533-8845
Fax: 717-533-7115
Website: https://www.igi-global.com E-mail: cust@igi-global.com

Library of Congress Cataloging-in-Publication Data

Names: Bubevski, Vojo, 1953- author
Title: Oil and gas risk assessment and management : emerging research and opportunities / Vojo Bubevski.
Description: Hershey, PA : IGI Global Scientific Publishing, [2025] | Includes bibliographical references and index. | Summary: "This book aims to provide advanced methods and tools to improve the financial risk management process in finance in general"-- Provided by publisher.
Identifiers: LCCN 2025008700 (print) | LCCN 2025008701 (ebook) | ISBN 9798337309590 hardcover | ISBN 9798337309606 paperback | ISBN 9798337309613 ebook
Subjects: LCSH: Petroleum industry and trade--Risk management | Gas industry--Risk management | Financial risk management
Classification: LCC HD9560.5 .B825 2025 (print) | LCC HD9560.5 (ebook) | DDC 338.2/728--dc23
LC record available at https://lccn.loc.gov/2025008700
LC ebook record available at https://lccn.loc.gov/2025008701

British Cataloguing in Publication Data
A Cataloguing in Publication record for this book is available from the British Library.

This book is dedicated to my wife Dina, with love!

Table of Contents

Preface

Most industries today recognise Six Sigma as a standard means to accomplish process and quality improvements and increase their customers' satisfaction. The financial industry has accepted and successfully applied Six Sigma, but only to improve its operations and provide higher-quality services to its customers. Six Sigma introductory topics for financial professionals were published in September 2003 (Stamatis 2003). Hayler and Nichols (2006) showed how American Express, Bank of America, and Wachovia have applied Six Sigma, Lean, and Process Management to their service-based operations by providing specific, real-world examples and offering step-by-step solutions. Also, Tarantino and Cernauskas (2009) provided an operational risk framework by using proven quality control methods such as Six Sigma and Total Quality Management (TQM) in financial risk management to forestall major risk management failures.

In the author's book "Novel Six Sigma Approaches to Risk Assessment and Management" published by IGI Global (Bubevski 2017), a new Six Sigma DMAIC (Define, Measure, Analyse, Improve, and Control) generic method for improving Risk Management was presented. Elaboration on applications of this new method to Risk Management was presented in the following fields: Finance, Oil and Gas, Research and Development, Software Engineering, Project Management, Agriculture, Production, and Retail.

Subsequently, the author published his original work "Six Sigma Improvements for Basel III and Solvency II in Financial Risk Management" (Bubevski 2018). The significant recognition of the original work (Bubevski 2018) encouraged the author to work on another book, which is the book presented herein. The book is enhanced with Sensitivity and What-If Analysis.

This book elaborates on comprehensive applications, as well as advanced novel concepts and tools for Financial Risk Management. The concepts and tools include Stochastic Models, Simulation, Optimisation, Sensitivity Analysis, and What-If Analysis.

The book is practical, and it only provides advanced methods and tools to improve the financial risk management process in Finance in general. That is, the book does not teach financial risk management concepts. Mostly, it is purposed for experienced financial managers in general, and specifically financial risk analysts and financial risk managers. In addition, the book will be very beneficial to academics in teaching and practicing Financial Risk Management. Also, it will be useful to the degree students studying the topics of Finance in general, and specifically, Financial Risk Management, Risk and Decision Analysis, and Operations Research providing simple examples for practicing on their subjects of study.

The book assumes a working knowledge of the subject. By applying the proposed approach in Finance, readers will substantially improve and facilitate the financial risk measurement and assessment, which will ultimately and systematically enhance financial risk management globally. This is an important objective, which if achieved, will gain significant benefits.

Financial risk managers and regulators of financial institutions define risk as the uncertainty of outcomes and the negative consequences that it may have on an institution, and both aim at enhancing the resiliency of institutions to adverse situations. As a result of their efforts, risks became better identified, assessed, and monitored, risk practices improved, and risk models became more widespread. Financial risks are defined according to the sources of uncertainty. The major classes of financial risks are credit risk, market risk, liquidity risk, interest rate risk, and foreign exchange risk.

Today, risk management has become a core central function for financial firms, banks, funds, and insurance companies. Financial risk management is a process of identification, assessment, and prioritization of risk followed by the coordination of actions and deployment of resources to minimize, monitor, and control the impact of undesired events. The objective of financial risk management is to ensure that uncertainty does not affect or has a minimal impact on, the achievement of the goals of a financial institution.

Financial crises can expose underlying faults in the financial institution's systems and processes. The 2008 financial crisis exposed the failure of a prevalent laissez-faire economic and regulatory philosophy that financial institutions could and should manage their own risk with little outside interference. Now, many see the danger of fragile financial service networks bringing systemic risk to the real economy. So, financial organizations face increasing regulations such as Basel III for banks, and Solvency II for insurance. To meet the requirements of the increased and rigorous regulation, financial organizations are striving to improve their formal risk assessment and management processes, which is their ultimate objective. The major focus of Basel III and Solvency II is the solvency risk.

To help financial organizations to achieve their ultimate objective and meet the Basel III requirements, this book broadly presents applications of advanced tools and methods for improving financial Risk Management, specifically elaborating on different aspects of financial risk analysis and management.

Bernstein stated, "*The risk will always be there, so we must explore many interesting tools that can help us to control risks we cannot avoid taking*" (Bernstein and Damodaran 1998). As inspired by Bernstein, the "Oil & Gas Risk Assessment and Management" was applied to Businesses to improve the process and help control financial risks.

In addition to conventional stochastic optimisation (Lee, C.F., Lee, A.C., and J. Lee 2010) and Monte Carlo simulation (Bratley et al 1983, Rubinstein & Kroese 2008), this book tactically applies the risk analysis concepts such as Sensitivity Analysis, and What-If Analysis, which significantly enhanced the controlling of financial risks.

The frontier of ALM is based on stochastic optimisation and simulation models that involve an asset allocation approach by considering the liabilities aspect as well. Specifically, an internal Monte Carlo Simulation model for Solvency II (i.e., an ALM-market risk simulation model) was presented by Bourdeau (2009).

The methods apply to internal models for Basel III. By using it, financial institutions can reduce financial risk, capital requirements, and Value at Risk (VAR), thus achieving higher business capabilities and competitiveness, which is their ultimate objective.

It should be noted that this book will demonstrate the application of the approach based on real-world published financial projects including projects' data. However, for elaboration, hypothetical scenarios are used to emulate real-world published projects. In the research and demonstration experiments, Microsoft™ Excel® was used for modelling; and Palisade™ @RISK® and RISKOptimizer® were used for Monte Carlo simulation and stochastic optimisation respectively. The terms simulation and Monte Carlo simulation are interchangeably used in the book.

This book elaborates on applications to Financial Risk Management. Financial Risk Management is improved with Sensitivity Analysis.

The book elaborates on the following 10 chapters i) Oil Drilling Schedule; ii) Oil Gas Forecast; iii) Correlation between Porosity and Water Saturation; iv) Exponential Decline; v) Forecasting Exponential Decline; vi) Oil Depletion Allowance; vii) Oil Pipeline Risk; viii) Oil Transportation with Weather Disruption; ix) Projecting Oil Prices; and x) Waterflood Project with Production Scenario.

REFERENCES

Bernstein, P. L., & Damodaran, A. (1998). *Investment Management*. John Wiley & Sons.

Bratley, P. F., & Bennett, L. (1983). *A Guide to Simulation*. Springer-Verlag. DOI: 10.1007/978-1-4684-0167-7

Bubevski, V. (2016). Risk Management: A novel Six Sigma Approach. In Darnel, B. (Ed.), *Risk Management: Past Present and Future*. Nova Science Publishers.

Bubevski, V. (2017). *Novel Six Sigma Approaches to Risk Assessment and Management*. IGI Global.

Bubevski, V. (2018). *Six Sigma Improvements for Basel III and Solvency II in Financial Risk Management*. IGI Global.

Hayler, R., & Nichols, M. D. (2006). Six Sigma for Financial Services: How Leading Companies Are Driving Results Using Lean, Six Sigma, and Process Management. McGraw-Hill.

Lee, C. F., Lee, A. C., & Lee, J. (Eds.). (2010). Handbook of Quantitative Finance and Risk Management. Springer. DOI: 10.1007/978-0-387-77117-5

Rubinstein, R. Y., & Kroese, D. P. (2008). *Simulation and the Monte Carlo Method*. John Wiley & Sons.

Stamatis, D. H. (2003). *Six Sigma for Financial Professionals*. Wiley.

Tarantino, A., & Cernauskas, D. (2009). *Risk Management in Finance: Six Sigma and Other Next-Generation Techniques*. Wiley.

Acknowledgment

I would like to thank you very much my daughter Ivana Bubevska for reviewing the manuscript and suggesting very relevant improvements. She has also substantially helped with the editing and formatting of the manuscript. Her contribution has been essential for the successful publication of the book.

Also, acknowledgments to Palisade Corporation for publishing the data of the real project for Risk Analysis. I have used these data for the experiments demonstrated in this book, which proved the concept of the applied approach. This substantially increased my confidence and allowed me to publish this book.

Introduction

FINANCIAL RISK MANAGEMENT

Generally, the risk is considered as a probability or threat of damage, injury, liability, loss, or any other negative occurrence that is caused by external or internal vulnerabilities, and that may be avoided through preemptive action. In Finance specifically, risk is defined as the randomness of the return of investments, including both positive and negative outcomes. From this perspective, a greater expected return is associated with greater variability of outcomes. However, from the aspect of financial regulators and risk managers, risk is defined as the uncertainty that has adverse consequences on earnings or wealth, or the uncertainty associated with negative outcomes only. Regulations (i.e., Basel III for Finance and Solvency II for Insurance) aim at enhancing the resiliency of financial firms and the financial system in stressed conditions. Risk managers are generally accountable for identifying, assessing, and controlling the likelihood and the consequences of adverse events for financial organisations.

The broad classes of financial risks are credit risk, market risk, liquidity risk, and interest rate risk, which are further divided into subclasses relative to the specific events that trigger losses.

Risk management is a process that necessitates that the risks of a financial institution are identified, assessed, and controlled. Nowadays, risk management has become a core central function for financial corporations including banks, funds, and businesses.

Risk processes include the identification, monitoring, and control of risks. Risk models serve for measuring and quantifying risk and provide the inputs for the management processes and decisions. To be effective, they should be implemented within a dedicated organisational framework that should be enterprise wide.

All risk processes imply that risk policies are properly defined and that the risk appetite of the firm is well defined. Within this framework, the common process for controlling risks is based on risk limits and risk delegations. Limits impose upper bounds on the potential loss of transactions, or of portfolios of transactions.

Limits aim at avoiding those adverse events, that affect a transaction or a portfolio of transactions and impair the credit standing of the firm. Financial institutions need to segment their activities into meaningful portfolios, for example by business unit, product, or type of clients. Limits of exposure are set for each segment and down to transactions, forming a hierarchy of limits and sub-limits. For example, credit risk limits are set by segment, then by a counterparty, and then by an individual transaction. For market risk, limits can be set for specific books of trades, then desks, and then trades.

Delegations serve for decentralisation of the risk decisions, within limits. Delegations are authorisations to act and take risks on behalf of the organisation. Delegations decentralise and simplify the risk process by allowing local managers to make decisions without referring to the upper levels of the organisation, within the scope of their delegations. For example, they simplify the risk process for transactions that are small enough to be dealt with by local procedures.

Any limit system requires one or several measures of risk used for determining whether a transaction, or a portfolio of transactions, complies with limits. Various risk metrics are used for setting limits for credit risk. The amount at risk, or exposure, is a simple measure of the amount that could be lost in the event of a default of the borrower. Other metrics capture other dimensions of credit risk. For example, trades might be allowed only for eligible borrowers based on their credit quality. Or limits can apply to regulatory capital for credit risk, which combines various components of credit risk, exposure, loss after recoveries, and credit quality.

Credit limit systems are based on common criteria, for example, i) Diversify the commitments across various dimensions such as customers, industries, and regions; ii) Avoid lending to any borrower an amount that would increase its debt beyond its borrowing capacity; iii) The equity of the borrower sets up some reasonable limit to its debt given acceptable levels of debt/equity ratios and repayment ability; iv) Set up a maximum risk level, for example, defined by the credit standing of borrowers, above which lending is prohibited; and v) Ensure a minimum diversification across counterparties and avoid concentrations of risk on a single borrower, an industry or a region.

To be comprehensive and consistent, the limit system has to be financial institution wide. Global limit systems aggregate all risks on any single counterparty, no matter which business unit initiates the risk, across all transactions with the financial organisation.

Generally, the financial risk assessment requires defining the risk and understanding how to measure it. Different risk models are used for risk assessment, e.g., the Capital Asset Pricing Model (CAPM), Arbitrage Pricing Model (APM), and other multifactor risk models (Damodaran 1998). Alternative measures of risk can also be used for risk assessment, e.g., Standard Deviation, Variance, Value at Risk (VAR), Conditional Value at Risk (CVAR), etc. (Clark 1998). Also, absolute risk measures are used for risk assessment such as Standard Deviation and Variance, as well as the risk measures relative to a market index (i.e., a benchmark), for example, Beta. Moreover, risk-adjusted measures can be used such as the Sharpe Ratio and Treynor Ratio (Jacob 1998). Moreover, Plantinga (2007) discussed methodologies for measuring and evaluating the performance of financial institutions for management purposes. He elaborated methods for i) Measuring returns on investment; and ii) Evaluating performance considering the Sharpe Ratio, Jensen's Alpha, Treynor Ratio, and Information Ratio, as well as the downside risk measures, i.e., Sortino Ratio and Fouse Index.

Miller (1992) argues that treatments of risk in the international management literature largely focus on uncertainties to the exclusion of other interrelated uncertainties. His paper develops a framework for categorizing the uncertainties faced by firms operating internationally and outlines both financial and strategic corporate risk management responses.

A paper by Hsieh (1993) demonstrates that when log price changes are not independent and identically distributed (IID), their conditional density may be more accurate than their unconditional density for describing short-term behaviour. Using the BDS test (i.e., Brock, Dechert, and Scheinkman test which detects nonlinear serial dependence in time series) of independence and identical distribution, daily log price changes in four currency futures contracts are found to be not IID. While there appear to be no predictable conditional mean changes, conditional variances are predictable and can be described by an autoregressive volatility model that seems to capture all the departures from independence and identical distribution. Based on this model, daily log price changes are decomposed into a predictable part, which is described parametrically by the autoregressive volatility model, and an unpredictable part, which can be modelled by an empirical density, either parametrically or non-parametrically. This two-step semi-nonparametric method yields a conditional density for daily log price changes, which has many uses in financial risk management.

Froot, Scharfstein, and Stein (1993) in their paper presented a general framework for analysing corporate risk management policies. By observing that if external sources of finance are costlier to corporations than internally generated funds, there will typically be a benefit to hedging. Hedging adds value to the extent that it helps ensure that a corporation has sufficient internal funds available to take advantage of attractive investment opportunities. The authors argue that this simple observation has wide-ranging implications for the design of risk management strategies. They delineate how these strategies should depend on such factors as shocks to investment and financing opportunities. They also discuss exchange rate hedging strategies for multinationals, as well as strategies involving "nonlinear" instruments like options.

Stulz (1996) in his paper presents a theory of corporate risk management that attempts to go beyond the "variance-minimisation" model that dominates most academic discussions on the subject. It argues that the primary goal of risk management is not to dampen swings in corporate cash flows or value but rather to protect against the possibility of costly lower-tail outcomes–situations that would cause financial distress or make a company unable to carry out its investment strategy. By eliminating downside risk and reducing the expected costs of financial trouble, risk management can also help a company achieve both its optimal capital structure and its optimal ownership structure. For, besides increasing corporate debt capacity, the reduction of downside risk also encourages larger equity stakes for managers by shielding their investments from "uncontrollable-s."

The paper also departs from standard finance theory in suggesting that some companies may have a comparative advantage in bearing certain financial market risks–an advantage that derives from information acquired through their normal business activities. Although such specialised information may lead some companies to take speculative positions in commodities or currencies, it is more likely to encourage "selective" hedging, a practice in which the risk manager's "view" of future price movements influences the percentage of the exposure that is hedged. To the extent that such view-taking becomes an accepted part of a company's risk management program, it is important to evaluate managers' bets on a risk-adjusted basis and relative to the market. If risk managers want to behave like money managers, they should be evaluated like money managers.

Alexander (1996) published a book discussing the mathematical applications in finance. During the past 20 years or so, and especially since the last financial crisis, the advances in mathematical applications to financial analysis and forecasting have been enormous. Mathematical methods are not only being used in forecasting but also in the vitally important area of risk management. This book is the definitive source for professionals seeking an introduction to the very latest thinking on risk analysis and risk management strategies. Each chapter contains an introductory survey of the area, followed by a technical exposition of the main ideas that are at the forefront of current research.

Froot and Stein (1998) developed a framework for analysing the capital allocation and capital structure decisions facing financial institutions. The model incorporates two key features: i) value-maximising banks have a well-founded concern with risk management, and ii) not all the risks they face can be frictionlessly hedged in the capital market. This approach allows showing how bank-level risk management considerations should factor into the pricing of those risks that cannot be easily hedged. The authors examine several applications, including the evaluation of proprietary trading operations, and the pricing of non-hedge able derivatives positions. They also compare the approach to the Risk-Adjusted Return on Capital (RAROC) methodology that has been adopted by many banks.

Christoffersen, Diebold, and Schuermann (1998) in their paper consider the question: "Is volatility forecast-ability important for long-horizon risk management, or is a traditional constant volatility assumption adequate?" The authors elaborate on this question, exploring the interface between long-horizon financial risk management and long-horizon volatility forecast-ability and whether long-horizon volatility is forecastable enough such that volatility models are useful for long-horizon risk management.

A paper published by Diebold, Hahn, and Tay (1999) provides a framework for evaluating and improving multivariate density forecasts. Among other things, the multivariate framework is used to evaluate the adequacy of density forecasts involving cross-variable interactions, such as time-varying conditional correlations. Also, provided are conditions under which a technique of density forecast "calibration" can be used to improve deficient density forecasts. The authors show how the calibration method can be used to generate good density forecasts from econometric models, even when the conditional density is unknown. Finally, motivated by recent advances in financial risk management, provided is a detailed application to multivariate high-frequency exchange rate density forecasts.

Lawton and Jankowski (2009) edited a collection of works of some of the most prominent industry professionals and academics focussing on investment performance evaluation. Also, Meier (2009) elaborated on how institutional investors evaluate the return on investment. Standard Deviation and risk measures versus the market were utilised including Alpha, Beta Excess Return, Information Ratio, Sharpe Ratio, and Tracking Error. In addition, Busse, Goyal, and Wahal (2010) used to aggregate and average estimates of alphas for performance measurement of institutional investment management considering the return on investment.

A handbook of quantitative finance and risk management edited by Lee, C.F., Lee, A.C., and J. Lee (2010) is a combination of economics, accounting, statistics, econometrics, mathematics, stochastic process, and computer science and technology. Increasingly, the tools of financial analysis are being applied to assess, monitor, and mitigate risk, especially in the context of globalisation, market volatility, and economic crisis. This three-volume handbook is one of the most comprehensive in the field, integrating the most current theory, methodology, policy, and practical applications. Including contributions from an international array of experts, the book is unparalleled in the breadth and depth of its coverage. In Volume 1, the handbook presents an overview of quantitative finance and risk management research, covering the essential theories, policies, and empirical methodologies used in the field. Chapters provide an in-depth discussion of portfolio theory and investment analysis. Volume 2 covers options and option pricing theory and risk management. Volume 3 presents a wide variety of models and analytical tools. Throughout, the handbook extensively offers illustrative case examples and worked equations. It is an essential reference for academics, educators, students, policymakers, and practitioners.

Homaifar (2004) published a comprehensive guide to managing global financial risk. From the balance of payment exposure to foreign exchange and interest rate risk to credit derivatives and other exotic options, futures, and swaps for mitigating and transferring risk, this book provides a simple yet comprehensive analysis of complex derivatives pricing and their application in risk management. The risk posed by foreign exchange transactions stems from the volatility of the exchange rate, the volatility of the interest rates, and factors unique to individual companies which are interrelated. To protect and hedge against adverse currency and interest rate changes, multinational corporations need to take concrete steps to mitigate these risks. This book offers a thorough treatment of the price, foreign currency, and interest rate risk management practices of multinational corporations in a dynamic global economy. It lays out the pros and cons of various hedging instruments, as well as the economic cost-benefit analysis of alternative hedging vehicles. Written in a detailed yet user–friendly manner, this resource provides treasurers and other financial managers with the tools they need to manage their various exposures to credit, price, and foreign exchange risk.

Hasan, Kapadia, and Siddique (2017) debate that rating downgrades can have adverse consequences on a firm due to the feedback effect, even when ratings lack informational content. In this paper, the authors consider whether the rating agency attempts to mitigate the feedback effect through its rating actions. Using Moody's issuer ratings over 1982–2009, they show that firms with greater external financing constraints are less likely to be downgraded. The issuer bias is robust, and its economic significance increases at times when economy-wide credit spreads are unusually high. The paper documents that severely constrained firms whose ratings are affirmed or upgraded have long-term positive excess equity returns.

Dash et al (2017) established that with the rise of computing power and new analytical techniques, banks can now extract deeper and more valuable insights from their ever-growing mountains of data. And they can do it quickly, as many key processes are now automated (and many more soon will be). For risk departments, which have been using data analytics for decades, these trends present unique opportunities to better identify, measure, and mitigate risk. Critically, they can leverage their vast expertise in data and analytics to help leaders shape the strategic agenda of the bank.

Financial Risk Management is a major aspect of Basel III and Solvency II. Jorion (2011), in his book on financial risk management, presented the utilisation of the Monte Carlo Simulation for options valuation and VAR calculation. He also generally elaborated on Optimal Hedging, applying the Optimal Hedge Ratio, i.e., the minimal variance hedge ratio. In addition, he specifically described the application of Optimal Hedging in two important cases: Duration Hedging and Beta Hedging.

The new regulation requirements introduced by Basel III and Solvency II focus on the solvency risk to impose a required amount of equity value based on the risk associated with the investments of asset portfolios. The banking and insurance industry is responding to these requirements by developing internal models based essentially on the VAR, parametric (GARCH, EGARCH), and simulation (Monte Carlo) models, extended to CVAR and Copulas.

Asset and Liability Management (ALM) originated from the duration analysis proposed by Macaulay (1938) and Redington (1952). Subsequently, ALM has evolved into a powerful and integrated tool for the analysis of assets and liabilities to value not only the interest rate risk but the liquidity risk, solvency risk, firm strategies, and asset allocation as well (Bloomsbury 2012).

The methods apply to internal models for Solvency II. By using it, financial institutions can reduce the solvency risk, capital requirements, and Value at Risk (VAR), thus achieving higher business capabilities and competitiveness, which is their ultimate objective.

The frontier of ALM is based on stochastic optimisation and simulation models that involve an asset allocation approach by considering the liabilities aspect as well. Specifically, an internal Monte Carlo Simulation model for Solvency II (i.e., an ALM-market risk simulation model) was presented by Bourdeau (2009).

In addition, Adam (2007) published a comprehensive guide to ALM from a quantitative aspect with economic explanations. He presented advanced ALM stochastic models for Solvency II and Basel II & III using optimisation and simulation methodologies.

Engelmann & Rauhmeier (2006) edited a book about Basel II. This book compiles articles by various authors addressing the estimation of three key risk parameters: the probability of default (PD), loss-given default (LGD), and exposure at default (EAD). The authors identify their intended audience as risk managers and quantitative risk or rating analysts working on credit risk and regulatory issues. These groups likely will find this book an accessible reference. The exposition related to regulatory issues is quite good and worthwhile for all.

Mitra and Schwaiger (2011) published a book that brings together state-of-the-art quantitative decision models for asset and liability management for pension funds, and banks. It considers new regulations and industry risks, covering new accounting standards for pension funds, Solvency II implementation for insurance companies, and Basel III accord for banks.

Editors Christodoulakis and Satchell (2007) collected papers that are beginning to appear by regulators, consultants, and academics, to provide the first collection that focuses on the quantitative side of model validation. Risk model validation is an emerging and important area of research and has arisen because of Basel I and II. These regulatory initiatives require trading institutions and lending institutions to compute their reserve capital in a highly analytic way, based on the use of internal risk models. It is part of the regulatory structure that these risk models be validated both internally and externally, and there is a great shortage of information as to best practices. The book covers the three main areas of risk: Credit Risk and Market and Operational Risk. Risk model validation is a requirement of Basel I and II. In this first collection of papers in this new and developing area of research, international authors cover model validation in credit, market, and operational risk.

Barfield (2011) covered the revised Basel Accord framework Basel III, introduced in the wake of the global financial crisis. The new measures are designed to update and strengthen the resilience of the international banking sector, and this book will cover in-depth what the new measures mean in practice. It could be essential reading for compliance, legal, and other senior management in banks, and their advisers.

Editors Cannata & Quagliariello (2011) presented expert contributions from those deeply and directly involved in the creation of the new global standards. Their book is a must-read for market practitioners and regulators who need to understand the emerging framework of financial regulation, its implications, and its impact. After three of the most tumultuous years in financial markets in living memory, the regulatory die was cast in December 2010. This book provides the reader with a comprehensive discussion of the contents of the regulatory reform, taking advantage of the knowledge of experts who contributed to shaping the new rules. With a foreword from Mario Draghi - an eminent banking official, and written by experts deeply involved in these reforms, this work provides a practical and global perspective on the new standards. The book combines technical rigor with an accessible style to provide the essential primer to the new regulatory blueprint and the rationale behind it. It discusses the technical aspects and disciplines of modern markets and provides summaries of the most important elements, the thinking behind them, how they will be implemented, and the potential repercussions.

This work focuses on the market practices that contributed to the financial turmoil and the subsequent policy response from the G20 and the Financial Stability Board that led to the proposals of the Basel Committee. Also, the book analyses the new definition of regulatory capital, the new framework for the trading book, changes to the counterparty credit risk capital rules, and the new measures for mitigating pro-cyclicality. In addition, it analyses the elements designed to complement the capital rules: the leverage ratio, a global minimum liquidity standard, initiatives regarding credit rating agencies; how to handle systemically important banks, and remuneration. Finally, it surveys the changing regulatory landscape, looking at crisis management and resolution, the impact of the new regulations, and the future architecture of financial supervision and regulation.

Bessis (2015) in his book Risk Management in Banking provided the industry's seminal reference that offers a comprehensive review of all aspects of the field. The text covers a complete range of risk topics in banking including asset-liability management, risk-based capital, value at risk, loan portfolio management, capital allocation, and other fundamental risk factors. All these topics are examined within the new mindset inspired by the financial crisis. This practical guide contains the latest information on topics such as ALM, Basel III, liquidity analysis, market risk, credit risk, derivatives, structured products, securitisations, and more. In this book, professionals will discover an easily navigable resource that is filled with research and practices that reflect the most recent changes in the field.

The Basel III handbook by Ramirez (2017) delves deep into the principles underpinning the capital dimension of Basel III to provide a more advanced understanding of real-world implementation. Going beyond the simple overview or model, this book merges theory with practice to help practitioners work more effectively within the regulatory framework and utilise the complex rules to more effectively allocate and enhance capital. A European perspective covers the CRD IV directive and associated guidance, but practitioners across all jurisdictions will find value in the strategic approach to decisions surrounding business lines and assets; an emphasis on analysis urges banks to shed unattractive positions and channel capital toward opportunities that fit their risk and return profile. Real-world cases demonstrate successful capital initiatives as models for implementation, and in-depth guidance on Basel III rules equips practitioners to more effectively utilise this complex regulatory treatment.

The specifics of Basel III implementation vary, but the underlying principles are effective around the world. This book expands upon existing guidance to provide a deeper working knowledge of Basel III utility, and the insight to use it effectively to i) Improve asset quality and risk and return profiles; ii) Adopt a strategic approach to capital allocation;

iii) Compare Basel III implementation varies across jurisdictions; iv) Examine successful capital enhancement initiatives from around the world.

There is a popular misconception about Basel III being extremely conservative and a deterrent to investors seeking attractive returns. Basel III presents both the opportunity and a framework for banks to improve their assets and enhance overall capital the key factor is a true, comprehensive understanding of the regulatory mechanisms. The Handbook of Basel III Capital Enhancing Bank Capital in Practice provides advanced guidance for advanced practitioners and real-world implementation insight.

The evolution of the Basel Accord is presented in Table 1.

Table 1. Evolution of the Basel accord

Basel I	•Minimum risk-based capital, the definition of capital
M R A	•Market risk treatment in the trading book; standard and internal model approaches
Basel II	•Credit Risk, Operational Risk –standard and internal model approaches •Pillars 2 and 3
Basel 2.5	•Enhanced Market Risk standards •Securitisation enhancements
Basel III	•Definition of capital, Capital buffers: pro-cyclicality and capital conservation; Leverage •Enhanced risk coverage; Liquidity framework
Review of Trading Book	•New Standardised Approach •New Trading Book Boundary •New Standards for Models

BASEL III

Basel III is a comprehensive set of reform measures, developed by the Basel Committee on Banking Supervision, to strengthen the regulation, supervision, and risk management of the banking sector. These measures aim to i) improve the banking sector's ability to absorb shocks arising from financial and economic stress, whatever the source; ii) improve risk management and governance; and iii) strengthen banks' transparency and disclosures.

Currently, the Basel Accord for bank regulation is Basel III. Issued by the Basel Committee on Banking Supervision, the Basel III standards on capital and liquidity, along with measures from July 2009 on the trading book and structured finance, are the centrepiece of the regulatory community's response to the crisis. Even though it was implemented in January 2013, Basel III must be fully phased in by January 2019.

The Basel Committee on Banking Supervision issued the second consultative paper on the fundamental review of trading book capital requirements. The revisions to the capital framework set out in this paper aim to contribute to a more resilient banking sector by strengthening capital standards for market risks. They form part of the Committee's broader agenda to reform regulatory standards for banks in response to the financial crisis. The revisions in this paper also reflect the Committee's increased focus on achieving a regulatory framework that can be implemented consistently by supervisors across jurisdictions. As such, they incorporate the lessons learned from the Committee's recent investigations into the variability of market risk-weighted assets.

The financial crisis exposed material weaknesses in the overall design of the framework for capitalising on trading activities. The level of capital required against trading book exposures proved insufficient to absorb losses. As an important response to the crisis, the Committee introduced a set of revisions to the market risk framework in July 2009 (part of the "Basel 2.5" package of reforms). At the time, the Committee recognised that the Basel 2.5 revisions did not fully address the shortcomings of the framework. In response, the Committee initiated a fundamental review of the trading book regime, beginning with an assessment of "what went wrong". The Committee published the first consultative paper in May 2012. Having reflected on the comments received, this paper sets out more detailed proposals for reforming the trading book regime, including the draft text for the Basel Accord.

The Committee has focused on the following key areas as part of its review:

1. The Basel Committee on Banking Supervision provides a forum for regular cooperation on banking supervisory matters. It seeks to promote and strengthen supervisory and risk management practices globally. The Committee comprises representatives from Argentina, Australia, Belgium, Brazil, Canada, China, France, Germany, Hong Kong SAR, India, Indonesia, Italy, Japan, Korea, Luxembourg, Mexico, the Netherlands, Russia, Saudi Arabia, Singapore, South Africa, Spain, Sweden, Switzerland, Turkey, the United Kingdom, and the United States. Observers on the Basel Committee are the European Banking Authority, the European Central Bank, the European Commission, the Financial Stability Institute, and the International Monetary Fund.
2. To view the first consultative paper, see Basel Committee on Banking Supervision, Fundamental review of the trading book, May 2012 (www.bis.org/publ/bcbs219.pdf). It is intended that this second consultative paper can be read as a standalone document, without the need for cross-reference with the first consultative paper.
3. See Basel Committee on Banking Supervision, Regulatory Consistency Assessment Programme (RCAP) – Analysis of risk-weighted assets for market risk, January 2013, and revised February 2013 (www.bis.org/publ/bcbs240.pdf).

The Basel Committee on Banking Supervision provides a forum for regular cooperation on banking supervisory matters. Its objective is to enhance understanding of key supervisory issues and improve the quality of banking supervision worldwide. This document sets out revised standards for minimum capital requirements for Market Risk by the Basel Committee on Banking Supervision ("the Committee"). The text herein is intended to replace the existing minimum capital requirements for market risk in the global regulatory framework, including amendments made after the June 2006 publication of Basel II: International Convergence of Capital Measurement and Capital Standards - Comprehensive Version. Consistent with the policy rationales underpinning the Committee's three consultative papers on the Fundamental Review of the Trading Book,1 the revised market risk framework consists of the following key enhancements:

1. A revised internal models' approach (IMA). The new approach introduces a more rigorous model approval process that enables supervisors to remove internal modelling permission for individual trading desks, more consistent identification and capitalization of material risk factors across banks, and constraints on the capital-reducing effects of hedging and diversification.
2. A revised standardized approach (SA). The revisions fundamentally overhaul the standardized approach to make it sufficiently risk-sensitive to serve as a credible fall-back for, as well as a floor too, the IMA, while still providing an appropriate standard for banks that do not require a sophisticated treatment for market risk.
3. A shift from Value-at-Risk (VAR) to an Expected Shortfall (ES) measure of risk under stress. The use of ES will help to ensure a more prudent capture of "tail risk" and capital adequacy during periods of significant financial market stress.
4. Incorporation of the risk of market illiquidity. Varying liquidity horizons are incorporated into the revised SA and IMA to mitigate the risk of sudden and severe impairment of market liquidity across asset markets. These replace the static 10-day horizon assumed for all traded instruments under VAR in the current framework.
5. A revised boundary between the trading book and banking book. The establishment of a more objective boundary will serve to reduce incentives to arbitrage between the regulatory banking and trading books, while still being aligned with banks' risk management practices.

The IPOL - EGOV Briefing (2016) describes the evolution of the Basel framework since the first standards were enacted and describes the ongoing revisions of the Basel III framework. The main findings of different impact assessments are reminded, as well as the different positions of various stakeholders. This is regularly updated and was initially prepared in advance of ECON's Open Coordinators and Banking Union Working Group meeting on 12 October 2016 with Mr. Bill Coen, Secretary-General of the Basel Committee on Banking Supervision.

Over the last decades, banking regulatory capital requirements have changed substantially. In 1988, the first Basel Accord introduced an international standard to compute banks' regulatory capital. Today, nearly

30 years later, the BCBS is preparing what has already been coined by some as 'Basel IV'.

Over the years, capital standards drafted by the BCBS have shifted from simplicity to risk sensitivity, probably at the expense of transparency and comparability of capital position across banks.

MODELLING TOOLS

Any appropriate modelling tools for Monte Carlo simulation and stochastic optimisation can be used to implement the approach. Specifically, in the research and demonstration experiments for this book, Microsoft™ Excel® was used for modelling; and Palisade™ @RISK® and RISKOptimizer® were used for Monte Carlo simulation and stochastic optimisation respectively.

For example, here is a significant parameter in finance: *Sharpe Ratio* is a portfolio performance measure compared to the *Free Risk Rate* to the risk associated with it. That is the gain per unit of risk taken. A higher Sharp Ratio indicates a better portfolio performance in response to the risk involved. *Sharpe Ratio* is calculated by using the following formula:

$$\text{Sharpe Ratio} = (\mu - r) / \sigma$$

Were, μ = *Mean Return* (for example, i.e., calculated by the Monte Carlo Simulation model); σ = *Standard-Deviation* (i.e., calculated by the Monte Carlo Simulation model); and r = *Risk-Free Rate*, which is estimated to be 5.35%.

It is important and should be emphasised that the approach is independent of the choice of tools. If the readers want to use the Palisade™ tolls, they should visit the Palisade™ website and download the free trial version of the tools, which lasts for 15 days. So, they can experiment and subsequently buy the tools if found useful (Winston 2000, 2001).

ABOUT THE FUTURE OF FINANCIAL RISK MANAGEMENT

The financial risk landscape is changing fast. Every day's headlines bring new reminders that the future is on its way as the financial risk evolves. New trends and new challenges are around every corner and new financial risk strategies, techniques, and regulations are required. The outlines of new trends, challenges, strategies, techniques, and regulations of financial risk management are presented below.

In an early paper by Li (2003), the future trends and challenges of financial risk management were considered at the beginning of the millennium. First, the historical developments and the early 2000s status of financial risk management were assessed. Then, key features of the financial industry in the digital economy were discussed. It is argued that technological innovations, particularly in computing and telecommunication, will continue to have an important influence on the then-future development of financial risk management. Based on past and then-present financial risk management as well as the general trends in the financial industry, some then-future trends and challenges of financial risk management in the digital economy were discussed. Finally, some implications for financial institutions, corporations, and emerging economies were given.

Alexander (2005) established that in 2005, the research on financial risk management applications of econometrics focused on the accurate assessment of individual market and credit risks with relatively little theoretical or applied econometric research on other types of risk, aggregation risk, data incompleteness, and optimal risk control. The author debates that consideration of the model risk arising from crude aggregation rules and inadequate data could lead to a new class of reduced-form Bayesian risk assessment models. Logically, these models should be set within a common factor framework that allows proper risk aggregation methods to be developed. The paper explains how such a framework could also provide the essential links between risk control, risk assessments, and the optimal allocation of resources.

The Institute of Risk Management (IRM) in their report Risk Agenda 2025 (IRM 2015) explores the future direction the profession of risk management is likely to take. In this report, they have gathered the wisdom of some of our key stakeholders and members on the opportunities and threats the profession faces, as well as how they are likely to impact risk management by 2025.

Härle, Havas & Samandari (2016) discuss the future of risk management for banks. The authors established that risk management in banking has been transformed over the past decade, largely in response to regulations that emerged from the global financial crisis and the fines levied in its wake. But important trends are afoot that suggest risk management will experience even more sweeping change in the next decade. The change expected in the risk function's operating model illustrates the magnitude of what lies ahead. Today, about 50 percent of the function's staff are dedicated to risk-related operational processes such as credit administration, while 15 percent work in analytics. "McKinsey Research" suggests that by 2025, these numbers will be closer to 25 and 40 percent, respectively. No one can draw a blueprint of what a bank's risk function will look like in 2025, or predict all forthcoming disruptions, be they technological advances, macroeconomic shocks, or banking scandals. However, the fundamental trends do permit a broad sketch of what will be required of the risk function of the future.

Koch et al (2017) published a discussion paper on Basel IV. Since Basel III was rolled out, the Basel Committee on Banking Supervision has been reviewing risk-measurement approaches internationally and among banks. One outcome of this review was the new standardized measurement approach (SMA) for operational risk, which was proposed in 2016. The committee also began a discussion on aggregated internal-rating model floors, concerned about the wide variation in the levels of risk-weighted assets (RWA) issued from banks' internal models. The committee finalized standards for minimum capital requirements for market risk—the fundamental review of the trading book (FRTB) in January 2016. The committee plans to make technical revisions to this framework in 2017–18, however, and the country-level implementation is still under discussion.

A structured review of Six Sigma and implications for future research were presented by Aboelmaged (2010). This study systematically analyzed the published work on Six Sigma from 417 referred journal articles in business and management disciplines, information systems and computer science, engineering, healthcare, etc. Conclusions from the analysis were that: i) Six Sigma research was rapidly growing, covering various disciplines and domains with a great focus on Six Sigma tools and techniques; ii) empirical research was dominant with more emphasis on a case study approach; and iii) the growing gap between manufacturing and service focused works confirmed the return of Six Sigma to manufacturing, i.e., its initial origin. Although a large volume of applications was published, Six Sigma is still under development and offers potential opportunities for future research and applications. To date, however, Six Sigma DMAIC has not been broadly applied to financial risk management specifically on an ongoing basis.

The "Comprehensive Applications to Banking Risk Assessment and Management" book proposed a generic structured approach to financial risk management, which is a recent concept (Bubevski 2017) and certainly has potential prospects for future research and applications.

RISK MANAGEMENT FUTURE DIRECTIONS

Eminent Risk Management scholars and practitioners are referenced considering the future direction for Risk Management in general across industries. Also, references to the future directions for specific industries, disciplines, and corporate businesses are provided including 1) Financial Risk Management; 2) Information Systems Security; 3) Energy Sector; 4) Project Management; 5) Construction Industry; 6) Supply Chain; 7) Agriculture; and 8) Six Sigma.

Continuous change is a universal principle. The universe is endlessly changing, and so is our world and everything in it. What was yesterday is not today, and what is today, won't be tomorrow. Consequently, the scenery of risk and risk management is rapidly changing as well. So, new strategies are constantly required to assess and control risk.

Albinson, Blau, and Chu (2016) published a generic report across industries about future risk management tendencies. They argue that organisations would respond to risk change by using cognitive technologies to supplement and, at times, even replace human decision-making. Also, they would deploy widespread controls as part of their operations to monitor and manage risk in real-time. In addition, improvements in behavioural sciences would help to comprehend risk insights, influence risk behaviours, and improve risk decision-making. Moreover, organisations would realise that 100% risk prevention is impossible, so investment in detecting risk events as they happen as well as containing and reducing the impact of risk events would increase. Finally, risk transfer instruments would progressively be used to protect organisations from a wider range of risks, e.g., cyber-attacks, climate change, geopolitical risks, terrorism, business disruptions, etc.

The report also claims that risk changes would influence changes within organizations. For example, the marketplace would reward organizations that take on strategic, high-risk inventions. Or, as risks become more measurable and tangible, organizations would be more able to determine an accurate upside value of risk.

Lastly, as businesses engage more deeply with many external stakeholders, they rely more heavily on them to identify, manage, and reduce risks together. The constant threat of disruption resulting from emerging technologies, business model transformations, and ecosystem changes, will force executives to make significant strategic choices to drive organizational success. To survive in a hyper-connected world, organization leaders would proactively address the accelerated and amplified risks to their reputation.

Another generic study addressing future research directions in management control systems (MCS) was published by Chenhall (2003). This article presented a critical review of findings from contingency-based studies over the past 20 years, resulting in proposals for applying MCS to organizational frameworks. The author argues that recent developments, including strategic risk management, are only just beginning to be understood by researchers. Likewise, product life cycles place demands for new product initiatives and alter cost structures. So, decreasing life cycles increases operating risk and requires increased capital investment.

Understanding how MCS innovations can assist management from these perspectives will probably become more and more important. Also, recent MCS research has recognized that managers have a 'strategic choice' to position their organizations in particular environments. For example, if the current product range is too uncertain, they may need to reformulate the product strategy in a more predictable market. This may limit potential opportunities and may require the organization to study its approaches to the trade-off between potential returns and acceptable risk.

Alexander (2005) discussed the future aspects of Financial Risk Management. The author claimed that current research on financial risk management focuses on the truthful assessment of individual market and credit risks. So, there is comparatively little theoretical or applied econometric research on other types of risk, aggregation risk, data incompleteness, and optimal risk control. The paper discussed that the model risk originating from crude aggregation rules and insufficient data could lead to a new class of reduced-form Bayesian risk assessment models. Logically, these models should be set within a common factor framework that allows proper risk aggregation methods to be developed. The paper explained how such a framework could also provide the essential links between risk control, risk assessments, and the optimal allocation of resources.

A study of future directions in information systems security was published by Crossler et al (2013). This study claimed that although the major weaknesses of information security are the system users within an organization, the emphasis of present security research is on technical matters. The study emphasized the future directions for "Behavioral InfoSec" research, arguing that this is a novel developing area. It presented the challenges currently faced, as well as the future directions that researchers should explore, for example, separating insider divergent behavior from insider misbehavior, approaches to understanding hackers, improving information security compliance, security cross-cultural research, and security data gathering and measurement matters.

Future directions in the energy sector were discussed by Edwards (2008). The article reviewed examples of Knowledge Management (KM) in the energy sector and identified key current issues. Important conclusions were made and future directions for research and implementation were identified. For example, in an uncertain future, enough diversity is required to successfully continue innovation, and organisations should retain the learning and knowledge. More specifically for the energy sector in the future, new sources of energy will require new processes as well as new technology, and perhaps differently trained and educated personnel. The theory should be further applied such as knowledge-based systems and the associated techniques of knowledge elicitation. Also, studying the wider theory of knowledge sharing and organisational learning would be required. For example, the movement of complexity theories into the mainstream and knowledge-based view of the organisation should be utilised.

Lyneis and Ford (2007) studied the application of system dynamics on projects, assessed project progress, and proposed directions for future development. Regarding future routes for risk management and project controls, the authors focus on several aspects of project management including i) project conditions required for project control decisions; ii) actions to take when a project is forecasted to miss performance targets; iii) amounts, durations, combinations, and order of application of measures to be applied to improve performance as much as is possible; iv) heuristics for managing project dynamics to improve performance; and v) qualitative and quantitative models required for these heuristics. They concluded that all these aspects should rigorously be studied using simulation models.

A study by Edwards and Bowen (1998) reviewed and analyzed the works on construction and project risk management published from 1960 to 1997, to find practical and research tendencies and associated emphases. The objective was to identify variations in the knowledge and conduct of construction and project risk. The paper suggested that research on the categories of construction risk deserves greater attention. It also deemed that chronological aspects of risk and risk communication are key fields for investigation.

Packendorff (1995) published a theoretical paper discussing new research directions in project management (PM). This study identified three key limitations of PM theoretical research: i) PM is understood as a general theory in its own right; ii) research on PM is not adequately experiential, and iii) projects are perceived as utensils. It claimed that a diversity of theoretical perspectives should be employed in future research on "temporary organizations" aiming to create mid-range theories on different kinds of projects.

Future directions of Supply Chain Risk Management (SCRM) were studied by Singhal, Agarwal, and Mittal (20011). They claimed that organizations have implemented outsourcing, global partnerships, and lean strategies to improve their efficiency; however, these strategies made them vulnerable to market uncertainties, dependencies, and disruptions. Additionally, natural disasters and manufactured crises have negatively affected the strategic, operational, and tactical performance of organizations. These issues have initiated academic and corporate interest to consider risk as a major problem. The authors employ a multi-layered top-town taxonomy to classify and codify the literature and put forward probable dimensions for future research to capture the basic elements of diversified risk issues related to the supply chain. They also studied the SCRM literature concentrating on coordination and decision-making.

Idrees (2009) discussed the future research directions in agriculture considering the agribusiness supply chain. The author proposed a Total Risk Management Process model arguing that an agriculture sector-specific framework can be developed by implementing this model. Also, future research in this area can address food or country-specific issues. This approach can be applied to the non-organic food industry as well. Although only the crop sector of agriculture was covered, other agriculture areas can be explored to further gain the benefits of this research.

Even though Six Sigma is not the subject of this book, it is significant. A structured review of Six Sigma and implications for future research were presented by Aboelmaged (2010). This study systematically analyzed the published work on Six Sigma from 417 referred journal articles in business and management disciplines, information systems and computer science, engineering, healthcare, etc. Conclusions from the analysis were that: i) Six Sigma research was rapidly growing, covering various disciplines and domains with a great focus on Six Sigma tools and techniques; ii) empirical research was dominant with more emphasis on a case study approach; and iii) the growing gap between manufacturing and service focused works confirmed the return of Six Sigma to manufacturing, i.e., its initial origin. Although a large volume of applications was published, Six Sigma is still under development and offers potential opportunities for future research and applications.

To date, however, Six Sigma has not been specifically applied to risk management on an ongoing basis. In conclusion, considering that Six Sigma is in expansion today and offers future opportunities for implementations (Aboelmaged 2010), Six Sigma has not only contemporary but prospects for utilisation across industries as well.

REFERENCES

Abbott, J. C. (2012). The Executive Guide to Six Sigma. Robert Houston Smith Publishers.

Aboelmaged, M. G. (2010). Six Sigma quality: A structured review and implications for future research. *International Journal of Quality & Reliability Management, 27*(3), 268–317. DOI: 10.1108/02656711011023294

Adam, A. (2007). Handbook of Asset and Liability Management: From Models to Optimal Return Strategies. John Wiley & Sons.

Albinson, N., Blau, A., & Chu, Y. (2016). *The future of risk: New game, new rules*. Deloitte. https://www2.deloitte.com/content/dam/Deloitte/us/Documents/risk/us-aers-the-future-of-risk-new-game-new-rules.pdf

Alexander, C. (1996). *The handbook of risk management and analysis*. John Wiley & Sons.

Alexander, C. (2005). *The Present and Future of Financial Risk Management*. Journal of Financial Econometrics. DOI: 10.1093/jjfinec/nbi003

Atkinson, P., & Blundell-Wignall, A. (2010). Thinking beyond Basel III – Necessary solutions for capital and liquidity. *OECD Market Trends, 98*(1).

Barfield, R. (2011). *A Practitioners Guide to Basel III and Beyond*. Sweet & Maxwell.

Basel Committee on Banking Supervision. (2014). Consultative Document: Fundamental review of the trading book: A revised market risk framework. Bank for International Settlements, Basel Committee on Banking Supervision.

Basel Committee on Banking Supervision. (2016). STANDARDS: Minimum capital requirements for market risk. Bank for International Settlements, Basel Committee on Banking Supervision.

BCBS. (2010a). *Basel III: A global regulatory framework for more resilient banks and banking systems*. BCBS.

BCBS. (2010b). *Basel III: International framework for liquidity risk measurement, standard, and monitoring*. BCBS.

BCBS. (2011). *Revisions to the Basel II market risk framework updated as of 31 December 2010.* BCBS.

Bessis, J. (2015). *Risk Management in Banking* (4th ed.). John Wiley & Sons, Ltd.

BIS. (2011). *Basel III: Long-term impact on economic performance and fluctuations.* Working paper No 338, February 2011.

Bloomsbury. (2012). *Asset Liability Management for Financial Institutions: Balancing Financial Stability with Strategic Objectives.* Bloomsbury Information Ltd.

Borror, C. M. (2009). *The Certified Quality Engineer Handbook* (3rd ed.). ASQ Quality Press.

Bourdeau, M. (2009). Market Risk Measurement Under Solvency II. In Cruz, M. (Ed.), *The Solvency II Handbook* (pp. 193–226). Risk Books – Incisive Media.

Bubevski, V. (2017). *Novel Six Sigma Approaches to Risk Assessment and Management.* IGI Global.

Busse, J. A., Goyal, A., & Wahal, S. (2010). Performance and Persistence in Institutional Investment Management. *The Journal of Finance*, *LXV*(2), 765–790. DOI: 10.1111/j.1540-6261.2009.01550.x

Cannata, F., & Quagliariello, M. (2011). *Basel III and Beyond.* Risk Books.

Chenhall, R.H. (2003). Management control systems design within its organizational context: findings from contingency-based research and directions for the future. *Accounting, Organizations and Society*, *28*, 127–168.

Christodoulakis, G. A., & Satchell, S. (Eds.). (2007). The Analytics of Risk Model Validation. Elsevier Science & Technology.

Christoffersen, P., Diebold, F. X., & Schuermann, T. (1998). *Horizon Problems and Extreme Events in Financial Risk Management. Economic Policy Review, 4*(3), 98-16.

Clark, R. G. (1998). Alternative Measures of Risk. In Bernstein, P. L., & Damodaran, A. (Eds.), *Investment Management* (pp. 81–98). John Wiley & Sons.

Cosimano, T. F., & Hakura, D. S. (2011). Bank Behavior in Response to Basel III: A Cross-Country Analysis. *IMF Working Paper*, WP/11/119, May 2011.

Crossler, R. E. (2013). *Future directions for behavioral information security research. Computers & Security*, 32.

Cruz, M. (2009). *The Solvency II Handbook*. Risk Books – Incisive Media.

Damodaran, A. (1998). Models of Risk. In Bernstein, P. L., & Damodaran, A. (Eds.), *Investment Management* (pp. 58–80). John Wiley & Sons.

Dash, R., Kremer, A., Nario, L., & Waldron, D. (2017). Risk analytics enters its prime. *McKinsey Working Papers on Risk*, Number 3, 2017, McKinsey & Company.

De Feo, J.A. & Barnard, W.W. (2005). *JURAN Institute's Six Sigma Breakthrough and Beyond*. McGraw-Hill Education.

Diebold, F. X., Hahn, J., & Tay, A. S. (1999, November). Multivariate Density Forecast Evaluation and Calibration in Financial Risk Management: High-Frequency Returns on Foreign Exchange. *The Review of Economics and Statistics, 81*(4), 661–673. DOI: 10.1162/003465399558526

Edwards, J. S. (2008). Knowledge management in the energy sector: Review and future directions. *International Journal of Energy Sector Management*, 2(2), 197–217. DOI: 10.1108/17506220810883216

Edwards, P.J., & Bowen, P.A. (1998). Risk and risk management in construction: a review and future directions for research. *Engineering, Construction, and Architectural Management*, 5(4), 339 – 349.

Engelmann, B., & Rauhmeier, R. (Eds.). (2006). *The Basel II Risk Parameters: Estimation, Validation, and Stress Testing*. Springer. DOI: 10.1007/3-540-33087-9

Froot, K.A., Scharfstein, D.S., & Stein, J.C. (1993). Risk Management: Coordinating Corporate Investment and Financing Policies. *The Journal of Finance*, *48*(5), 1629-1658.

Froot, K.A., & Stein, J. (1998). Risk management, capital budgeting, and capital structure policy for financial institutions: An integrated approach. *Journal of Financial Economics*, *47*(1), 55–82.

GDV. (2005). *Discussion Paper for a Solvency II Compatible Standard Approach*. Gesamtverband der Deutschen Versicherungswirtschaft. https://www.gdv.de/Downloads/English/Documentation_Sol_II.pdf

Härle, P., Havas, A., & Samandari, H. (2016). The future of bank risk management. *McKinsey Working Papers on Risk*, Number 3, July 2016, McKinsey & Company.

Hasan, M. N., Kapadia, N., & Siddique, A. (2017, December). Issuer bias in corporate ratings toward financially constrained firms. *The Journal of Credit Risk*, *13*(4), 1–35. DOI: 10.21314/JCR.2017.226

Homaifar, G. A. (2004). *Managing Global Financial and Foreign Exchange Rate Risk*. Wiley.

Hsieh, D. A. (1993). *Implications of Nonlinear Dynamics for Financial Risk Management*. Journal of Financial and Quantitative Analysis.

Idrees, F. (2009). *Total Risk Management Process in Agrifood Supply Chain*. https://www.ifama.org/resources/files/2009-Symposium/1008_paper.pdf

IPOL - Egov Briefing. (2016). *Upgrading the Basel standards: from Basel III to Basel IV*. European Parliament. https://www.europarl.europa.eu/RegData/etudes/BRIE/2016/587361/IPOL_BRI(2016)587361_EN.pdf

IRM. (2015). Perspectives on the future of risk. *The Institute of Risk Management (IRM) – Risk Agenda 2025*. https://www.theirm.org/media/3105903/IRM_Risk_Agenda_2025_v8.pdf

Jacob, N. L. (1998). Evaluating Investment Performance. In Bernstein, P. L., & Damodaran, A. (Eds.), *Investment Management* (pp. 329–371). John Wiley & Sons.

Jorion, P. (2011). *Financial Risk Manager Handbook*. John Wiley & Sons.

Keller, P. (2011). *Six Sigma Demystified* (2nd ed.). McGraw-Hill Education.

Koch, S., Schneider, R., Schneider, S., & Schröck, G. (2017). Bringing Basel IV into focus. *McKinsey Working Papers on Risk*, Number 4, November 2017, McKinsey & Company.

Lawton, P., & Jankowski, T. (2009). Investment Performance Measurement: Evaluating and Presenting Results. CFA Institute.

Lee, C. F., Lee, A. C., & Lee, J. (Eds.). (2010). Handbook of Quantitative Finance and Risk Management. Springer. DOI: 10.1007/978-0-387-77117-5

Li, S. (2003). Future trends and challenges of financial risk management in the digital economy. *Managerial Finance*, *29*(5/6), 111–125. DOI: 10.1108/03074350310768797

Lyneis, J. M., & Ford, D. N. (2007). *System Dynamics Applied to Project Management. System Dynamics Review*, *23*(2-3), 157–189.

Macaulay, F. R. (1938). *Some Theoretical Problems Suggested by the Movements of Interest Rates*. National Bureau of Economic Research.

Meier, J. P. (2009). Investment Performance Appraisal. In *Investment Performance Measurement: Evaluating and Presenting Results*. CFA Institute.

Miller, K.D. (1992). A Framework for Integrated Risk Management in International Business. *Journal of International Business Studies*, *23*(2), 311–331.

Mitra, G., & Schwaiger, K. (2011). *Asset and Liability Management Handbook*. Palgrave Macmillan.

Montgomery, D. C. (2004). *Introduction to Statistical Quality Control*. John Wiley & Sons, Inc.

Neef, D. (2003). Strategy and Risk Management: An Integrated Practical Approach. Taylor & Francis Ltd.

Packendorff, J. (1995). Inquiring into the temporary organization: New directions for project management research. *Scandinavian Journal of Management*, *11*(4).

Plantinga, A. (2007). *Performance Measurement and Evaluation*. Munich Personal RePEc Archive (MPRA), MPRA Paper No 5048, September 2007.

Rael, R. (2017). Managing Corporation Reputation and Risk: A Strategic Approach Using Knowledge Management. John Wiley & Sons.

Ramirez, J. (2017). *Liquidity Management: Handbook of Basel III Capital: Enhancing Bank Capital in Practice*. John Wiley & Sons.

Redington, F. M. (1952). Review of the Principles of Life Office Valuations. *Journal of the Institute of Actuaries, 78*(3), 286-340.

Singhal, P., Agarwal, G., & Mittal, M. L. (2011). Supply chain risk management: Review, classification and future research directions. *International Journal of Business Science and Applied Management*, *6*(3), 15–42. DOI: 10.69864/ijbsam.6-3.75

Siviy, J. M., Penn, L. M., & Stoddard, R. W. (2007). *CMMI® and Six Sigma: Partners in Process Improvement*. Addison-Wesley Professional.

SST. (2004). *White Paper of the Swiss Solvency Test*. Swiss Federal Office of Private Insurance. http://www.naic.org/documents/committees_smi_int_solvency_switzerland_sst_wp.pdf

Stulz, R. M. (1996). *Rethinking Risk Management*. Journal of Applied Corporate Finance.

Tarantino, A., & Cernauskas, D. (2009). *Risk Management in Finance: Six Sigma and Other Next-Generation Techniques*. Wiley.

Winston, W. L. (2000). *Decision Models Using Simulation and Optimization*. Palisade Corporation.

Winston, W. L. (2001). *Decision Models Using Simulation and Optimization II*. Palisade Corporation.

Chapter 1
Oil Drilling Schedule

ABSTRACT

The Initial Oil Drilling Schedule Model With Uncertainty estimates a schedule of capital expenditures and production and shows how this schedule depends on the anticipated volumes of oil recovery. The Initial model here does this for a 5-year planning period. The uncertainties, treated here as normal, are the inputs to the amount of recovery (area, net pay, and recovery rate). These are multiplied to get the recoverable amount. The Oil Drilling Schedule Basic @RISK Model expands on the Initial Model With Uncertainty. Each of the inputs to the reserve size (area, net pay, and recovery rate) is modeled with triangular distributions. (The parameters of these distributions would come from experts' knowledge about the current site and similar historical sites.) These lead to the histogram of Recoverable shown. This looks like a lognormal shape. In general, when random quantities are multiplied, the resulting product typically has a lognormal shape.

INTRODUCTION

Oil Drilling Schedule

Directional drilling is a technique used by oil extraction companies to access oil in underground reserves. Directional drilling is also called directional boring. Most oil wells are positioned above the targeted res-

DOI: 10.4018/979-8-3373-0959-0.ch001

ervoir, so accessing them involves drilling vertically from the surface through to the well below.

However, directional drilling is different because it involves drilling at a non-vertical angle. (Directional drilling is used to describe any drilling that doesn't go straight down.)

The main benefit of directional drilling is that it enables companies to exploit multiple oil reservoirs with a single well, thereby reducing the total cost of drilling while also limiting the environmental impact of drilling.

Key Features

- Directional drilling is the practice of accessing an underground oil or gas reserve by drilling in a non-vertical direction.
- Directional drilling is also called directional boring.
- Directional drilling increases the efficiency of oil and gas extraction and can also lessen the environmental impact of drilling.
- Although directional drilling has been used since the 1920s, modern technological improvements to the technique have increased its accuracy and safety.
- The main benefit of directional drilling is that it enables companies to exploit multiple oil reservoirs with a single well.

The practice of directional drilling has been used since the 1920s throughout the oil and gas industry. In its early years, directional drilling involved using the same basic equipment as vertical wells, except the drilling itself was done at a non-vertical angle.

Modern directional drilling techniques have refined this process by using drill bits that can bend to better accommodate non-vertical angles. Additional technologies, such as the use of hydraulic jets that adjust and guide the drill direction, have further improved the efficiency and reliability of this process.

Today, drill operators can use computers to adjust the angle of the drill bit in real-time and can even use GPS signals to pinpoint the exact location of an oil and gas field. Using advanced software programs, engineers can create 3-D models of the oil fields to determine the optimal location for the well, as well as the best possible entry point for directional drilling.

Directional drilling is also used in the installation of utility pipelines and conduits.

Furthermore, directional drilling can be much more cost-effective. Oil rigs and their staff sometimes have day rates that are upwards of hundreds of thousands of dollars. With directional drilling, one rig alone may be able to work up to five or ten square miles (compared to having a dozen or more vertical rigs).

Directional drilling can be especially useful in situations where the underground reservoir has an abnormal shape and vertical entry is considered impractical. Directional drilling may also be preferable if there have been concerns expressed by residents living near the surface drill sites.

By limiting the number of surface wells used, directional drilling reduces soil disturbance and can make the oil extraction process less disruptive to nearby residents and other stakeholders in the vicinity. By reducing the fractures to existing rock formations, directional drilling also reduces the contamination of groundwater pollution, further protecting the ecosystem and adjacent areas.

Because directional drilling can permit a single location to be used to access multiple underground reservoirs, it can enable oil companies to explore smaller and less-proven reserves that would otherwise not be economical to access. Depending on the location, directional drilling can produce greater amounts of oil and gas.

In addition to allowing companies to access reserves that might otherwise be inaccessible, directional drilling can also contribute to site safety. By creating boreholes far in advance of the mine face in question, directional drilling can allow companies to reduce the risk of gas ruptures while developing a new well.

On the other hand, directional drilling can make operating wells more complex, particularly if the well is dug at an inclination of 40 degrees or greater. In addition, as with all construction equipment, directional drilling damages the existing ground (although the impact can be minimized). Many directional drilling rigs are very heavy, run-on tracks, and tend to damage the areas where they traverse and travel.

Pros of Directional Drilling

- Reduces soil disturbance
- Makes the oil extraction process less disruptive to nearby residents and other stakeholders in the vicinity
- Reduces the fractures to existing rock formations
- Reduces the contamination of groundwater pollution
- Protects the ecosystem and adjacent areas
- Contributes to site safety by reducing the risk of gas ruptures while developing a new well

Cons of Directional Drilling

- Can make operating wells more complex
- As with all construction equipment, directional drilling damages the existing ground (although the impact can be minimised)

The maximum length and diameter of directional drilling are determined by the specific site where the drilling is taking place. However, some horizontal drilling rigs have an outside range of up to 9,843 feet.

The cost of directional drilling varies depending on the project. Projects may be priced based on a lump sum, or they may be priced per foot.

Many different factors contribute to the cost of directional drilling, including the soil conditions, the length and depth of the bore, and the location of the job site.

LITERATURE

Piersol et al. (2021): This work has been selected by scholars as being culturally important and is part of the knowledge base of civilisation as we know it. This work is in the public domain in the United States of America, and possibly other nations. Within the United States, you may freely copy and distribute this work, as no entity (individual or corporate) has a copyright on the body of the work. Scholars believe, and we concur, that this work is important enough to be preserved, reproduced, and made generally available to the public. To ensure a quality reading experience, this work has been proofread and republished using a format that seamlessly blends the original graphical elements with text in an easy-to-read typeface. We appreciate your support of the preservation process and thank you for being an important part of keeping this knowledge alive and relevant. Budhu (2015): An accessible, clear, concise, and contemporary course in geotechnical engineering, this key text: i) Strikes a balance between theory and practical applications for an introductory course in soil mechanics; ii) Keeps mechanics to a minimum for the students to appreciate the background, assumptions and limitations of the theories; iii) Discusses implications of the key ideas to provide students with an understanding of the context for their application; iv) Gives a modern explanation of soil behaviour is presented particularly in soil settlement and soil strength; and v) Offers substantial on-line resources to support teaching and learning.

Patterson (2019): Lists of Offshore Drilling Recruitment Companies and Agencies. Offshore drilling companies account for a significant portion of the energy generated in the form of oil and gas across the world. An offshore drilling company obtains crude oil and gasoline from the seabed and supplies it to the global market. The offshore drilling companies are expected to maintain steady growth for the period of forecast owing to the steep demand for crude oil and gas all around the world. Presently, almost 100 countries produce crude oil and gas, however, almost half of the global crude oil production comes from the top five oil-producing countries. Offshore drilling of oil has witnessed a decline in the past two decades, but recent market trends suggest there is going to be growth for the list of offshore drilling companies due to surging prices of crude oil and high demand for fossil fuel across the globe for the coming five years. The global market for offshore drilling of oil is estimated to surpass a value of $125 billion by the end of 2023 growing at a CAGR of more than 4.5% for the coming five years. Russia and Saudi are the two largest oil-producing countries in the world with a 13% market share for global crude oil production. The United States is the third largest oil producer with a 12% market share, followed by Iraq and Iran with a share of 6% and 5% respectively. An offshore drilling company is capable of extracting petroleum from as deep as 1,500 meters from the seabed.

Patterson (2022): For those people who are searching for an oil rig job with no experience, it might be very difficult to know where to start. However, it's not as difficult as most people think. In this guide, I explain how to get a job on an oil rig and provide important career information, including the typical work environment and skills in this career. HowExpert Press (Author) et al. (2017): If you want to learn about oil drilling as a beginner, then check out this book! How to drill an oil and gas well from A to Z, or in a shorter form from one to seven. The first step is to determine what type of rock we will be drilling. The second step is to refine this preliminary well configuration by determining the exact dimensions required for casing strings. Afterward, the third stage is to select the appropriate bits, bottom hole assembly (BHA), and drill string for each hole section. The fourth step is a big one, selecting a rig, which goes hand in hand with the abovementioned characteristics of drilling a well. Eventually, we get a shortlist and go to the market to close the best fit-for-purpose rig contract. The fifth step is the huge logistics framework that surrounds a drilling operation to ensure it goes smoothly and most important of all, for safety to prevail. The sixth step is to plug and abandon the well. Gladly, strict regulations have been put in place to ensure industry best practices are always followed. Finally, the seventh step encompasses all the previous six, which is to assess and mitigate the environmental impact of all the operations. Safety is, from the beginning until the end of oil and gas drilling, the number one priority.

Piersol et al. (2021): This work has been selected by scholars as being culturally important and is part of the knowledge base of civilisation as we know it. This work is in the public domain in the United States of America, and possibly other nations. Within the United States, you may freely copy and distribute this work, as no entity (individual or corporate) has a copyright on the body of the work. Scholars believe, and we concur, that this work is important enough to be preserved, reproduced, and made generally available to the public. To ensure a quality reading experience, this work has been proofread and republished using a format that seamlessly blends the original graphical elements with text in an easy-to-read typeface. We appreciate your support of the preservation process and thank you for being an important part of keeping this knowledge alive and relevant. Budhu (2015): A concise, and contemporary course in geotechnical engineering, this key text: i) Strikes a balance between theory and practical applications; ii) Keeps mechanics to a minimum for the students; iii) Discusses implications of the key ideas to provide students with an understanding of the context for their application; iv) Gives a modern explanation of soil; and v) Offers substantial on-line resources.

Selley (1978): Academic Journal Offprint from: - Quartal Journal Geological Society, 135, Part 1, 1978. 13pp, 16figs, Printed Card Cover, VGC. Hawkins (1978): Academic Journal Offprint from: - Quartal Journal Geological Society, 135, Part 1, 1978. 17pp, 10figs, 3 b/wpls, Printed Card Cover, VGC. ELABORATION

Simulation 1 Calculations (Define)

The Known Inputs are presented in Table 1:

Table 1. Known inputs

Year	1	2	3	4	5
Min capital expenditures ($MM)	30	40	30	0	0
Max capital expenditures ($MM)	50	75	75	40	20
Min number of wells	8	8	4	0	0
Max number of wells	10	10	10	5	5

The Uncertain Inputs on Reserve Size (*but treated here as known*) are presented in Table 2:

Table 2. Uncertain inputs on reserve size

Area (acres)	=@RiskNormal(2000,200)
Net Pay (feet)	=@RiskNormal(150,15)
Recovery Rate (STB/Acre-Foot)	=@RiskNormal(120,12)

The Outputs are presented in Table 3:

Table 3. Outputs

Recoverable (MMSTB)	=@RiskOutput("Recoverable STB (MM)") + PRODUCT(C10,C11,C12)/10^6
Relative Size	=@RiskOutput()+MIN(1,MAX(0,(C15-E15)/(F15-E15)))

The *fixed* numbers were found by simulating to estimate the 1st and 99th percentiles of the recoverable amount. They are used to generate the relative size shown in Table 4:

Table 4. The 1st and 99th percentiles of the recoverable STB (MM)

1st Percentile	99th Percentile
18	142

The Capital Expenditures for five years and Total are shown in Table 5:

Table 5. Capital expenditures of five years with total

Year	1	2	3	4	5	5
Capital Expend ($MM)	= @Risk Output(," CapEx Series",1)+ C4+ $C$16* (C5-C4)	=@Risk Output(," CapEx Series",2)+ D4+ $C$16* (D5-D4)	=@Risk Output(," CapEx Series",3)+ E4+ $C$16* (E5-C4)	=@Risk Output(," CapEx Series",4)+ F4+ $C$16* (F5-F4)	=@Risk Output(," CapEx Series",5)+ G4+ $C$16* (G5-G4)	=@Risk Output(" Total CapEx")+ SUM(C19 : G19)
Number of Wells	=@Risk Output(," NWells Series",1) +C6+$C$16* (C7-C6)	=@Risk Output(," NWells Series",2) +D6+$C$16* (D7-D6)	=@Risk Output(,"NWells Series",3) +E6+$C$16* (E7-E6)	=@Risk Output(,"NWells Series",4) +F6+$C$16* (F7-F6)	=@Risk Output(,"NWells Series",2) +G6+$C$16* (G7-G6)	

Simulation 2 Calculations (Define)

The Known Inputs are presented in Table 6:

Table 6. Known inputs

Year	1	2	3	4	5
Min capital expenditures ($MM)	30	40	30	0	0
Max capital expenditures ($MM)	50	75	75	40	20
Min number of wells	8	8	4	0	0
Max number of wells	10	10	10	5	5

The Uncertain Inputs on Reserve Size (*but treated here as known*) are presented in Table 7:

Table 7. Uncertain inputs on reserve size

Area (acres)	=@RiskTriang(F10,G10,H10)
Net Pay (feet)	=@RiskTriang(F11,G11,H11)
Recovery Rate (STB/Acre-Foot)	=@RiskTriang(F12,G12,H12)

The Triangular Distribution Parameter in Table 8:

Table 8. Triangular distribution parameter

Distribution	Min	Most likely	Max
Triangular	1000	2000	4000
Triangular	80	150	350
Triangular	80	120	200

The Outputs are presented in Table 9, and the *fixed* numbers were found by simulating to estimate the 1st and 99th percentiles of the recoverable amount, generating the relative size shown in Table 10.

Table 9. Outputs

Recoverable (MMSTB)	=@RiskOutput("Recoverable STB (MM)") + PRODUCT(C10,C11,C12)/10^6
Relative Size	50%

Table 10. The 1st and 99th percentiles of the recoverable STB (MM)

1st Percentile	99th Percentile
18	142

The Capital Expenditures for five years and Total are shown in Table 11:

Table 11. Capital expenditures of five years with total

Year	1	2	3	4	5	5
Capital Expend ($MM)	= @Risk Output(," CapEx Series",1) + C4+ $C$16* (C5-C4)	=@Risk Output(," CapEx Series",2) + D4+ $C$16* (D5-D4)	=@Risk Output(," CapEx Series",3) + E4+ $C$16* (E5-C4)	=@Risk Output(," CapEx Series",4) + F4+$C$16* (F5-F4)	=@Risk Output(," CapEx Series",5) + G4+$C$16* (G5-G4)	=@Risk Output(" Total CapEx") +SUM (C19:G19)
Number of Wells	=@Risk Output(," NWells Series",1) +C6+ $C$16* (C7-C6)	=@Risk Output(," NWells Series",2) +D6+ $C$16* (D7-D6)	=@Risk Output(," NWells Series",3) +E6+ $C$16* (E7-E6)	=@Risk Output(," NWells Series",4) +F6+ $C$16* (F7-F6)	=@Risk Output(," NWells Series",2) +G6+ $C$16* (G7-G6)	

Simulation1: Risk Evaluation and Sensitivity Analysis

Recoverable STB (MM) Analysis and Evaluation

Figure 1 displays the Recoverable STB (MM) distribution.

Figure 1. Recoverable STB (MM) distribution

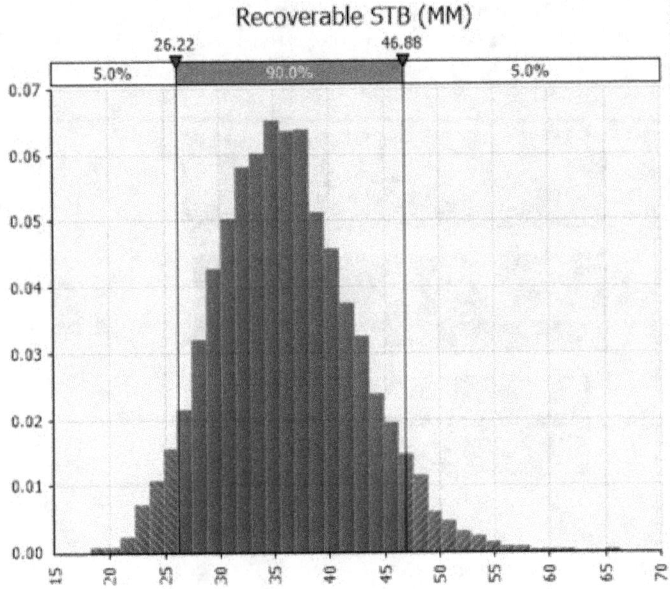

Statistics	Recoverable STB (M...
Cell	C15
Minimum	18.191
Maximum	66.221
Mean	35.997
90% CI	±0.145
Mode	37.639
Median	35.657
Std Dev	6.242
Skewness	0.3211
Kurtosis	3.1390
Values	5000
Errors	0
Filtered	0
Left X	26.22
Left P	5.0%
Right X	46.88
Right P	95.0%
Dif. X	20.657
Dif. P	90.0%

The Recoverable STB Minimum is 18.191 STB (MM) and the Maximum is 66.221 STB (MM). The Recoverable STB *Mean* is 35.997 STB (MM), and the *Standard Deviation* is 6.246 STB (MM). There is a 5% probability that the Recoverable STB will be below 26.22 STB (MM), a 90% probability will be in the range of 26.22 STB (MM) – 46.88 STB (MM); and a 5% probability that it will be above 46.88 STB (MM) as shown on the graph.

Sensitivity Analysis

Sensitivity analysis provides for identifying and quantifying the main contributors to variability and risk based on the probability distribution.

The Inputs Ranked by Effect on Output Mean are given in Figure 2.

The graph illustrates that the effect of the top variable Net Pay (feet), on the Recoverable STB is a change in the range of 29.499 MM to 42.376 MM, which are respectively left and right from the Baseline of 35.997 MM, which is marked on the graph. Other variables are less influential as their associated effect has smaller arrays.

Figure 2. Recoverable STB (MM) inputs ranked by effect on output mean

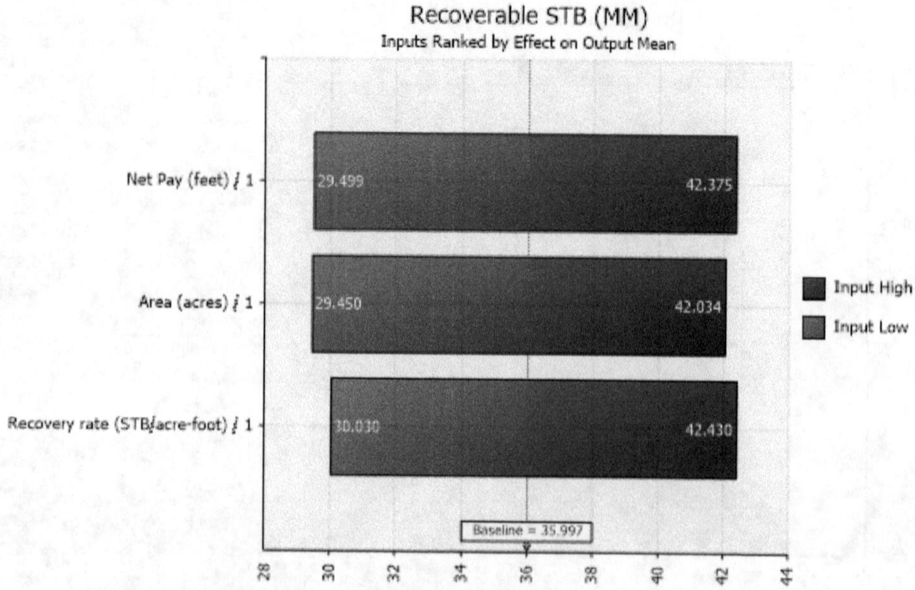

Total Capital Expenditure ($MM) Analysis and Evaluation

Figure 3 displays the Total Capital Expenditure distribution. The Total Capital Expenditure Minimum is $100.247 MM, and the Maximum is $162.221 MM. The Total Capital Expenditure *Mean* is $123.222 MM, and the *Standard Deviation* is $8.055 MM. There is a 5% probability that the Total Capital Expenditure will be below $110.6 MM, a 90% probability that it will be in the range of $110.6 MM – $137.3 MM; and a 5% probability that it will be above $137.3 MM as shown on the graph.

Figure 3. Total capital expenditure distribution

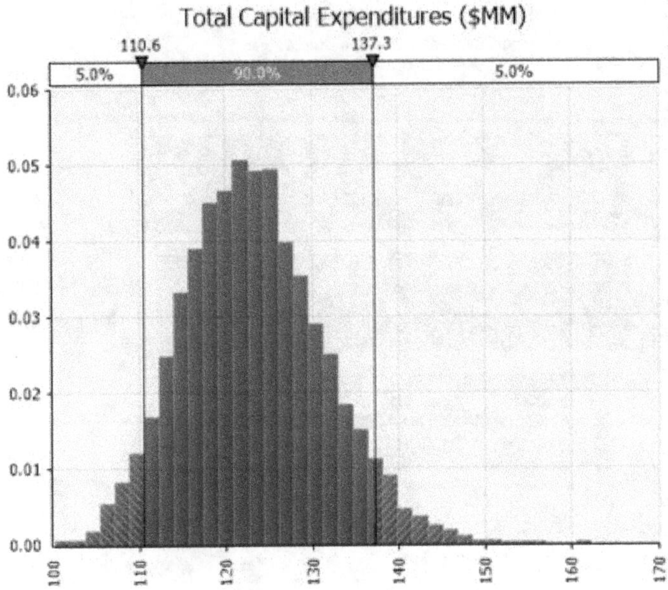

Statistics	Total Capital Expen...
Cell	H19
Minimum	100.247
Maximum	162.221
Mean	123.222
90% CI	±0.187
Mode	125.341
Median	122.783
Std Dev	8.055
Skewness	0.3211
Kurtosis	3.1390
Values	5000
Errors	0
Filtered	0
Left X	110.6
Left P	5.0%
Right X	137.3
Right P	95.0%
Dif. X	26.654
Dif. P	90.0%

Sensitivity Analysis

Sensitivity analysis provides for identifying and quantifying the main contributors to variability and risk based on the probability distribution.

The Inputs Ranked by Effect on Output Mean are given in Figure 4.

The graph illustrates that the effect of the top variable Net Pay (feet) / 1, on the Total Capital Expenditure is a change in the range of $114.84 MM to $131.45 MM, which are respectively left and right from the Baseline of $123.222 MM, which is marked on the graph. Other variables are less influential as their associated effect has smaller arrays.

Figure 4. Total capital expenditures inputs ranked by effect on output mean

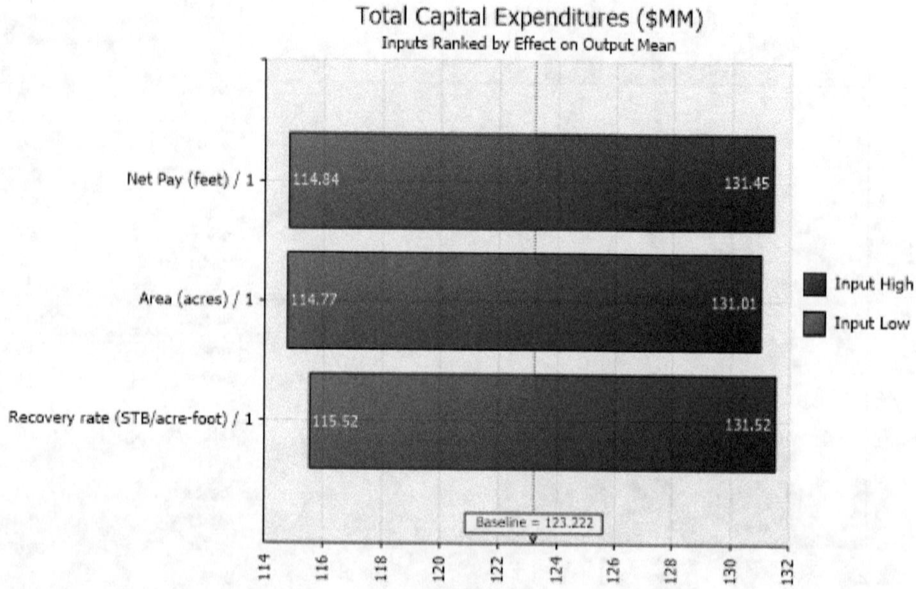

Capital Expenditure and Number of Wells for Year 1 Analysis and Evaluation

Figure 5 displays the Capital Expenditure Year 1 distribution. The Capital Expenditure Year 1 Minimum is $30.0308 MM, and the Maximum is $37.7776 MM. The Capital Expenditure Year 1 *Mean* is $32.9028 MM, and the *Standard Deviation* is $1.0069 MM. There is a 5% probability that the Capital Expenditure Year 1 will be below $31.33 MM, a 90% probability will be in the range of $31.33 MM – $34.66 MM; and a 5% probability that it will be above $34.66 MM as shown on the graph.

Figure 5. Capital expenditure year 1 distribution

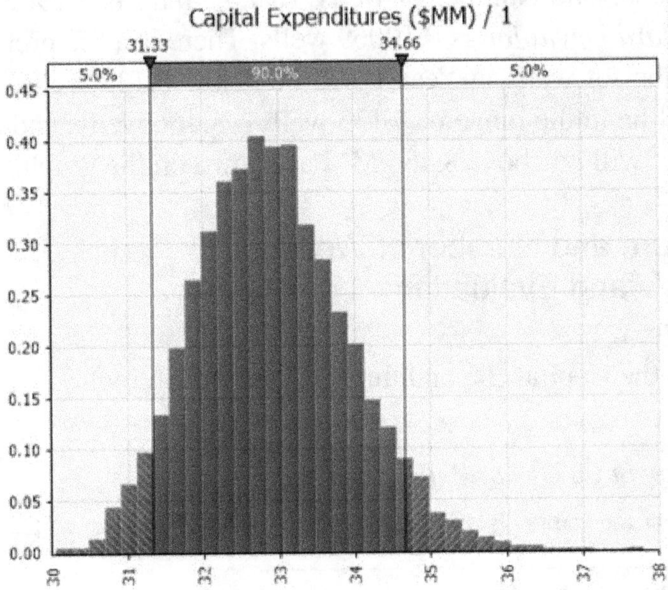

Statistics	Capital Expenditure...
Cell	C19
Minimum	30.0308
Maximum	37.7776
Mean	32.9028
90% CI	± 0.0234
Mode	33.1677
Median	32.8479
Std Dev	1.0069
Skewness	0.3211
Kurtosis	3.1390
Values	5000
Errors	0
Filtered	0
Left X	31.33
Left P	5.0%
Right X	34.66
Right P	95.0%
Dif. X	3.3317
Dif. P	90.0%

Figure 6 displays the number of wells in the Year 1 distribution.

Figure 6. Number of wells year 1 distribution

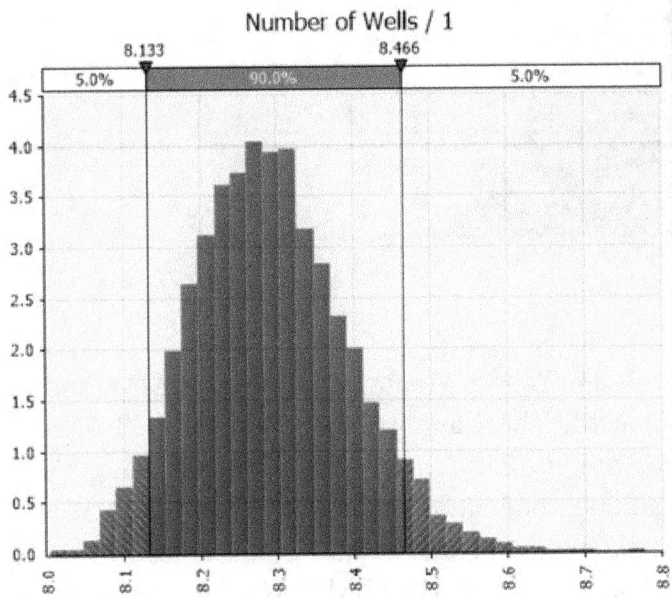

Statistics	Number of Wells / 1
Cell	C20
Minimum	8.00308
Maximum	8.77776
Mean	8.29028
90% CI	± 0.00234
Mode	8.31677
Median	8.28479
Std Dev	0.10069
Skewness	0.3211
Kurtosis	3.1390
Values	5000
Errors	0
Filtered	0
Left X	8.133
Left P	5.0%
Right X	8.466
Right P	95.0%
Dif. X	0.33317
Dif. P	90.0%

The Number of wells Year 1 Minimum is 8.00308 wells, and the Maximum is 8.77776 wells. The Number of wells Year 1 *Mean* is 8.29028 wells, and the *Standard Deviation* is 0.10069 wells. There is a 5% probability that the number of wells in Year 1 will be below 8.133 wells, a 90% probability will be in the range of 8.133 wells – 8.466 wells; and a 5% probability that it will be above 8.466 MM as shown on the graph.

Capital Expenditure and Number of Wells for Year 2 Analysis and Evaluation

Figure 7 displays the Capital Expenditure Year 2 distribution.

Figure 7. Capital expenditure year 2 distribution

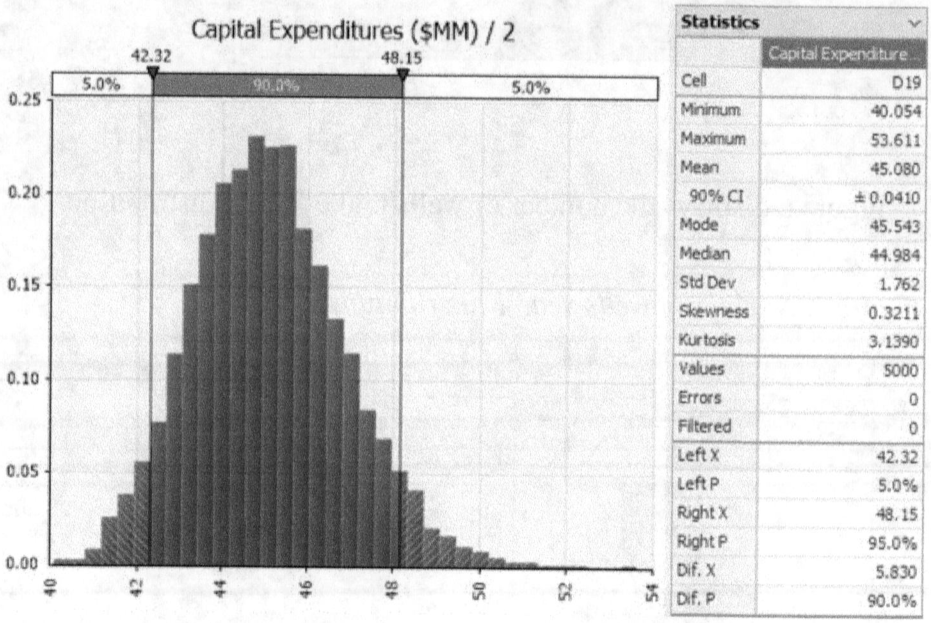

The Capital Expenditure Year 2 Minimum is $40.054 MM, and the Maximum is $53.611 MM. The Capital Expenditure Year 2 *Mean* is $45.080 MM, and the *Standard Deviation* is $1.762 MM. There is a 5% probability that the Capital Expenditure Year 2 will be below $42.32 MM, a 90% probability will be in the range of $42.32 MM – $48.15 MM; and a 5% probability that it will be above $48.15 MM as shown on the graph.

Figure 8 displays the Number of wells Year 2 distribution.

The Number of wells Year 2 Minimum is 8.00308 wells, and the Maximum is 10 wells. The Number of wells Year 2 *Mean* is 8.77776 wells, and the *Standard Deviation* is 0.10069 wells. There is a 5% probability that the number of wells in Year 2 will be below 8.133 wells, a 90% probability will be in the range of 8.133 wells – 8.466 wells; and a 5% probability that it will be above 8.466 wells as shown on the graph.

Figure 8. Number of wells year 2 distribution

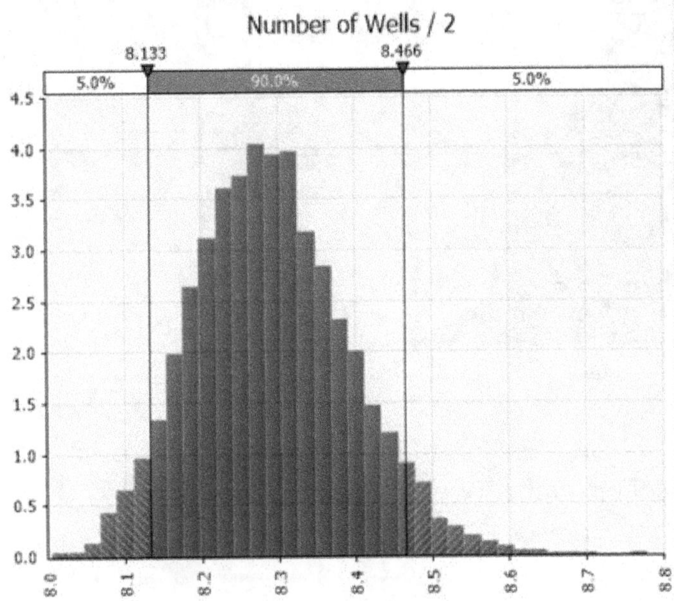

Statistics	Number of Wells / 2
Cell	D20
Minimum	8.00308
Maximum	8.77776
Mean	8.29028
90% CI	± 0.00234
Mode	8.31677
Median	8.28479
Std Dev	0.10069
Skewness	0.3211
Kurtosis	3.1390
Values	5000
Errors	0
Filtered	0
Left X	8.133
Left P	5.0%
Right X	8.466
Right P	95.0%
Dif. X	0.33317
Dif. P	90.0%

Capital Expenditure and Number of Wells for Year 3 Analysis and Evaluation

Figure 9 displays the Capital Expenditure Year 3 distribution.

The Capital Expenditure Year 3 Minimum is $30.069 MM, and the Maximum is $47.500 MM. The Capital Expenditure Year 3 *Mean* is $36.531 MM, and the *Standard Deviation* is $2.265 MM. There is a 5% probability that the Capital Expenditure Year 3 will be below $32.98 MM, a 90% probability will be in the range of $32.98 MM – $40.48 MM; and a 5% probability that it will be above $40.48 MM as shown on the graph.

Figure 9. Capital expenditure year 3 distribution

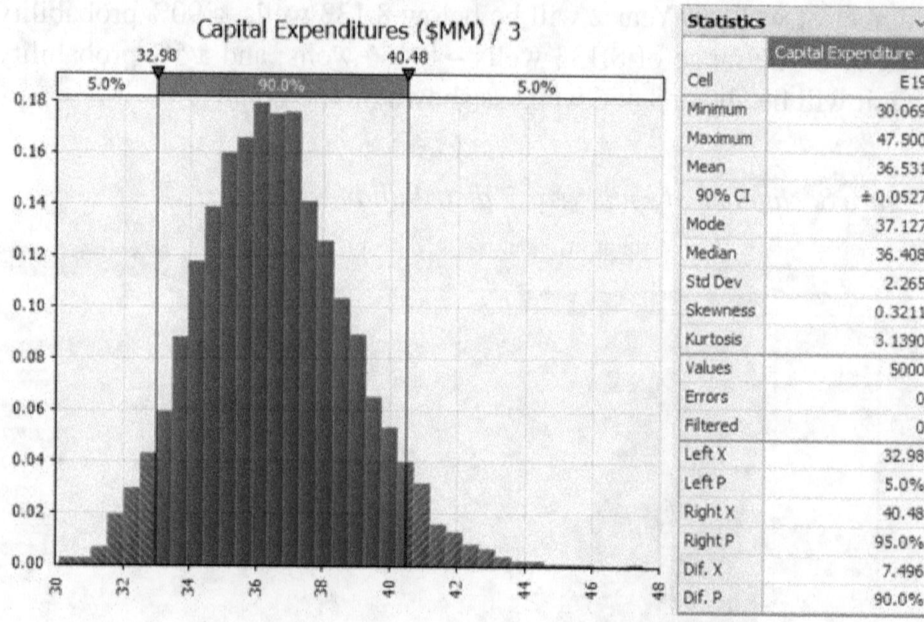

Figure 10 displays the Number of wells Year 3 distribution.

Figure 10. Number of wells year 3 distribution

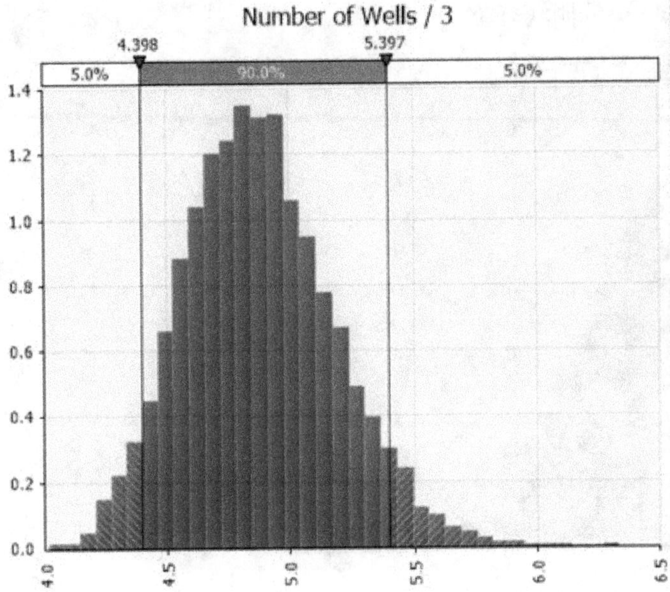

Statistics	Number of Wells / 3
Cell	E20
Minimum	4.0093
Maximum	6.3333
Mean	4.8708
90% CI	± 0.00703
Mode	4.9503
Median	4.8544
Std Dev	0.3021
Skewness	0.3211
Kurtosis	3.1390
Values	5000
Errors	0
Filtered	0
Left X	4.398
Left P	5.0%
Right X	5.397
Right P	95.0%
Dif. X	0.9995
Dif. P	90.0%

The Number of wells Year 3 Minimum is 4.0093 wells and the Maximum is 6.3333 wells. The Number of wells Year 3 *Mean* is 4.8708 wells and the *Standard Deviation* is 0.3021 wells. There is a 5% probability that the number of wells in Year 3 will be below 4.398 wells, a 90% probability will be in the range of 4.398 wells – 5.397 wells; and a 5% probability that it will be above 5.397 wells as shown on the graph.

Capital Expenditure and Number of Wells for Year 4 Analysis and Evaluation

Figure 11 displays the Capital Expenditure Year 4 distribution.

Figure 11. Capital expenditure year 4 distribution

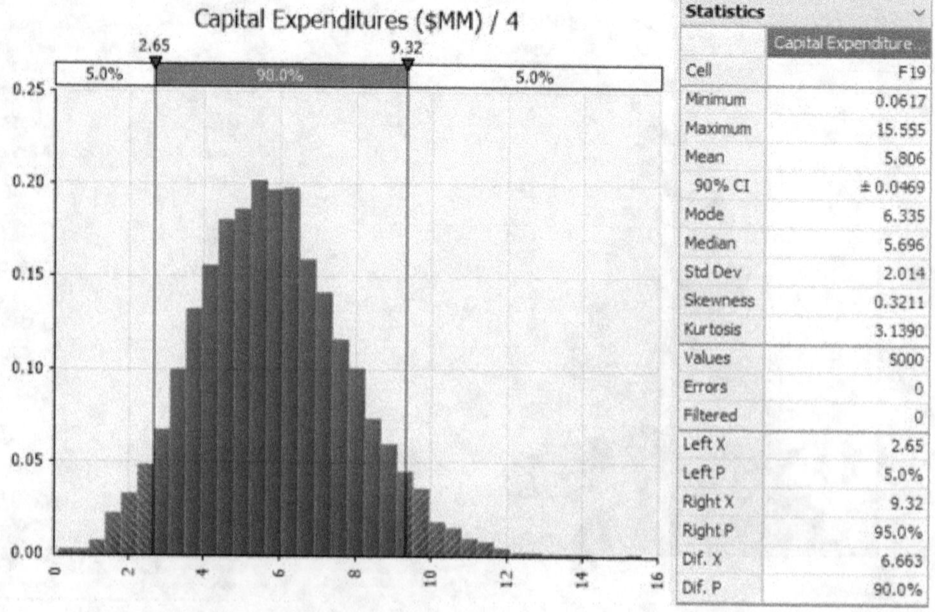

The Capital Expenditure Year 4 Minimum is 0.0617 MM, and the Maximum is $15.555 MM. The Capital Expenditure Year 4 *Mean* is $5.806 MM, and the *Standard Deviation* is $2.014 MM. There is a 5% probability that the Capital Expenditure Year 4 will be below $2.65 MM, a 90% probability will be in the range of $2.65 MM – $9.32 MM; and a 5% probability that it will be above $9.32 MM as shown on the graph.

Figure 12 displays the Number of wells Year 4 distribution.

The Number of wells Year 4 Minimum is 0.00771 wells, and the Maximum is 1.9444 wells. The Number of wells Year 4 *Mean* is 0.7257 wells, and the *Standard Deviation* is 0.2517 wells. There is a 5% probability that the number of wells in Year 4 will be below 0.331 wells, a 90% probability will be in the range of 0.331 wells – 1.164 wells; and a 5% probability that it will be above 1.164 wells as shown on the graph.

Figure 12. Number of wells Year 4 distribution

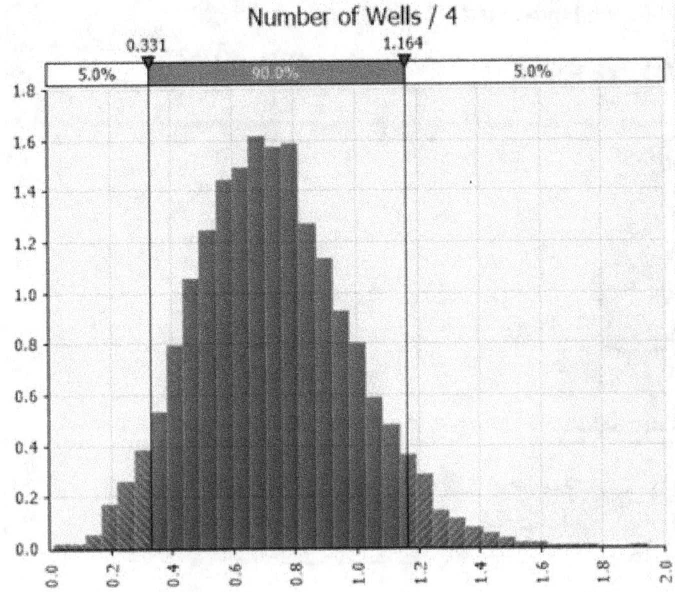

Statistics	Number of Wells / 4
Cell	F20
Minimum	0.00771
Maximum	1.9444
Mean	0.7257
90% CI	± 0.00586
Mode	0.7919
Median	0.7120
Std Dev	0.2517
Skewness	0.3211
Kurtosis	3.1390
Values	5000
Errors	0
Filtered	0
Left X	0.331
Left P	5.0%
Right X	1.164
Right P	95.0%
Dif. X	0.8329
Dif. P	90.0%

Capital Expenditure and Number of Wells for Year 5 Analysis and Evaluation

Figure 13 displays the Capital Expenditure Year 5 distribution.

The Capital Expenditure Year 5 Minimum is 0.0308 MM, and the Maximum is \$7.776 MM. The Capital Expenditure Year 5 *Mean* is \$2.9028 MM, and the *Standard Deviation* is \$1.0069 MM. There is a 5% probability that the Capital Expenditure Year 5 will be below \$1.33 MM, a 90% probability will be in the range of \$1.33 MM – \$4.66 MM; and a 5% probability that it will be above \$4.66 MM as shown on the graph.

Figure 13. Capital expenditure year 5 distribution

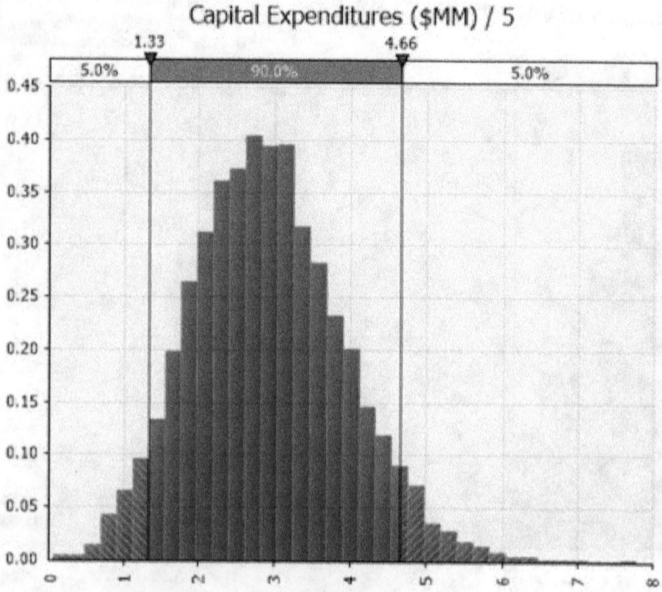

Statistics	Capital Expenditure...
Cell	G19
Minimum	0.0308
Maximum	7.7776
Mean	2.9028
90% CI	± 0.0234
Mode	3.1677
Median	2.8479
Std Dev	1.0069
Skewness	0.3211
Kurtosis	3.1390
Values	5000
Errors	0
Filtered	0
Left X	1.33
Left P	5.0%
Right X	4.66
Right P	95.0%
Dif. X	3.3317
Dif. P	90.0%

Figure 14 displays the Number of wells Year 5 distribution.

Figure 14. Number of wells year 5 distribution

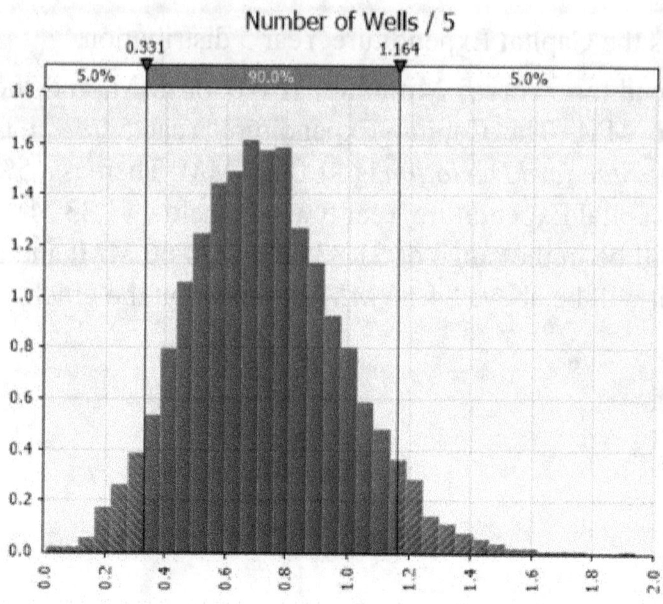

Statistics	Number of Wells / 5
Cell	G20
Minimum	0.00771
Maximum	1.9444
Mean	0.7257
90% CI	± 0.00586
Mode	0.7919
Median	0.7120
Std Dev	0.2517
Skewness	0.3211
Kurtosis	3.1390
Values	5000
Errors	0
Filtered	0
Left X	0.331
Left P	5.0%
Right X	1.164
Right P	95.0%
Dif. X	0.8329
Dif. P	90.0%

The Number of wells Year 5 Minimum is 0.00771 wells, and the Maximum is 1.9444 wells. The Number of wells Year 5 *Mean* is 0.7257 wells, and the *Standard Deviation* is 0.2517 wells. There is a 5% probability that the number of wells in Year 5 will be below 0.331 wells, a 90% probability will be in the range of 0.331 wells – 1.164 wells; and a 5% probability that it will be above 1.164 wells as shown on the graph.

Capital Expenditures Time Series

The Capital Expenditures Time Series is presented in Figure 15 including five years.

Figure 15. Capital expenditures time series

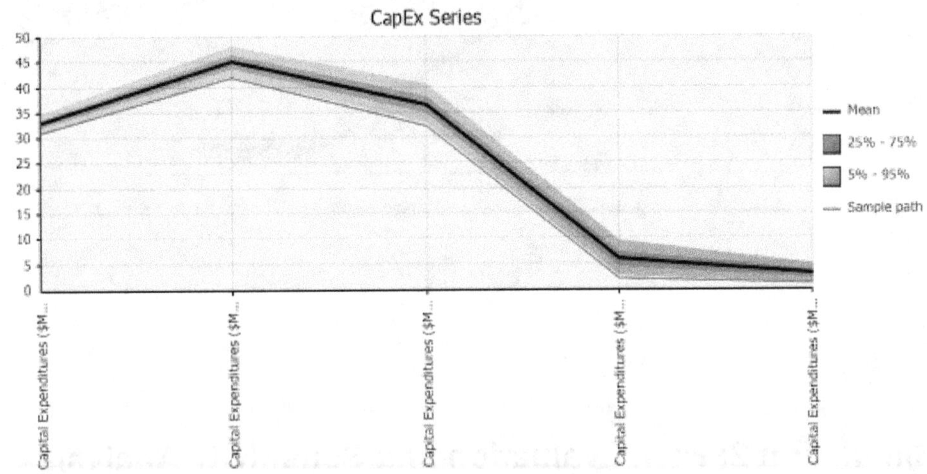

The Capital Expenditures Time Series values are Year 1: $32.903 MM; Year 2: $45.081 MM; Year 3: $36.532 MM; Year 4: $5.806 MM; and Year 5: $2.903 MM.

Number of wells Time Series

The Number of wells Time Series is presented in Figure 16 including five years.

The Number of wells Time Series values are Year 1: 8.290 wells; Year 2: 8.290 wells; Year 3: 4.871 wells; Year 4: 0.726 wells; and Year 5: 0.726 wells.

Figure 16. Number of wells time series

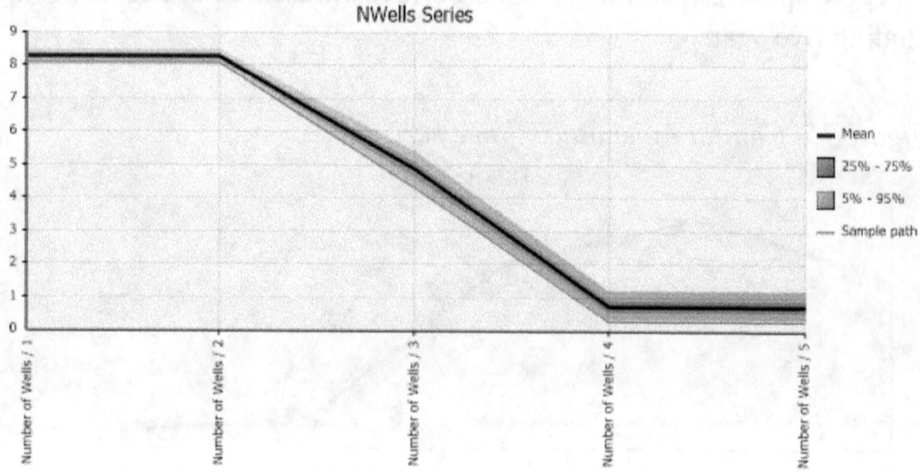

Simulation 2: Risk Evaluation and Sensitivity Analysis

Recoverable STB (MM) Analysis and Evaluation

Figure 17 displays the Recoverable STB (MM) distribution. The Recoverable STB Minimum is 12.01 STB (MM) and the Maximum is 205.35 STB (MM). The Recoverable STB *Mean* is 60.02 STB (MM) and the *Standard Deviation* is 26 STB (MM). There is a 5% probability that the Recoverable STB will be below 25.7 STB (MM), a 90% probability will be in the range of 25.7 STB (MM) – 111.7 STB (MM); and a 5% probability that it will be above 111.7 STB (MM) as shown on the graph.

Figure 17. Recoverable STB (MM) distribution

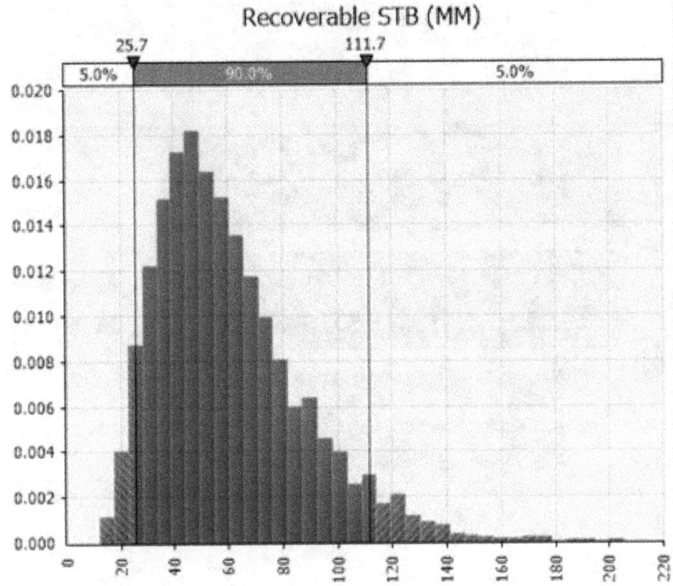

Statistics	Recoverable STB (M...
Cell	C15
Minimum	12.01
Maximum	205.35
Mean	60.02
90% CI	± 0.625
Mode	46.41
Median	54.98
Std Dev	26.86
Skewness	1.0657
Kurtosis	4.5331
Values	5000
Errors	0
Filtered	0
Left X	25.7
Left P	5.0%
Right X	111.7
Right P	95.0%
Dif. X	85.95
Dif. P	90.0%

Sensitivity Analysis: Sensitivity analysis provides for identifying and quantifying the main contributors to variability and risk based on the probability distribution.

The Inputs Ranked by Effect on Output Mean are given in Figure 18.

Figure 18. Recoverable STB inputs ranked by effect on output mean

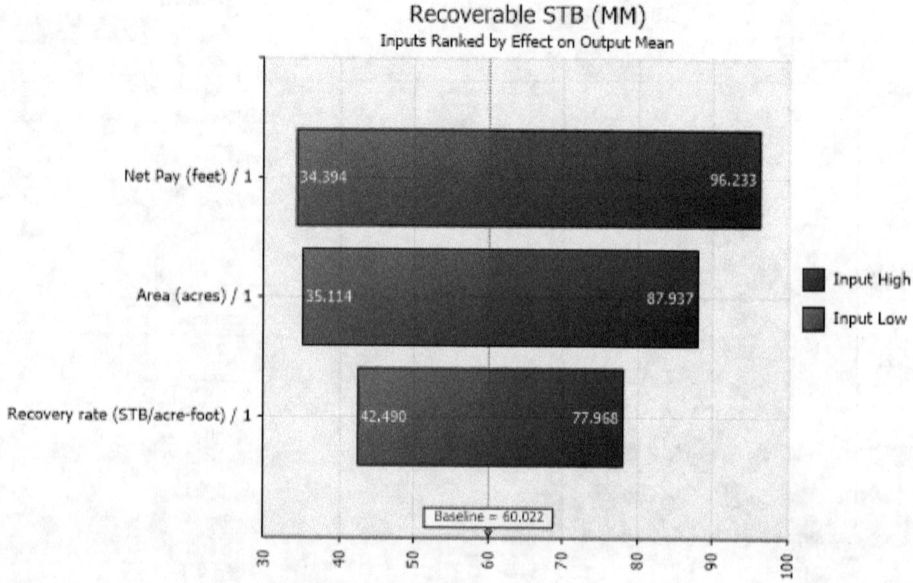

Total Capital Expenditure ($MM) Analysis and Evaluation

Figure 19 displays the Total Capital Expenditure distribution. The Total Capital Expenditure Minimum is $100 MM, and the Maximum is $260 MM. The Total Capital Expenditure *Mean* is $154.01 MM, and the *Standard Deviation* is $33.75 MM. There is a 5% probability that the Total Capital Expenditure will be below $109.9 MM, a 90% probability that it will be in the range of $109.9 MM – $220.9 MM; and a 5% probability that it will be above $220.9 MM as shown on the graph.

Figure 19. Total capital expenditure distribution

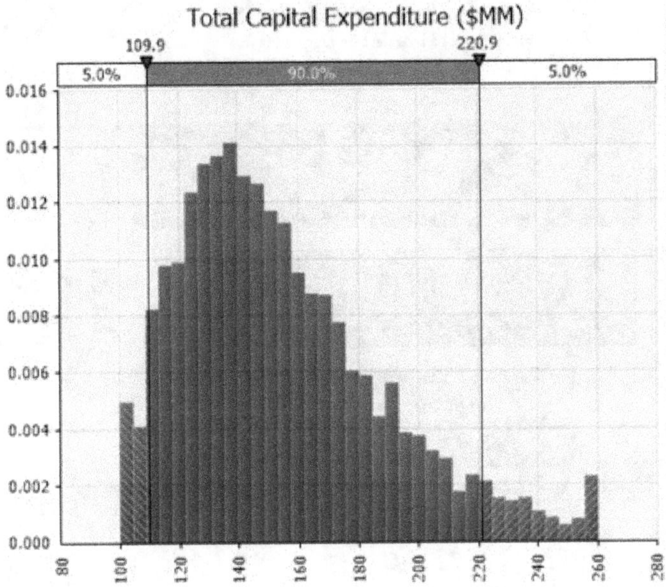

Statistics	Total Capital Expen...
Cell	H19
Minimum	100
Maximum	260
Mean	154.01
90% CI	± 0.785
Mode	260
Median	147.71
Std Dev	33.75
Skewness	0.8767
Kurtosis	3.4716
Values	5000
Errors	0
Filtered	0
Left X	109.9
Left P	5.0%
Right X	220.9
Right P	95.0%
Dif. X	110.90
Dif. P	90.0%

Sensitivity Analysis

Sensitivity analysis provides for identifying and quantifying the main contributors to variability and risk based on the probability distribution.

The Inputs Ranked by Effect on Output Mean are given in Figure 20.

The graph illustrates that the effect of the top variable Net Pay (feet) / 1, on the Total Capital Expenditure is a change in the range of $121.33 MM to $198.81 MM, which are respectively left and right from the Baseline of $154.009 MM, which is marked on the graph. Other variables are less influential as their associated effect has smaller arrays.

Figure 20. Capital expenditure inputs ranked by effect on output mean

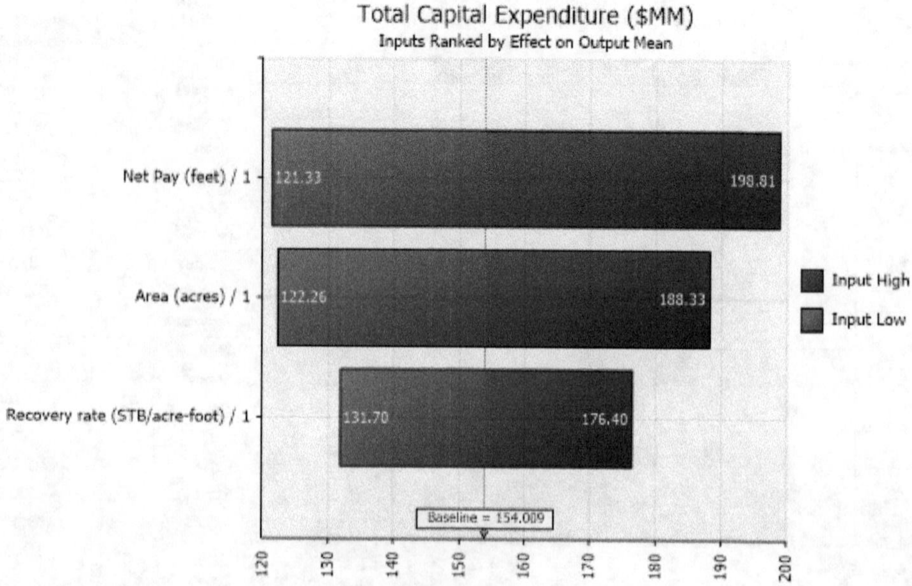

Capital Expenditure and Number of Wells for Year 1 Analysis and Evaluation

Figure 21 displays the Capital Expenditure Year 1 distribution.

The Capital Expenditure Year 1 Minimum is $30 MM, and the Maximum is $50 MM. The Capital Expenditure Year 1 *Mean* is $36.751 MM, and the *Standard Deviation* is $4.218 MM. There is a 5% probability that the Capital Expenditure Year 1 will be below $31.24 MM, a 90% probability will be in the range of $31.24 MM – $45.11 MM; and a 5% probability that it will be above $45.11 MM as shown on the graph.

Figure 21. Capital expenditure year 1 distribution

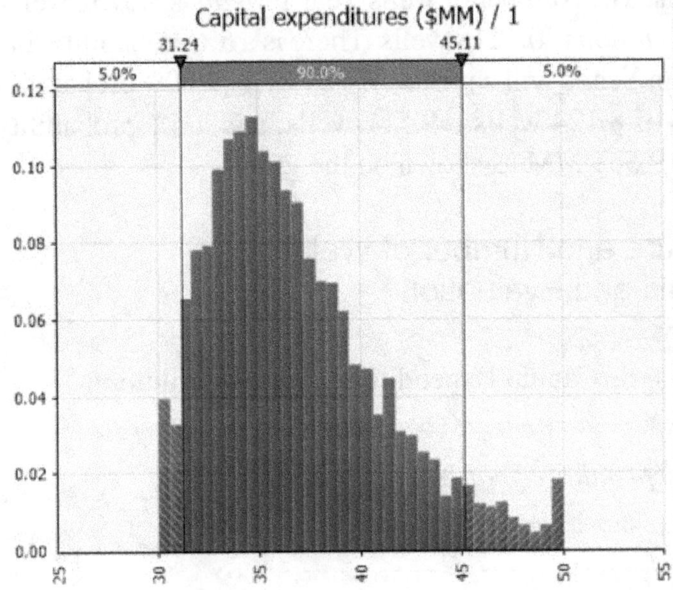

Statistics	Capital expenditure...
Cell	C19
Minimum	30
Maximum	50
Mean	36.751
90% CI	± 0.0982
Mode	50
Median	35.964
Std Dev	4.219
Skewness	0.8767
Kurtosis	3.4716
Values	5000
Errors	0
Filtered	0
Left X	31.24
Left P	5.0%
Right X	45.11
Right P	95.0%
Dif. X	13.863
Dif. P	90.0%

Figure 22 displays the number of wells in the Year 1 distribution.

Figure 22. Number of wells year 1 distribution

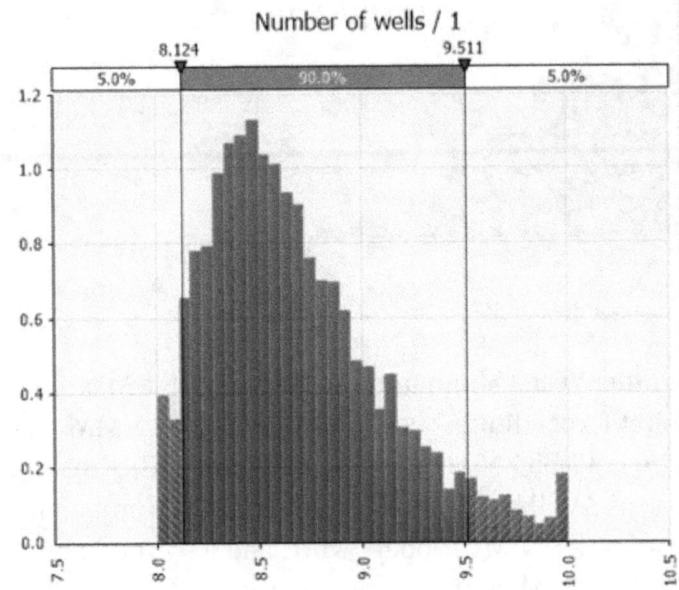

Statistics	Number of wells / 1
Cell	C20
Minimum	8
Maximum	10
Mean	8.6751
90% CI	± 0.00982
Mode	10
Median	8.5964
Std Dev	0.4219
Skewness	0.8767
Kurtosis	3.4716
Values	5000
Errors	0
Filtered	0
Left X	8.124
Left P	5.0%
Right X	9.511
Right P	95.0%
Dif. X	1.3863
Dif. P	90.0%

The Number of wells Year 1 Minimum is eight (8) wells, and the Maximum is ten (10) wells. The Number of wells Year 1 *Mean* is 8.6751 wells, and the *Standard Deviation* is 0.4219 wells. There is a 5% probability that the number of wells in Year 1 will be below 8.124 wells, a 90% probability will be in the range of 8.124 wells – 9.511 wells; and a 5% probability that it will be above 9.551 MM as shown on the graph.

Capital Expenditure and Number of Wells for Year 2 Analysis and Evaluation

Figure 23 displays the Capital Expenditure Year 2 distribution.

Figure 23. Capital expenditure year 2 distribution

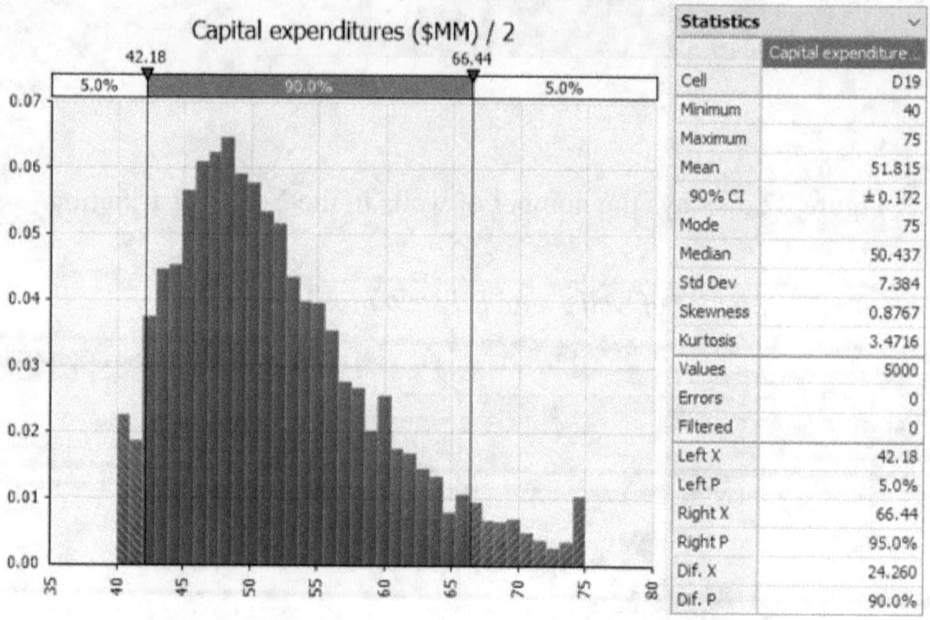

The Capital Expenditure Year 2 Minimum is $40 MM, and the Maximum is $75 MM. The Capital Expenditure Year 2 *Mean* is $51.815 MM, and the *Standard Deviation* is $7.384 MM. There is a 5% probability that the Capital Expenditure Year 2 will be below $42.18 MM, a 90% probability will be in the range of $42.18 MM – $66.44 MM; and a 5% probability that it will be above $66.44 MM as shown on the graph.

Figure 24 displays the Number of wells Year 2 distribution.

The Number of wells in Year 2 Minimum is 8 wells and the Maximum is 10 wells. The Number of wells Year 2 *Mean* is 8.6751 wells, and the *Standard Deviation* is 0.4219 wells. There is a 5% probability that the number of wells in Year 2 will be below 8.124 wells, a 90% probability will be in the range of 8.124 wells – 9.511 wells; and a 5% probability that it will be above 9.511 wells as shown on the graph.

Figure 24. Number of wells year 2 distribution

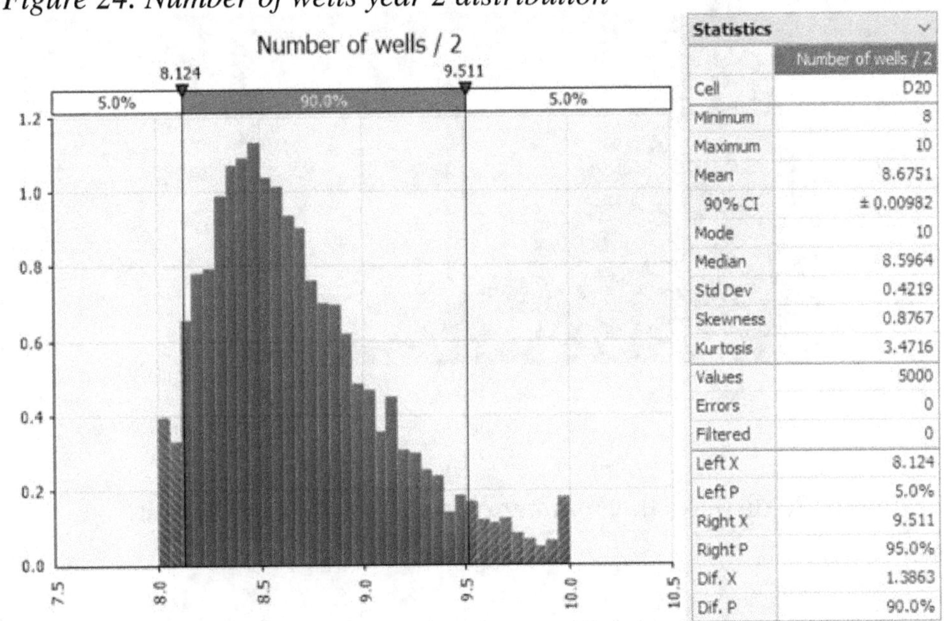

Capital Expenditure and Number of Wells for Year 3 Analysis and Evaluation

Figure 25 displays the Capital Expenditure Year 3 distribution.

The Capital Expenditure Year 3 Minimum is \$30 MM, and the Maximum is \$75 MM. The Capital Expenditure Year 3 *Mean* is \$46.190 MM, and the *Standard Deviation* is \$9.493 MM. There is a 5% probability that the Capital Expenditure Year 3 will be below \$32.08 MM, a 90% probability will be in the range of $32.80 MM – $63.99 MM; and a 5% probability that it will be above $63.99 MM as shown on the graph.

Figure 25. Capital expenditure year 3 distribution

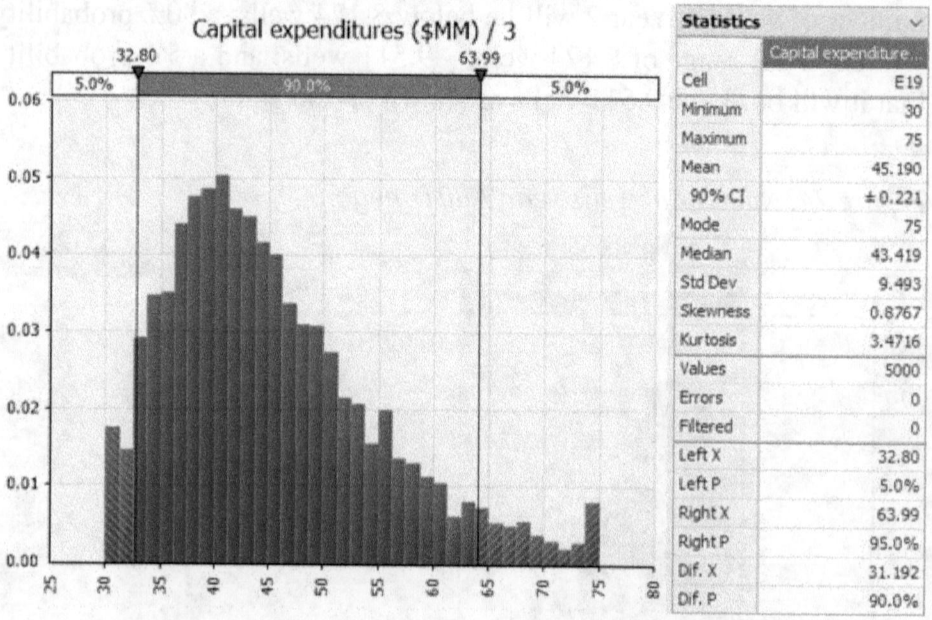

Figure 26 displays the Number of wells Year 3 distribution.

Figure 26. Number of wells year 3 distribution

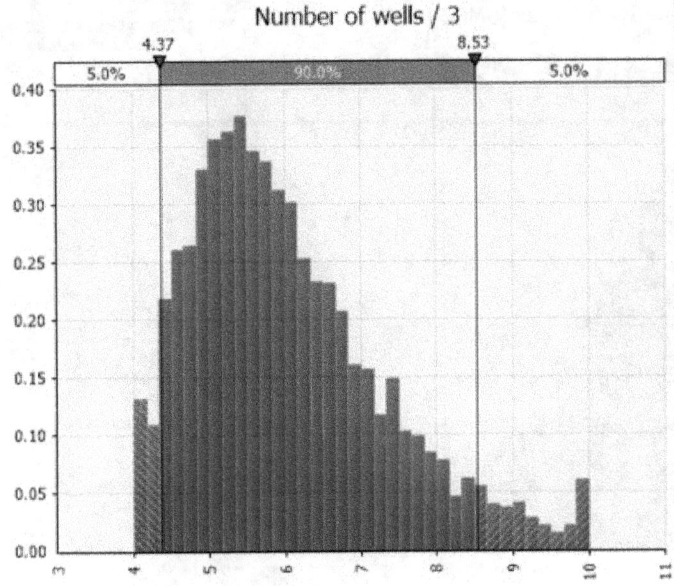

Statistics	Number of wells / 3
Cell	E20
Minimum	4
Maximum	10
Mean	6.0254
90% CI	± 0.0294
Mode	10
Median	5.7892
Std Dev	1.2658
Skewness	0.8767
Kurtosis	3.4716
Values	5000
Errors	0
Filtered	0
Left X	4.37
Left P	5.0%
Right X	8.53
Right P	95.0%
Dif. X	4.1589
Dif. P	90.0%

The Number of wells Year 3 Minimum is 4 wells, and the Maximum is 10 wells. The Number of wells Year 3 *Mean* is 6.0254 wells, and the *Standard Deviation* is 1.2658 wells. There is a 5% probability that the number of wells in Year 3 will be below 4.37 wells, a 90% probability will be in the range of 4.37 wells – 8.53 wells; and a 5% probability that it will be above 8.53 wells as shown on the graph.

Capital Expenditure and Number of Wells for Year 4 Analysis and Evaluation

Figure 27 displays the Capital Expenditure Year 4 distribution.

Figure 27. Capital expenditure year 4 distribution

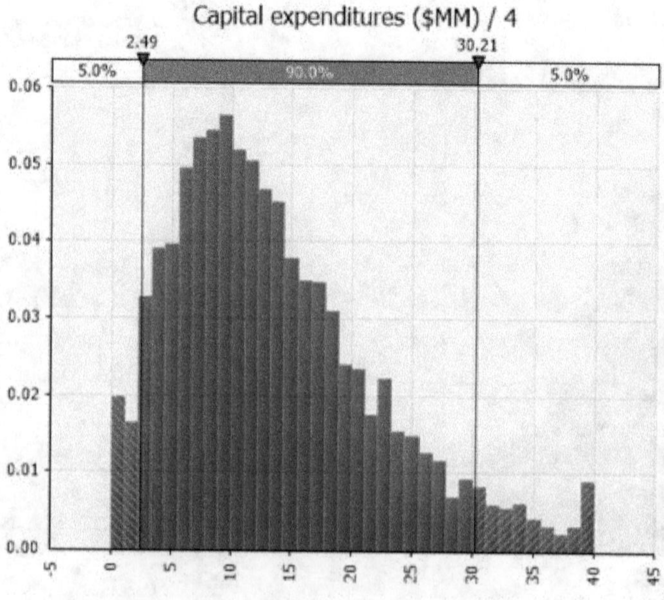

Statistics	Capital expenditure...
Cell	F19
Minimum	0
Maximum	40
Mean	13.502
90% CI	±0.196
Mode	40
Median	11.928
Std Dev	8.439
Skewness	0.8767
Kurtosis	3.4716
Values	5000
Errors	0
Filtered	0
Left X	2.49
Left P	5.0%
Right X	30.21
Right P	95.0%
Dif. X	27.726
Dif. P	90.0%

The Capital Expenditure Year 4 Minimum is zero (0) MM, and the Maximum is $40 MM. The Capital Expenditure Year 4 *Mean* is $13.502 MM, and the *Standard Deviation* is $8.439 MM. There is a 5% probability that the Capital Expenditure Year 4 will be below $2.49 MM, a 90% probability will be in the range of $2.49 MM – $30.21 MM; and a 5% probability that it will be above $30.21 MM as shown on the graph.

Figure 28 displays the Number of wells Year 4 distribution.

The Number of wells Year 4 Minimum is zero (0) wells, and the Maximum is 5 wells. The Number of wells Year 4 *Mean* is 1.6878 wells, and the *Standard Deviation* is 1.0548 wells. There is a 5% probability that the number of wells in Year 4 will below 0.31 wells, a 90% probability will be in the range of 0.31 wells – 3.78 wells; and a 5% probability that it will be above 3.78 wells as shown on the graph.

Figure 28. Number of wells year 4 distribution

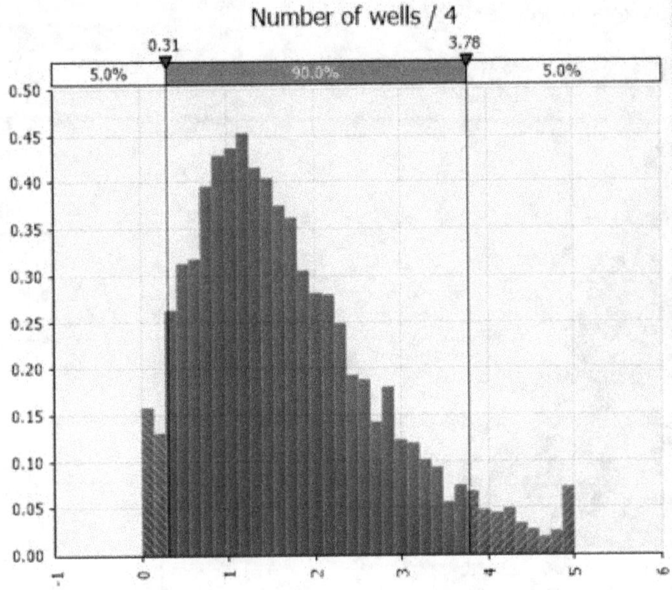

Statistics	Number of wells / 4
Cell	F20
Minimum	0
Maximum	5
Mean	1.6878
90% CI	± 0.0245
Mode	5
Median	1.4910
Std Dev	1.0548
Skewness	0.8767
Kurtosis	3.4716
Values	5000
Errors	0
Filtered	0
Left X	0.31
Left P	5.0%
Right X	3.78
Right P	95.0%
Dif. X	3.4657
Dif. P	90.0%

Capital Expenditure and Number of Wells for Year 5 Analysis and Evaluation

Figure 29 displays the Capital Expenditure Year 5 distribution.

The Capital Expenditure Year 5 Minimum is zero (0) MM, and the Maximum is \$20 MM. The Capital Expenditure Year 5 *Mean* is \$6.751 MM, and the *Standard Deviation* is \$4.219 MM. There is a 5% probability that the Capital Expenditure Year 5 will be below \$1.24 MM, a 90% probability will be in the range of \$1.24 MM – \$15.11 MM; and a 5% probability that it will be above \$15.11 MM as shown on the graph.

Figure 29. Capital expenditure year 5 distribution

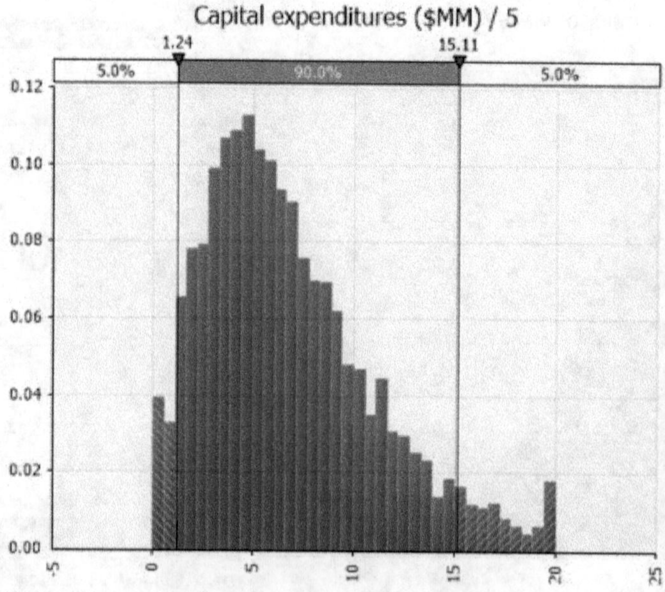

Statistics	Capital expenditure...
Cell	G19
Minimum	0
Maximum	20
Mean	6.751
90% CI	± 0.0982
Mode	20
Median	5.964
Std Dev	4.219
Skewness	0.8767
Kurtosis	3.4716
Values	5000
Errors	0
Filtered	0
Left X	1.24
Left P	5.0%
Right X	15.11
Right P	95.0%
Dif. X	13.863
Dif. P	90.0%

Figure 30 displays the Number of wells Year 5 distribution.

Figure 30. Number of wells year 5 distribution

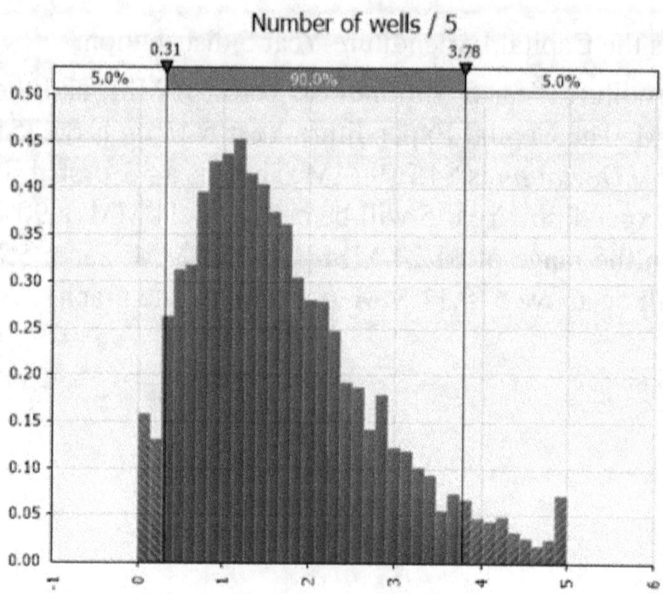

Statistics	Number of wells / 5
Cell	G20
Minimum	0
Maximum	5
Mean	1.6878
90% CI	± 0.0245
Mode	5
Median	1.4910
Std Dev	1.0548
Skewness	0.8767
Kurtosis	3.4716
Values	5000
Errors	0
Filtered	0
Left X	0.31
Left P	5.0%
Right X	3.78
Right P	95.0%
Dif. X	3.4657
Dif. P	90.0%

The Number of wells Year 5 Minimum is zero (0) wells, and the Maximum is 5 wells. The Number of wells Year 5 *Mean* is 1.6878 wells, and the *Standard Deviation* is 1.0548 wells. There is a 5% probability that the number of wells in Year 5 will be below 0.31 wells, a 90% probability will be in the range of 0.31 wells – 3.78 wells; and a 5% probability that it will be above 3.78 wells as shown on the graph.

Capital Expenditures Time Series

The Capital Expenditures Time Series is presented in Figure 31 including five years.

Figure 31. Capital expenditures time series

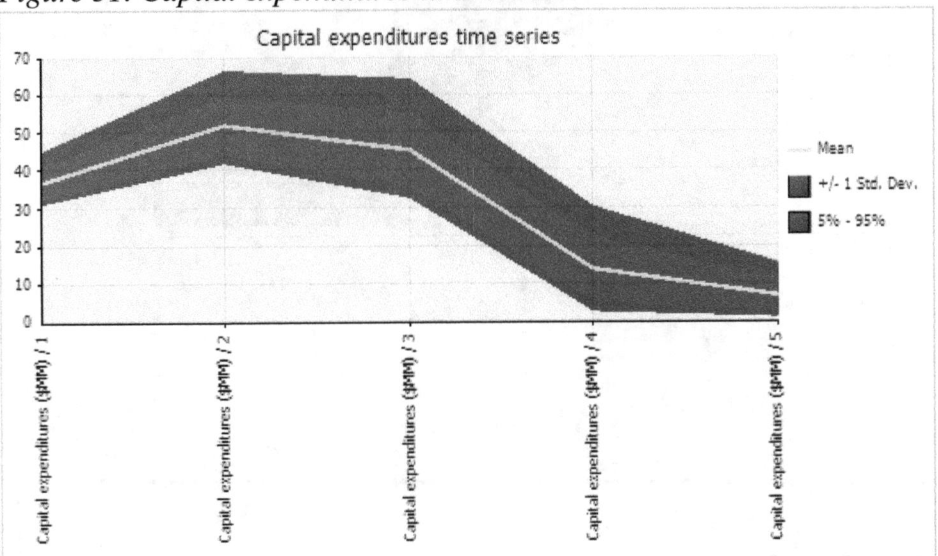

The Capital Expenditures Time Series values are Year 1: $36.798 MM; Year 2: $51.897 MM; Year 3: $42.296 MM; Year 4: $13.596 MM; and Year 5: $6.798 MM.

Number of wells Time Series

The Number of wells Time Series is presented in Figure 32 including five years.

The Number of wells Time Series values are Year 1: 8.680 wells; Year 2: 8.680 wells; Year 3: 8.039 wells; Year 4: 1.700 wells; and Year 5: 1.700 wells.

Figure 32. Number of wells time series

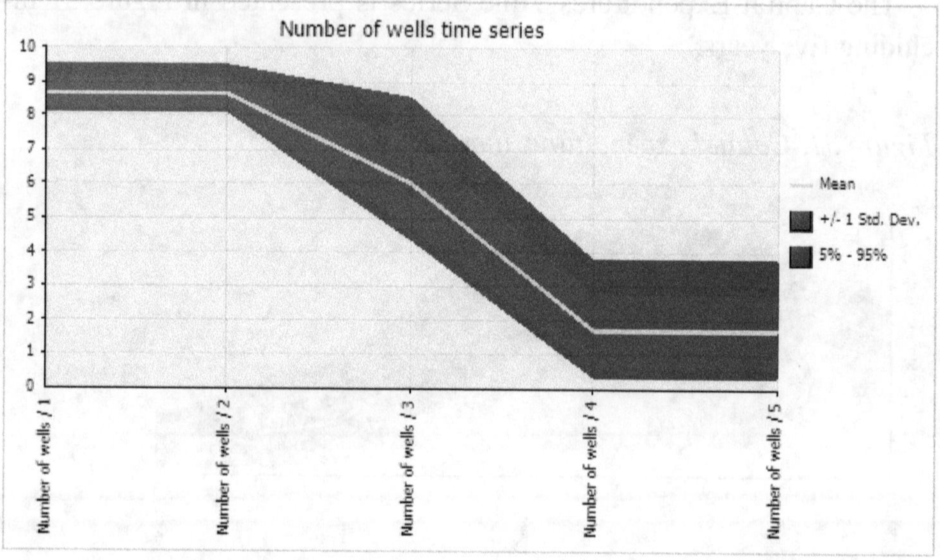

CONCLUSION

Oil Drilling Schedule Models

Initial Oil Drilling Schedule Model With Uncertainty

It is important in the oil industry to estimate a schedule of capital expenditures and production and to see how this schedule depends on the anticipated volumes of oil recovery. The initial model here does this for a

5-year planning period. The uncertainties, treated here as normal, are the inputs to the amount of recovery (area, net pay, and recovery rate). These are multiplied (and scaled) to get the recoverable amount in cell C15.

Given this recoverable amount, the model assumes that each year's capital expenditures in row 19 are some fractions of the way from the minimum possible expenditures that year to the maximum possible expenditures that year. The same statement applies to the number of wells drilled in row 20. The fraction used is the relative size of cell C16. It is the percentage of the way from the minimum recoverable amount to the maximum recoverable amount, and for this deterministic model, the value 50% is used. This will be changed into a more realistic model that includes uncertainty.

Oil Drilling Schedule Basic @RISK Model

This model expands on the initial model in the file *Initial Oil Drilling Schedule Model with Uncertainty*. Now, each of the inputs to the reserve size (area, net pay, and recovery rate) is modeled with triangular distributions. (The parameters of these distributions would come from experts' knowledge about the current site and similar historical sites.) These lead to the histogram of Recoverable shown. Not surprisingly, this looks like a lognormal shape. In general, when random quantities are *multiplied*, the resulting product typically has a lognormal shape.

The approximate 1st and 99th percentiles of this distribution are recorded in cells E15 and F15, and they are used to generate the uniformly distributed relative size in cell C16.

Because a few generated values of Recoverable will be outside the 1st and 99th percentile limits, the formula in C16 uses MIN and MAX functions to ensure that the relative size is never below 0% or above 100%.

The main point of this example is to generate the time series in rows 19 and 20, so the whole range C19:G19 is designated as an @RISK output range, and similarly for the range C20:G20. Then the Summary Trend graphs shown can be obtained from the Browse Results button. They show clearly how the means and amounts of variation change through time.

REFERENCES

Budhu, M. (2015). Soil Mechanics Fundamentals. Wiley-Blackwell.

Hawkins, R. (1978). Relationship between diagenesis, porosity reduction, and oil emplacement in late Carboniferous sandstone reservoirs, Bothamsall Oilfield, E Midlands. *Quartal Journal Geological Society, 135*(Part 1).

Patterson, M. C. (2019). The Oil Rig Guide: Lists of Offshore Drilling Employment Companies and Agencies: Offshore Job, Oil and Gas, Oil Platform, Offshore Career, Manage address book. Independent Publisher.

Patterson, M. C. (2022). The *Oil Rig Guide: A Comprehensive Guide on The Fundamentals of Oil Rig and How to Get a Job in Oil Rig*. Independent Publisher.

Piersol. (2021). Porosity, Total Liquid Saturation, and Permeability of Illinois Oil Sands; Report of Investigations No. 67. Hassell Street Press.

Selley, R. (1978). *Porosity gradients in North Sea oil-bearing sandstones*. *Quartal Journal Geological Society, 135*(Part 1). DOI: 10.1144/gsjgs.135.1.0119

Chapter 2
Oil and Gas Forecast

ABSTRACT

Initial Oil and Gas Forecast Model With Uncertainty makes forecasts of production-revenues-expenses for a multi-year period in the face of much uncertainty. It creates forecasts for 10 years, with all of the input required. The NPV of about $10.4 million is a best guess, but with all the uncertainty that exists. Oil and Gas Forecast Basic @RISK Model introduces essential improvements. Each of the input cells is modeled with a specific probability distribution. The values are generated once and then used each year. The decline in oil and gas production is constant from year to year. The model assumes constant trends in oil and gas prices. The annual operating expenses vary around 3% of the initial capital expenditure plus $3 per barrel of oil. Oil and Gas Forecast Sensitivity Analysis considers the uncertain inputs the NPV output is most sensitive to, illustrating one of the options in @RISK sensitivity analysis.

INTRODUCTION

Oil and Gas Forecast

The decline curve is a method for estimating reserves and predicting the rate of oil or gas production. It typically shows the pace at which production is expected to decline over the lifetime of an energy asset.

DOI: 10.4018/979-8-3373-0959-0.ch002

- The decline curve is a method for estimating reserves and predicting the rate of oil or gas production.
- The decline curve is a method used to determine the estimated ultimate recovery (EUR) for an oil or gas reserve.
- Primarily based on good conditions, three types of decline curves can apply to the future trend: exponential, hyperbolic, and harmonic.

Knowing the decline curve can help a producer estimate the number of oil reserves that can come from a well over its lifetime, the present and future value of a well, and the rate at which assets should depreciate on a company's books. In aggregate, the decline curve can also help determine the rate of production for a total reservoir or even multiple reservoirs.

The decline curve is a method used to determine the estimated ultimate recovery (EUR) for an oil or gas reserve. This calculation rests on a set of equations that U.S. geologist J.J. Arps developed in 1945. It is of the utmost importance that drilling projects meet an acceptable EUR threshold for a project to be considered viable and profitable.

In theory, the decline curve can apply to most wells in the industry. Underlying the decline curve equations is an expectation that well-production typically follows a three-part pattern.

1. In the initial phase production phase, the flow of oil or gas remains relatively steady, as pressure stays nearly constant.
2. Next is a transient period in which the flow of oil or gas declines rapidly, as the quantity of recoverable assets and pressure in the wellbore decreases.
3. Lastly, assets deplete to a level at which they approach the well's defined boundaries.

Arps decline curve equations most often apply to the boundary-defined production phase.

Calculating the decline curve involves a curve-fitting exercise to interpolate the future rate of production based on past production levels. Therefore, a somewhat lengthy period of time-series data is needed to estimate the projected trend. Also, the decline-curve equations assume that multiple variables involved in production and operations stay constant during the lifetime of a good asset. Primarily based on good conditions, three types of decline curves can apply to the future trend: exponential, hyperbolic, and harmonic.

Analysing the decline curve can be a more straightforward way to estimate production levels relative to more complex simulations. However, using the decline curve also can be less accurate than simulations.

Using the decline curve has several shortcomings, including that it can underestimate oil reserves, underestimate production rates, and overestimate reservoir performance. Because it relies on past data, the decline curve does not consider the labour, equipment, and technology changes that could affect production rates. It also cannot account for the likelihood of geologic changes that more complex models may be able to include to a degree. However, the Arps equations are still in use today.

Five of the Biggest Risks Faced by Oil and Gas Companies

Andrew Beattie was part of the original editorial team at Investopedia and has spent twenty years writing on a diverse range of financial topics including business, investing, personal finance, and trading.

Whenever an investor approaches a new industry, it is good to know what the risks are that a company in that sector must face to be successful. General risks apply to every stock, such as management risk, but there are also more concentrated risks that affect that specific industry. In this article, we'll look at the biggest risks faced by oil and gas companies.

- Despite the risks, there is still a very real energy demand, and oil and gas play a major part in filling that demand.
- A long-term risk for oil and gas companies is a dwindling natural supply.
- Short-term risks include political stances and supply and demand.
- Oil and gas companies remain some of the most heavily traded public companies.

- Natural resource pricing relies heavily on the underlying cost of procuring and refining the resource, as well as the price of the completed commodity itself.

Political Risk

The primary way that politics can affect oil is in the regulatory sense, but it's not necessarily the only way.

Typically, an oil and gas company is covered by a range of regulations that limit where, when, and how extraction is done. This interpretation of laws and regulations can also differ from state to state. That said, political risk generally increases when oil and gas companies are working on deposits abroad.

Oil and gas companies tend to prefer countries with stable political systems and a history of granting and enforcing long-term leases. However, some companies simply go where the oil and gas are, even if a particular country doesn't quite match their preferences. Numerous issues may arise from this, including sudden nationalisation and/or shifting political winds that change the regulatory environment. Depending on what country the oil is being extracted from, the deal a company starts with is not always the deal it ends up with, as the government may change its mind after the capital is invested, to make more profit for itself.

Political risk can be obvious (such as developing in countries with an unstable dictatorship and a history of sudden nationalization), or more subtle, (as found in nations that adjust foreign ownership rules to guarantee that domestic corporations gain an interest). An important approach that a company takes in mitigating this risk includes careful analysis and building sustainable relationships with international oil and gas partners —if it hopes to remain in business for the long run.

Geological Risk

Many of the easy-to-get oil and gas are already tapped out or in the process of being tapped out. Exploration has moved on to areas that involve drilling in less friendly environments, such as on a platform in the middle of an undulating ocean. There is a wide variety of unconventional oil and gas extraction techniques that have helped squeeze out resources in areas where it would have otherwise been impossible.

Geological risk refers to both the difficulty of extraction and the possibility that the accessible reserves in any deposit will be smaller than estimated. Oil and gas geologists work hard to minimize geological risk by testing frequently, so estimates are rarely substantially "off." They use the terms "proven," "probable" and "possible" before reserve estimates, to express their level of confidence in the findings.

Price Risk

Beyond the geological risk, the price of oil and gas is the primary factor in deciding whether a reserve is economically feasible. Basically, the higher the geological barriers to easy extraction, the more price risk a given project faces. This is because unconventional extraction usually costs more than a vertical drill down to a deposit.

This doesn't mean that oil and gas companies automatically cease operations on a project that becomes unprofitable due to a price dip. Often, these projects can't be quickly shut down and then restarted. Instead, O&G companies attempt to forecast the likely prices over the term of the project to decide whether to begin. Once a project has begun, price risk is a constant companion.

Supply and Demand Risks

Supply and demand shocks are a very real risk for oil and gas companies. As mentioned above, operations take a lot of capital and time to get going, and they are not easy to shut down when prices go south or ramp up when they go north. The uneven nature of production is part of what makes the price of oil and gas so volatile. Other economic factors also play into this, as with the 2008 financial crises, and macroeconomic factors can dry up capital or otherwise affect the industry independently of the usual price risks.

Cost Risks

All of these preceding risks feed into the biggest of them all: operational costs. The more onerous the regulation and the more difficult the drill, the more expensive a project becomes. Couple this with uncertain prices due to worldwide production beyond any one company's control, and you have some real cost concerns.

This is not the end, however, as many oil and gas companies struggle to find and retain the qualified workers that they need during boom times, so payroll can quickly rise to add another cost to the overall picture. These costs, in turn, have made oil and gas a very capital-intensive industry, with fewer players all the time.

LITERATURE

Sun (2015): In recent years, production decline-curve analysis has become the most widely used tool in the industry for oil and gas reservoir production analysis. However, most curve analysis is done by computer today, promoting a "black box" approach to engineering and leaving engineers with little background in the fundamentals of decline analysis. Advanced Production Decline Analysis and Application starts from the basic concept of advanced production decline analysis and thoroughly discusses several decline methods, such as Arps, Fetkovich, Blasingame, Agarwal-Gardner, NPI, transient, long linear flow, and FMB. A practical systematic introduction to each method helps the reservoir engineer understand the physical and mathematical models, solve the type curves and match up analysis, analyse the processes and examples, and reconstruct all the examples by hand, giving way to mastering the fundamentals behind the software. An appendix explains the nomenclature and major equations, and as a bonus, online computer programs are available for download. Poston & Poe (2020): Long ago, engineers recognized the characteristic decline of oil and gas well performance and attempted to predict its course by fitting equations to the production history. This book covers the production characteristics and associated interpretation analyses of petroleum reservoirs in a complete, thorough, and consistent manner.

Production decline-curve analyses are the most widely used tool in the industry for oil and gas reservoir production analyses. This book will serve as an authoritative reference on modern production decline-curve analyses, including details of some recent advances in the technology. Decline curves are probably the most widely used and least understood production forecasting technique currently in use in the industry. Analysis of decline curves provides an unsophisticated reservoir evaluation tool, but profound economic decisions often rest on the outcome of the prediction. A simplistic view of decline-curve analysis can lead to wide misuse, often caused by misunderstandings. There has been no single reference book on the meaning of production decline curves, their application, and their use and misuse. The authors have endeavoured to provide such a reference. Belyadi et al. (2016): Hydraulic Fracturing in Unconventional Reservoirs: Theories, Operations, and Economic Analysis introduces the basic characteristics and theories surrounding hydraulic fracturing and the main process of fracturing in shale, including the main workflow, the details in case analysis, and the fundamental differences between theory, study, and practical operation. The book takes the complex nature of hydraulic fracturing in unconventional reservoirs and applies a practical approach that can be used as a workflow for designing fracture treatments in various shale basins across the world. Providing the audience with theories, best practices, operation and execution, and economic analysis of hydraulic fracturing in unconventional reservoirs, this reference guides the engineer and manager through broad topics including an introduction to unconventional reservoirs, advanced shale reservoir characterization, and shale gas in place calculation as well as expanding to basic theories of hydraulic fracturing and advanced topics in shale reservoir stimulation. Rounding out with coverage of the environmental aspects and practice problems on design and economic analysis, the book delivers the critical link needed between academia and industry for all aspects of hydraulic fracturing operations. May (2017): This is a book about investing in oil and gas wells in the United States. (Sixth Edition). E (2021): The author Y.E. has worked for twenty years for major world oil groups including the American oil company Chevron, the British and Dutch oil company Royal Dutch Shell, and the Chinese oil company Sinopec. In this book, we discover the different oil cargo commercial life cycle stages in the middle of the oil market. Note that his work has permitted him to create a unique online course with no equivalent about professional commercial oil trading and shipping operations. From commercial negotiation to the maritime delivery of cargo with the support of practical examples from the oil trading environment, we learn the different stages of this life cycle as well as the prospects for adapting the oil sector to the energy challenges to come especially environmental. Elaboration

Simulation 1 Calculations with Risk Normal Distribution The Known Input are presented in Table 1.

Table 1. Known input

Discount Rate	10%

The Uncertain Inputs on Reserve Size (*but treated here as known*) are presented in Table 2:

Table 2. Uncertain inputs

Capital expenditures ($)	=@RiskNormal($1200000,$120000)
Year 1 oil production (STB)	=@RiskNormal(32000,3200)
Year 1 gas production (MSCF)	=@RiskNormal(22500,2250)
Annual decline rate in oil production	=@RiskNormal(12%,1.2%)
Annual decline rate in gas production	=@RiskNormal(25%,2.5%)
Year 1 price of oil ($/STB)	=@RiskNormal(87.5,8.75)
Year 1 price of gas ($/MSCF)	=@RiskNormal(3.5,0.35)
Annual trend in oil price	=@RiskNormal(1%,0.1%)
Annual trend in gas price	=@RiskNormal(1%,0.1%)

The Coefficients for Parameters of annual operating Expenses are presented in Table 3:

Table 3. Coefficients for parameters of annual operating expenses

Capital expenditures coefficient	=@RiskNormal(F17,G17)
Oil production coefficient	=@RiskNormal(F18,G18)

The *fixed* numbers were found to estimate the Normal Distribution parameters in Table 4. The Economic Model Outputs of 10 years and the Total are shown conceptually in Table 5 including only Years 1, 2, 3, and 10.

Table 4. The normal distributions parameters

Normal	**3.00%**	**0.35%**
Normal	$3.00	$0.35

Table 5. Economic model outputs for years 1, 2, 3, and 10

End of year	**1**	**2**	**3**	**10**
Oil production (STB)	=C7	=C22*EXP(-$C9)	=D22*EXP(-$C9)	=K22*EXP(-$C9)
Gas production (MSCF)	=C8	=C23*EXP(-$C10)	=D23*EXP(-$C10)	=K23*EXP(-$C10)
Price of oil	=C11	=C24*EXP(-$C13)	=D24*EXP(-$C13)	=K24*EXP(-$C13)
Price of gas	=C12	=C25*EXP(-$C10)	=D25*EXP(-$C10)	=K25*EXP(-$C10)
Oil revenue	=C22*C24	D22*D24	E22*E24	=L22*L24
Gas revenue	=C23*C25	D23*D25	E23*E25	=L23*L25
Operating expenses	=$C$17*$C$6 +$C$18*C22	=$C$17*$C$6 +$C$18*D22	=$C$17*$C$6 +$C$18*E22	=$C$17*$C$6 +$C$18*L22
Net cash	=C26+C27-C28	=D26+D27-D28	=E26+E27-E28	=L26+L27-L28

The Net Present Value (NPV) is presented in Table 6:

Table 6. Net Present Value (NPV)

Net Present Value (NPV)	=@RiskOutput("NPV")+-C6+NPV(C3,C29:L29)

Simulation 2 Calculations with Miscellaneous Distributions

The Known Input are presented in Table 7:

Table 7. Known input

Discount Rate	10%

The Uncertain Inputs on Reserve Size (*but treated here as known*) are presented in Table 8:

Table 8. Uncertain inputs

Capital expenditures ($)	=@RiskTriang(F6,G6,H6)
Year 1 oil production (STB)	=@RiskLognorm(F7,G7)
Year 1 gas production (MSCF)	=@RiskLognorm(F8,G8)
Annual decline rate in oil production	=@RiskLognorm(F9,G9)
Annual decline rate in gas production	=@RiskLognorm(F10,G10)
Year 1 price of oil ($/STB)	=@RiskTriang(F11,G11,H11)
Year 1 price of gas ($/MSCF)	=@RiskTriang(F12,G12,H12)
Annual trend in oil price	=@RiskNormal(F13,G13)
Annual trend in gas price	=@RiskNormal(F14,G14)

The Coefficients for Parameters of Uncertain Inputs are in Table 9:

Table 9. Coefficients for parameters of uncertain inputs

Distribution	Parameter1	Parameter2	Parameter3
Triangular	$1,000,000	$1,200,000	$1,400,000
Lognormal	32000	8000	
Lognormal	22500	6000	
Lognormal	12.0%	2.5%	
Lognormal	25.0%	3.0%	

continued on following page

Table 9. Continued

Distribution	Parameter1	Parameter2	Parameter3
Triangular	$80.00	$87.50	$95.00
Triangular	$3.25	$3.50	$3.75
Normal	1%	1%	
Normal	1%	1%	

Coefficients for Parameters of annual operating Expenses are in Table 10:

Table 10. Coefficients for parameters of annual operating expenses

Capital expenditures coefficient	=@RiskTriang(F17,G17,H17)
Oil production coefficient	=@RiskTriang(F18,G18,H18)

The Triangular Distribution parameters. They are shown in Table 11:

Table 11. The triangular distribution parameters

Triangular	2.90%	3.00%	3.10%
Triangular	$2.50	$3.00	$3.50

The Economic Model Outputs of 10 years and Total are shown in Table 12 including only Year 1, Year 2, and Year 10, which are sufficient to understand the concept.

Table 12. Economic model outputs for years 1, 2, 3, and 10

Year	1	2	3	10
Oil STB	=@RiskOutput(,"Oil Production",1)+C7	=@RiskOutput(,"Oil Production",2)+C22*EXP(-$C9)	=@RiskOutput(,"Oil Production",3)+D22*EXP(-$C9)	=@RiskOutput(,"Oil Production",10)+K22*EXP(-$C9)
Gas MSCF	=@RiskOutput(,"Gas Production",1)+C8	=@RiskOutput(,"Gas Production",2)+C23*EXP(-$C10)	=@RiskOutput(,"Gas Production",3)+D23*EXP(-$C10)	=@RiskOutput(,"Gas Production",10)+K23*EXP(-$C10)
Price of Oil	=@RiskOutput(, B24,1)+C11	=@RiskOutput(, B24,2)+C24*(1+$C13)*(1+@RiskNormal(0,0.005))	=@RiskOutput(,B24,3)+D24*(1+$C13)*(1+@RiskNormal(0,0.005))	=@RiskOutput(,B24,10)+K24*(1+$C13)*(1+@RiskNormal(0,0.005))

continued on following page

Table 12. Continued

Year	1	2	3	10
Price of gas	=@RiskOutput (,B25,1)+C12	=@RiskOutput (,B25,2)+C25*(1+$C14)* (1+@RiskNormal(0,0.005))	=@RiskOutput(,B25,3) +D25*(1+$C14)* (1+@RiskNormal(0,0.005))	=@RiskOutput(,B25,10) +K25*(1+$C14)* (1+@RiskNormal(0,0.005))
Oil Reven.	=@RiskOutput (,B26,1)+C22*C24	=@ RiskOutput(,B26,2)+D22*D24	=@ RiskOutput(,B26,3)+E22*E24	=@ RiskOutput(,B26,10)+L22*L24
Gas Reven.	=@RiskOutput (,B27,1)+C23*C25	=@ RiskOutput(,B27,2)+D23*D25	=@ RiskOutput(,B27,3)+E23*E25	=@ RiskOutput(,B27,10)+L23*L25
Operating expense	=@RiskOutput(,B28,1) +$C$17*$C$6+$C$18*C22	=@RiskOutput(,B28,2) +$C$17*$C$6+$C$18*D22	=@RiskOutput(,B28,3) +$C$17*$C$6+$C$18*E22	=@RiskOutput(,B28,10) +$C$17*$C$6+$C$18*L22
Net cash	=@RiskOutput(,B29,1) +C26+C27-C28	=@RiskOutput(,B29,2)+ D26+D27-D28	=@ RiskOutput(,B29,3)+E26+E27-E28	=@RiskOutput(,B29,10) +L26+L27-L28

The Net Present Value (NPV) is presented in Table 13:

Table 13. Net Present Value (NPV)

Net Present Value (NPV)	=@RiskOutput("NPV")+-C6+NPV(C3,C29:L29)

Simulation 3: Sensitivity Analysis Calculations with Miscellaneous Distributions

The Known Input are presented in Table 14:

Table 14. Known input

Discount Rate	10%

The Uncertain Inputs on Reserve Size (*but treated here as known*) are presented in Table 15:

Table 15. Uncertain inputs

Capital expenditures ($)	=@RiskTriang(F6,G6,H6)
Year 1 oil production (STB)	=@RiskLognorm(F7,G7)
Year 1 gas production (MSCF)	=@RiskLognorm(F8,G8)
Annual decline rate in oil production	=@RiskLognorm(F9,G9)
Annual decline rate in gas production	=@RiskLognorm(F10,G10)
Year 1 price of oil ($/STB)	=@RiskTriang(F11,G11,H11)
Year 1 price of gas ($/MSCF)	=@RiskTriang(F12,G12,H12)
Annual trend in oil price	=@RiskNormal(F13,G13)
Annual trend in gas price	=@RiskNormal(F14,G14)

The Coefficients for Parameters of Uncertain Inputs are in Table 16:

Table 16. Coefficients for parameters of uncertain inputs

Distribution	Parameter1	Parameter2	Parameter3
Triangular	$1,000,000	$1,200,000	$1,400,000
Lognormal	32000	8000	
Lognormal	22500	6000	
Lognormal	12.0%	2.5%	
Lognormal	25.0%	3.0%	
Triangular	$80.00	$87.50	$95.00
Triangular	$3.25	$3.50	$3.75
Normal	1%	1%	
Normal	1%	1%	

Coefficients for Parameters of annual operating Expenses are in Table 17, and Triangular Distribution parameters are in Table 18.

Table 17. Coefficients for parameters of annual operating expenses

Capital expenditures coefficient	=@RiskTriang(F17,G17,H17)
Oil production coefficient	=@RiskTriang(F18,G18,H18)

Table 18. The triangular distribution parameters

Triangular	2.90%	3.00%	3.10%
Triangular	$2.50	$3.00	$3.50

The Economic Model Outputs of 10 years and Total are shown in Table 19 including only Year 1, Year 2, and Year 10, which are sufficient to understand the concept.

Table 19. Economic model outputs for years 1, 2, 3, and 10

Year	1	2	3	10
Oil STB	=@RiskOutput(, "Oil Production",1)+C7	=@RiskOutput(,"Oil Production",2)+C22*EXP(-$C9)	=@RiskOutput(,"Oil Production",3) +D22*EXP(-$C9)	=@RiskOutput(,"Oil Production",10)+K22*EXP(-$C9)
Gas MSCF	=@RiskOutput(, "Gas Production",1)+C8	=@RiskOutput(,"Gas Production",2)+C23*EXP(-$C10)	=@RiskOutput(,"Gas Production",3) +D23*EXP(-$C10)	=@RiskOutput(,"Gas Production",10)+K23*EXP(-$C10)
Price of Oil	=@RiskOutput(, B24,1)+C11	=@RiskOutput(,B24,2)+ C24*(1+$C13)*(1+ @RiskNormal(0,0.005))	=@RiskOutput(,B24,3) +D24*(1+$C13)* (1+@RiskNormal(0,0.005))	=@RiskOutput(,B24,10) +K24*(1+$C13)* (1+@RiskNormal(0,0.005))
Price of gas	=@RiskOutput (,B25,1)+C12	=@RiskOutput(,B25,2)+ C25*(1+$C14)*(1+@ RiskNormal(0,0.005))	=@RiskOutput(,B25,3) +D25*(1+$C14)* (1+@RiskNormal(0,0.005))	=@RiskOutput(,B25,10) +K25*(1+$C14)* (1+@RiskNormal(0,0.005))
Oil revenue	=@RiskOutput (,B26,1)+C22*C24	=@RiskOutput (,B26,2)+D22*D24	=@RiskOutput (,B26,3)+E22*E24	=@RiskOutput (,B26,10)+L22*L24
Gas revenue	=@RiskOutput (,B27,1)+C23*C25	=@RiskOutput (,B27,2)+D23*D25	=@RiskOutput (,B27,3)+E23*E25	=@RiskOutput (,B27,10)+L23*L25
Operating expense	=@RiskOutput(,B28,1)+ $C$17*$C$6+$C$18*C22	=@RiskOutput(,B28,2)+ $C$17*$C$6+$C$18*D22	=@RiskOutput(,B28,3) +$C$17*$C$6+$C$18*E22	=@RiskOutput(,B28,10) +$C$17*$C$6+$C$18*L22
Net cash	=@RiskOutput(,B29,1)+ C26+C27-C28	=@RiskOutput(,B29,2) +D26+D27-D28	=@RiskOutput(,B29,3) +E26+E27-E28	=@RiskOutput (,B29,10)+L26+L27-L28

The Net Present Value (NPV) is presented in Table 20:

Table 20. Net Present Value (NPV)

Net Present Value (NPV)	=@RiskOutput("NPV")+-C6+NPV(C3,C29:L29)

Simulation 1: NPV Risk Evaluation and Sensitivity Analysis with Risk Normal Distribution

Net Present Value (NPV) Analysis and Evaluation

Figure 1 displays the NPV distribution. The NPV Minimum is \$4,603,105.89 and the Maximum is \$16,738,351.92. The NPV *Mean* is \$10,387,748.06 and the *Standard Deviation* is \$1,716,084.31. There is a 5% probability that the NPV will be below \$7.71 MM, a 90% probability will be in the range of \$7.71 MM – \$13.36 MM; and a 5% probability that it will be above \$13.36 MM as shown on the graph.

Figure 1. NPV distribution

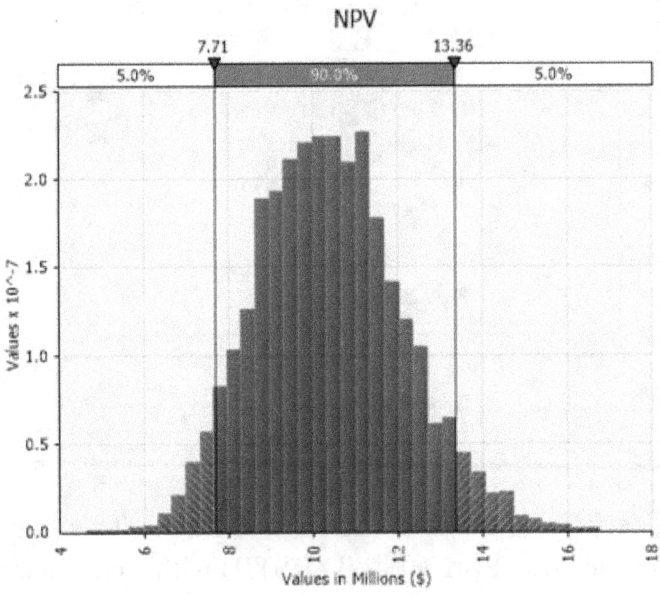

Statistics	NPV
Cell	C30
Minimum	\$4,603,105.89
Maximum	\$16,738,351.92
Mean	\$10,387,748.06
90% CI	± \$39,926.51
Mode	\$11,074,450.45
Median	\$10,327,011.17
Std Dev	\$1,716,084.31
Skewness	0.2513
Kurtosis	3.0269
Values	5000
Errors	0
Filtered	0
Left X	\$7,706,408.75
Left P	5.0%
Right X	\$13,361,783.57
Right P	95.0%
Dif. X	\$5,655,374.81
Dif. P	90.0%

Sensitivity Analysis

Sensitivity analysis provides for identifying and quantifying the main contributors to variability and risk based on the probability distribution.

The Inputs Ranked by Effect on Output Mean are given in Figure 2.

The graph illustrates that the effect of the top variable Year 1 oil production (STB), on the NPV, is a change in the range of $8,328,819.56 to $12,385,832; Also, the next variable is the Year 1 price of oil ($/STB), on the NPV is a change in the range of $8,373,535.86 to $12,382,294.78. The ranges are respectively left and right from the Baseline of $10,387,748.06, which is marked on the graph. Also, Other variables are less influential as their associated effect has much smaller figures.

Figure 2. NPV inputs ranked by effect on output mean

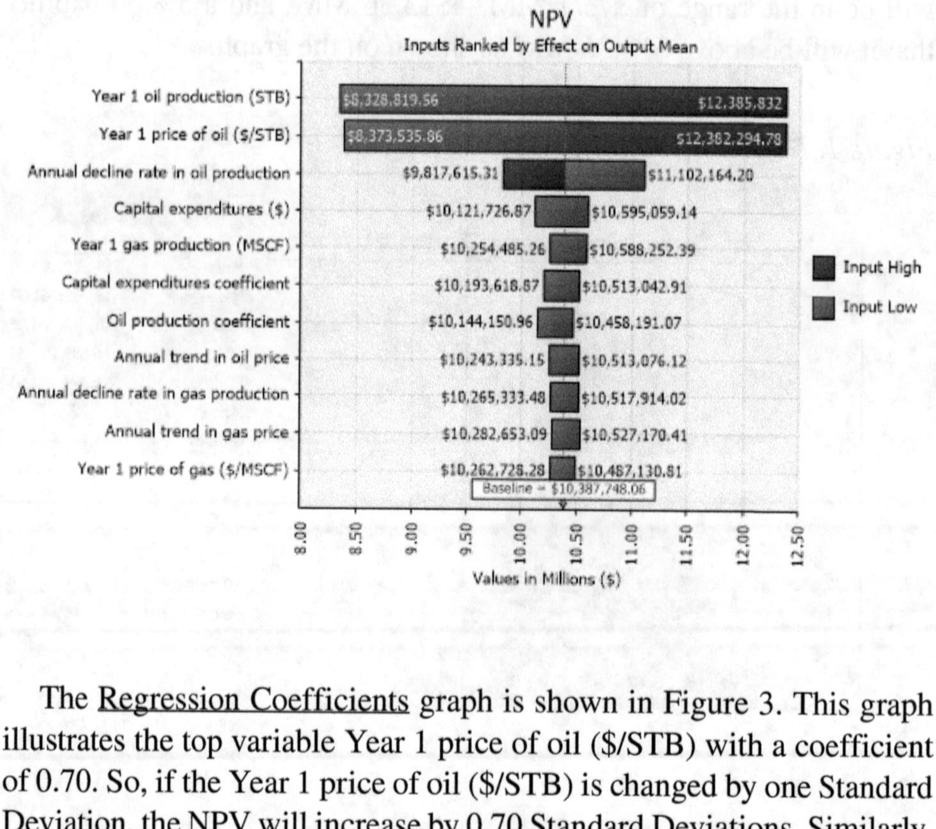

The Regression Coefficients graph is shown in Figure 3. This graph illustrates the top variable Year 1 price of oil ($/STB) with a coefficient of 0.70. So, if the Year 1 price of oil ($/STB) is changed by one Standard Deviation, the NPV will increase by 0.70 Standard Deviations. Similarly, if the next variable Year 1 oil production (STB), with a coefficient of 0.67, is changed by one Standard Deviation, the NPV will increase by 0.67 Standard Deviations. The other variables are less influential.

Figure 3. NPV regression coefficients

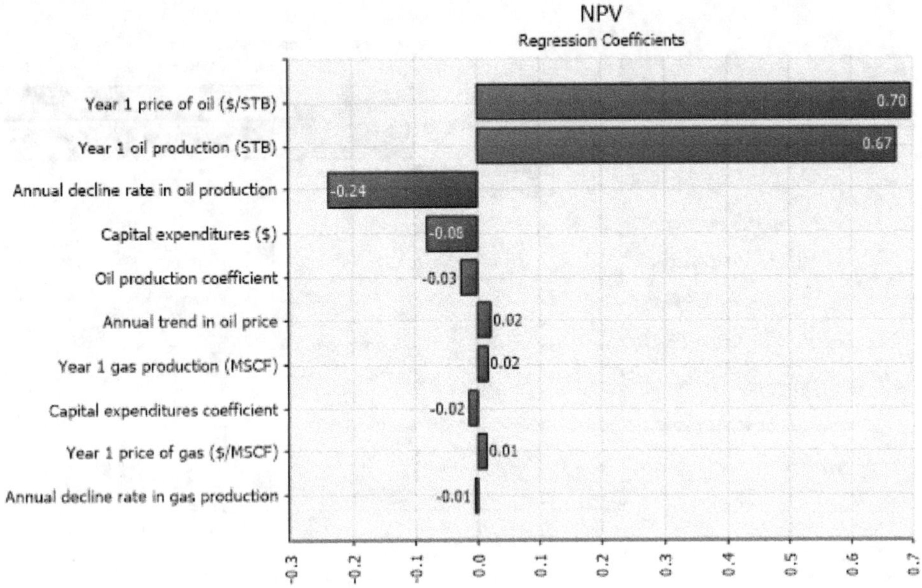

The Regression-Mapped-Values graph is shown in Figure 4. This graph illustrates the top variable Year 1 price of oil ($/STB) with a value of $1,197,854.78. Therefore, if the Year 1 price of oil ($/STB) changes by one Standard Deviation, the NPV will return $1,197,854.78. The other variables are less influential.

Figure 4. NPV regression mapped values coefficients

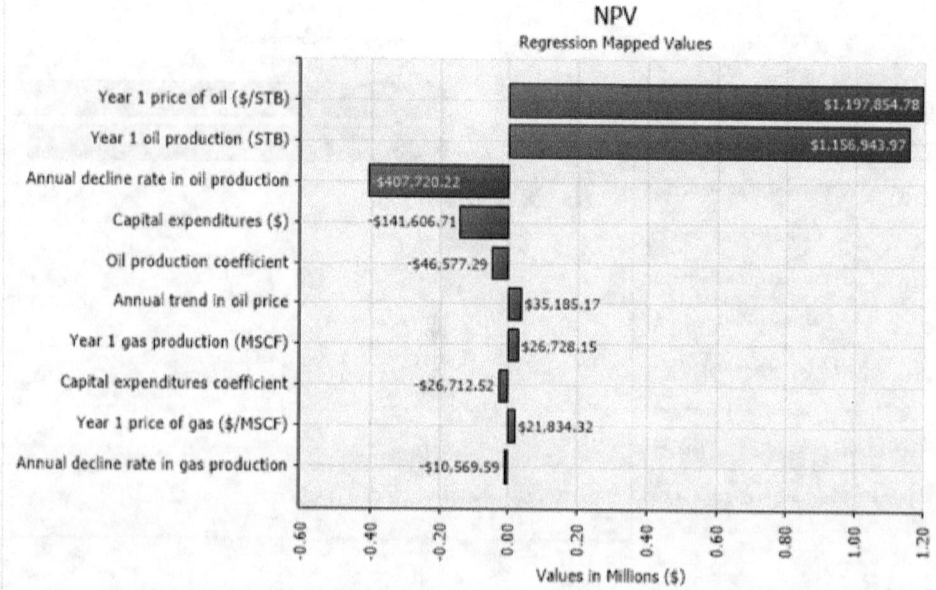

The Correlation Coefficients are presented in Figure 5.

Figure 5. NPV correlation coefficients

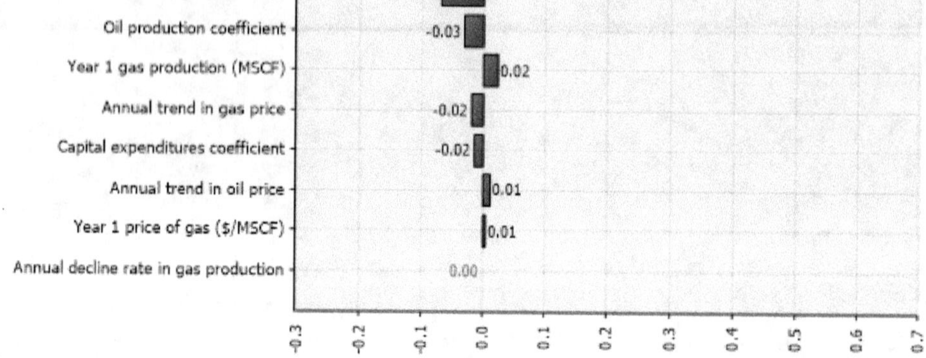

The graph shows that if the top variable top variable Year 1 price of oil ($/STB), with a correlation coefficient of 0.68, increases by one unit, the NPV will increase by 0.68 units. Other variables are less influential as the correlation coefficient is smaller.

The Contribution to Variance graph is presented in Figure 6.

Figure 6 illustrates that the top variable Year 1 price of oil ($/STB) has a contribution of 47.2% to the variance of the NPV. The other variables are less influential as the contribution to variances is smaller.

Figure 6. NPV contribution to variance

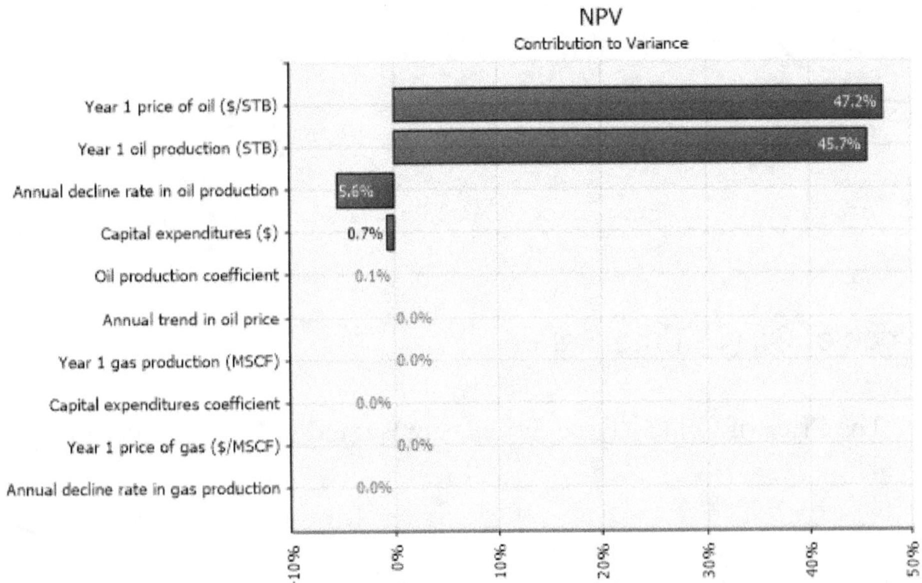

The Change in Output Mean Across the Range of Input Values graph is presented in Figure 7.

Figure 7 illustrates that the top variable Year 1 oil production (STB) (in Red), has a contribution of change increase from $8,328,819.56 to $12,385,832 with a Baseline of $10,387,748.06, to the variance of Average Rate STB/YR. Other variables are less influential as the contribution to variance is smaller.

Figure 7. NPV change in output mean across range of input values

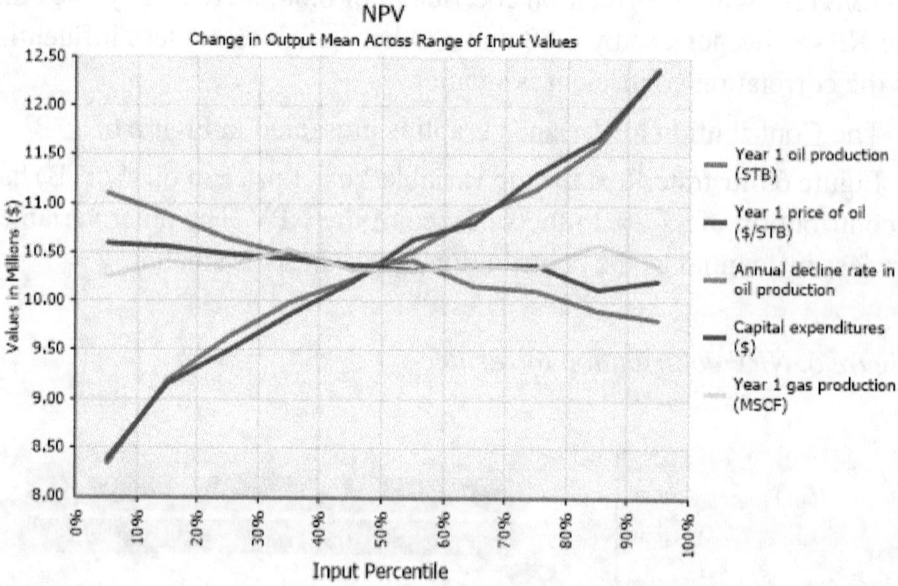

Price of Oil ($) Time Series

The Price of Oil ($) Time Series is presented in Figure 8 including 10 years.

Figure 8. Price of oil ($) time series

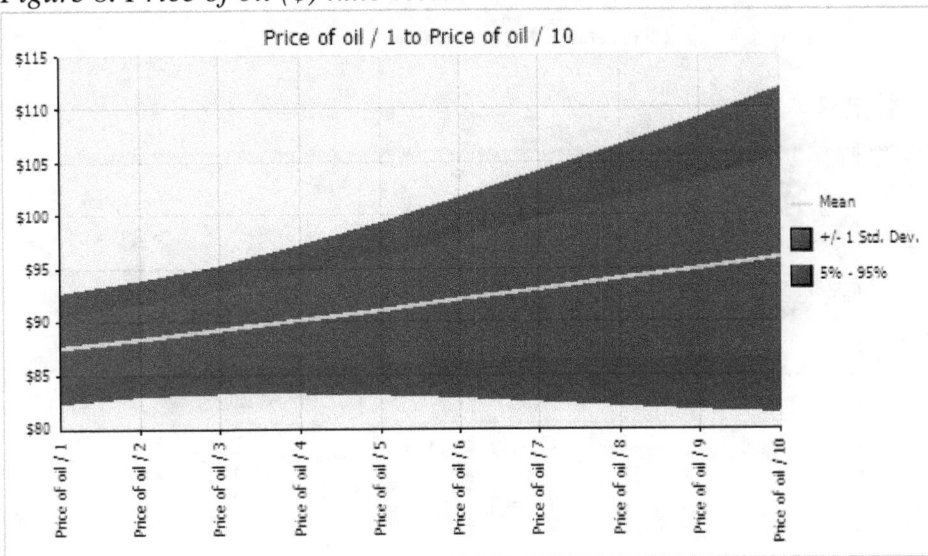

The Oil Price ($) Time Series values are: Year 1: $87.50; Year 2: $88.38; Year 3: $89.26; Year 4: $90.15; Year 5: $91.05; Year 6: $91.96; Year 7: $92.88; Year 8: $93.81; Year 9: $94.75; and Year 10: $95.70.

The Oil Revenue ($) Time Series is presented in Figure 9 including 10 years.

The Oil Revenue ($) Time Series values are: Year 1: $2,800,000; Year 2: $2,508,211; Year 3: $2,246,829; Year 4: $2,012,687; Year 5: $1,802,944; Year 6: $1,615,058; Year 7: $1,446,753; Year 8: $1,295,986; Year 9: $1,160,931; and Year 10: $1,039,950.

Figure 9. Oil revenue ($) time series

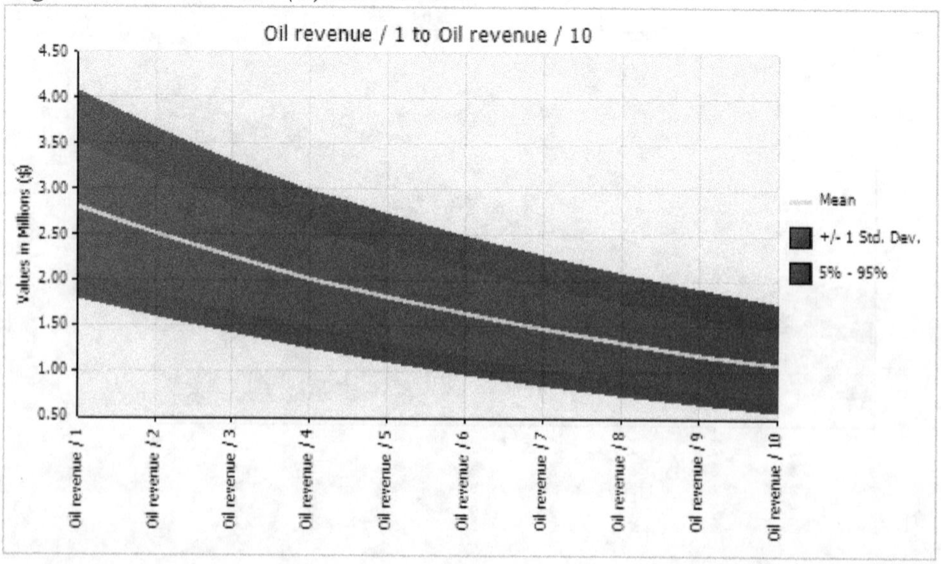

Operating Expenses ($) Time Series

The Operating Expenses ($) Time Series is presented in Figure 10. The Operating Expenses ($) Time Series values are: Year 1: $132,000; Year 2: $121,114; Year 3: $111,516; Year 4: $102,977; Year 5: $95,403; Year 6: $88,686; Year 7: $82,728; Year 8: $77,444; Year 9: $71,758; and Year 10: $68,601.

Figure 10. Operating expenses ($) time series

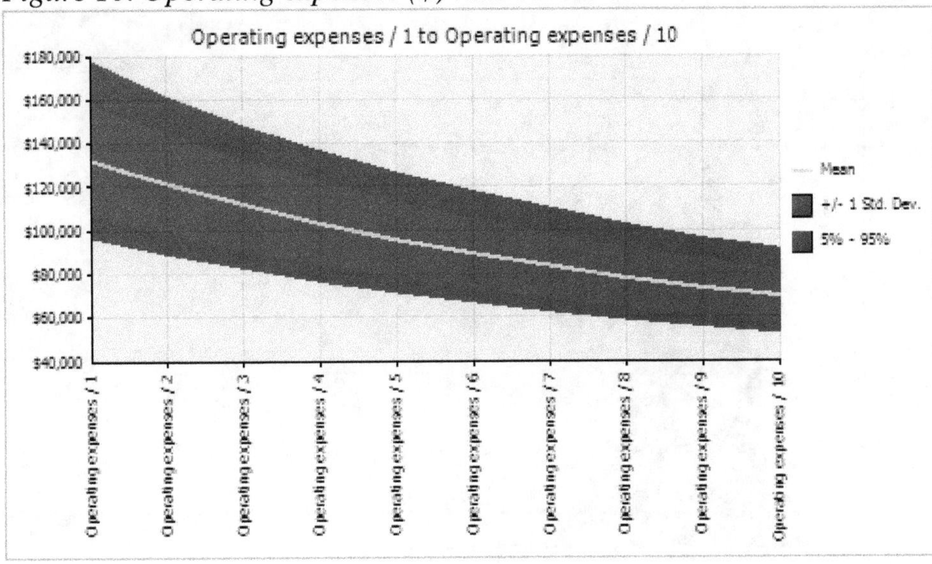

Simulation 2: NPV Risk Evaluation and Economic Outputs with Miscellaneous Distributions

NPV Analysis and Evaluation

Figure 11 displays the NPV distribution.

Figure 11. NPV distribution

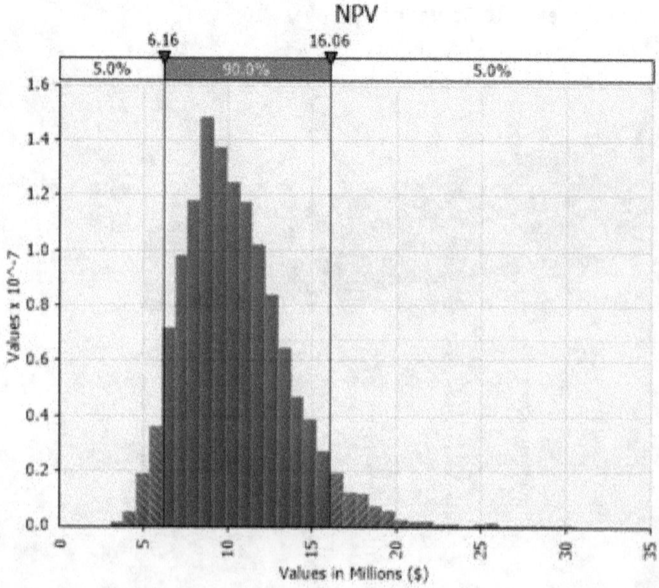

Statistics	NPV
Cell	C30
Minimum	$3,026,098.30
Maximum	$30,627,944.46
Mean	$10,442,117.47
90% CI	± $72,277.20
Mode	$8,937,565.03
Median	$10,029,532.58
Std Dev	$3,106,551.93
Skewness	0.8685
Kurtosis	4.5369
Values	5000
Errors	0
Filtered	0
Left X	$6,164,997.79
Left P	5.0%
Right X	$16,059,858.54
Right P	95.0%
Dif. X	$9,894,860.75
Dif. P	90.0%

The NPV Minimum is $3,026,098.30 and the Maximum is $30,627,944.46. The NPV *Mean* is $10,442,117.47 and the *Standard Deviation* is $3,106,551.93. There is a 5% probability that the NPV will be below $6.16 MM, a 90% probability will be in the range of $6.16 MM – $16.06 MM; and a 5% probability that it will be above $16.06 MM as shown on the graph.

Oil Production (STB) Time Series

The Oil Production (STB) Time Series is presented in Figure 12 including 10 years.

Figure 12. Oil production (STB) time series

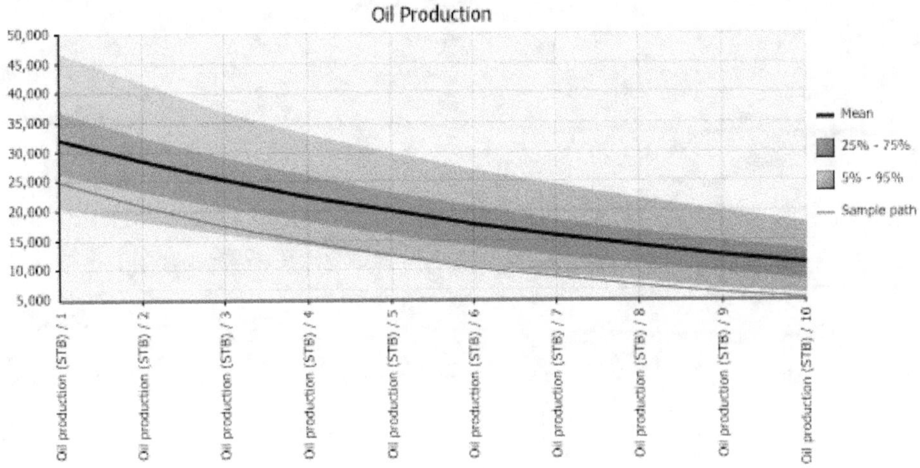

The Oil Production (STB) Time Series values are Year 1: 32,000 STB; Year 2: 28,381 STB; Year 3: 25,172 STB; Year 4: 22,326 STB; Year 5: 19,801 STB; Year 6: 17,562 STB; Year 7: 15,576 STB; Year 8: 13,815 STB; Year 9: 12,253 STB; and Year 10: 10,867 STB.

Gas Production (MSCF) Time Series

The Gas Production (MSCF) Time Series is presented in Figure 13 including 10 years.

Figure 13. Gas production (MSCF) time series

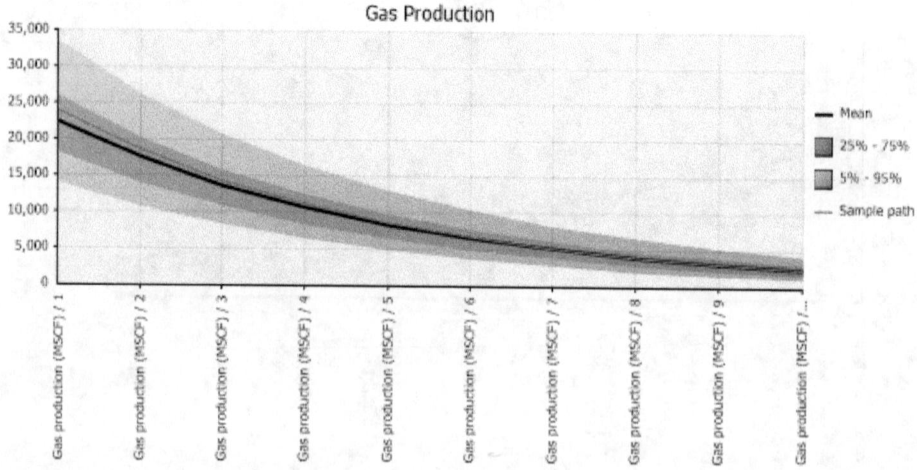

The Oil Production (MSCF) Time Series values are Year 1: 22,500 MSCF; Year 2: 17,523 MSCF; Year 3: 13,647 MSCF; Year 4: 10,628 MSCF; Year 5: 8,277 MSCF; Year 6: 6.446 MSCF; Year 7: 5,020 MSCF; Year 8: 3,910 MSCF; Year 9: 3,045 MSCF; and Year 10: 2,371 MSCF.

Oil Price ($) Time Series

The Oil Price ($) Time Series is presented in Figure 14 including 10 years.

The Oil Price ($) Time Series values are: Year 1: $87.50; Year 2: $88.38; Year 3: $89.26; Year 4: $90.15; Year 5: $91.05; Year 6: $91.96; Year 7: $92.88; Year 8: $93.81; Year 9: $94.75; and Year 10: $95.70.

Figure 14. Oil price ($) time series

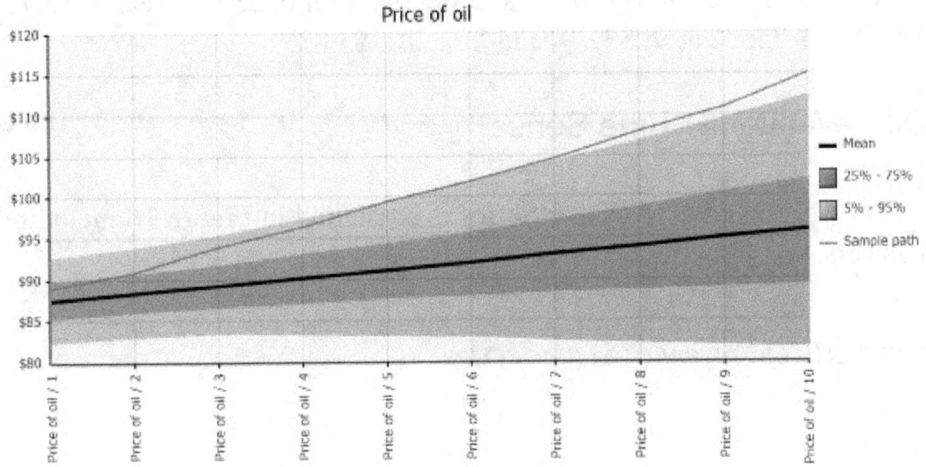

Gas Price ($) Time Series

The Gas Price ($) Time Series is presented in Figure 15 including 10 years.

Figure 15. Gas price ($) time series

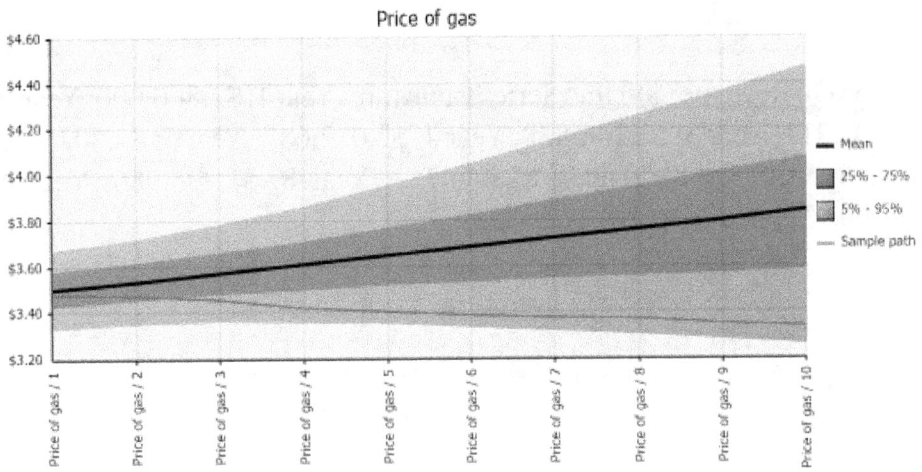

The Gas Price ($) Time Series values are: Year 1: $3.50; Year 2: $3.54; Year 3: $3.57; Year 4: $3.61; Year 5: $3.64; Year 6: $3.68; Year 7: $3.72; Year 8: $3.75; Year 9: $3.79; and Year 10: $3.83.

Oil Revenue ($) Time Series

The Oil Revenue ($) Time Series is presented in Figure 16 including 10 years.

Figure 16. Oil revenue ($) time series

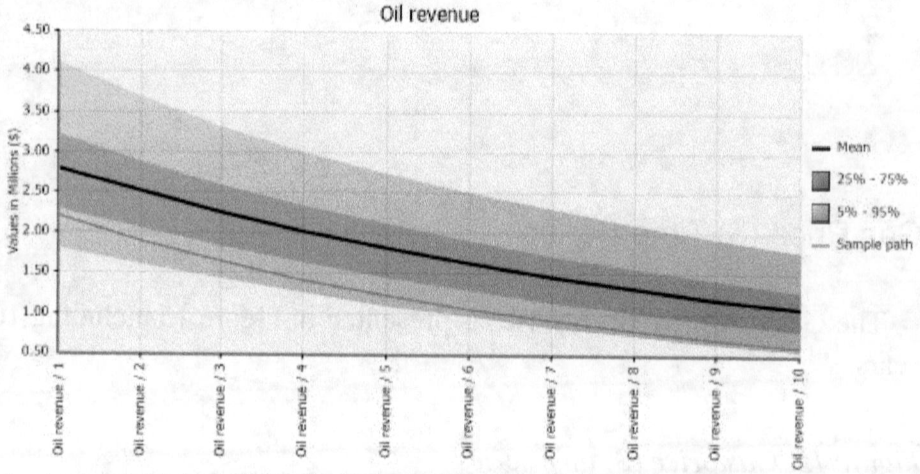

The Oil Revenue ($) Time Series values are: Year 1: $2,800,000; Year 2: $2,508,211; Year 3: $2,246,829; Year 4: $2,012,687; Year 5: $1,802,944; Year 6: $1,615,058; Year 7: $1,446,753; Year 8: $1,295,986; Year 9: $1,160,931; and Year 10: $1,039,950.

Gas Revenue ($) Time Series

The Gas Revenue ($) Time Series is presented in Figure 17.

The Gas Revenue ($) Time Series values are: Year 1: $78,750; Year 2: $61,944; Year 3: $48,724; Year 4: $38,326; Year 5: $30,147; Year 6: $23,713; Year 7: $18,653; Year 8: $14,672; Year 9: $11,541; and Year 10: $9,078.

Figure 17. Gas revenue ($) time series

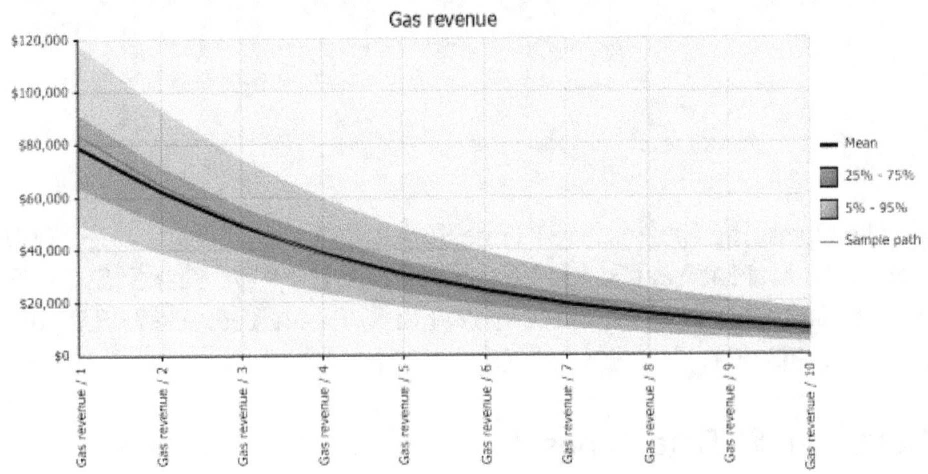

Operating Expenses ($) Time Series

The Operating Expenses ($) Time Series is presented in Figure 18.

Figure 18. Operating expenses ($) time series

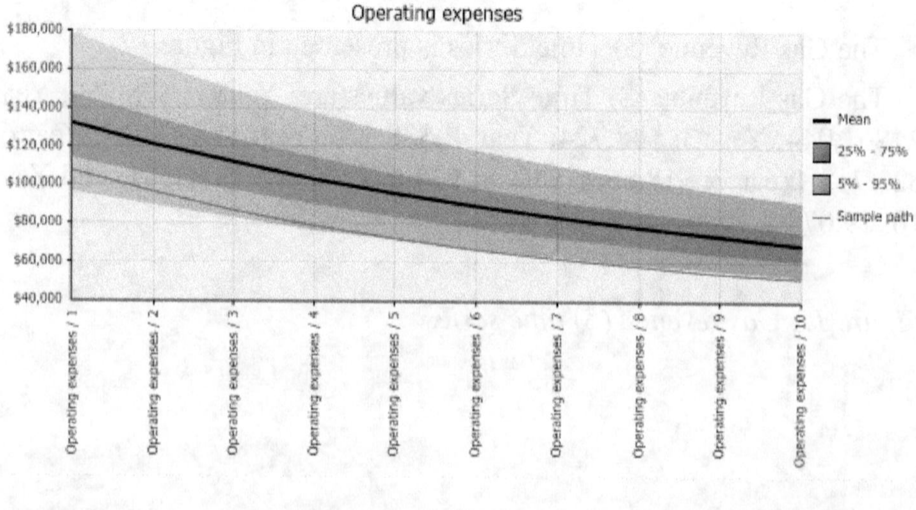

The Operating Expenses ($) Time Series values are: Year 1: $132,000; Year 2: $121,114; Year 3: $111,516; Year 4: $102,977; Year 5: $95,403; Year 6: $88,686; Year 7: $82,728; Year 8: $77,444; Year 9: $71,758; and Year 10: $68,601.

Net Cash ($) Time Series

The Net Cash ($) Time Series is presented in Figure 19 including 10 years.

Figure 19. Net cash ($) time series

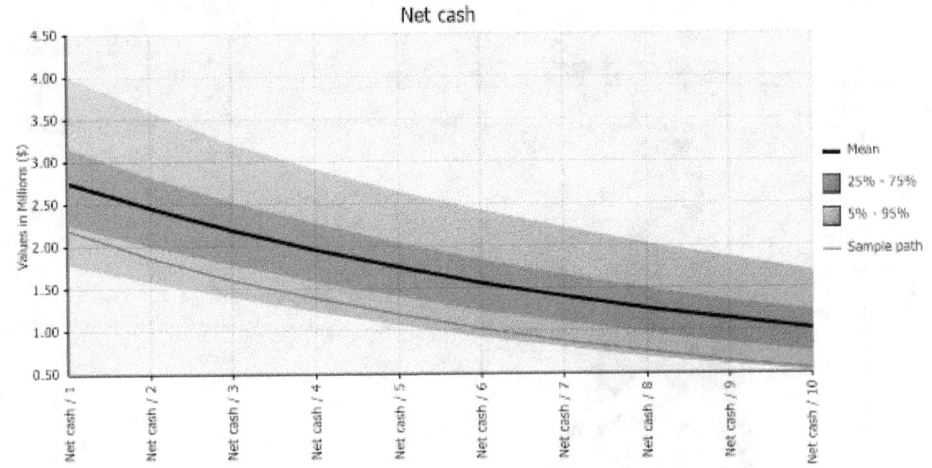

The Gas Price ($) Time Series values are: Year 1: $1,746,750; Year 2: $2,449,011; Year 3: $2,184,038; Year 4: $1,948,036; Year 5: $1,737,687; Year 6: $1,550,086; Year 7: $1,382,677; Year 8: $1,233,214; Year 9: $1,099,714; and Year 10: $980,426.

Simulation 3: NPV Distribution and Sensitivity Analysis with miscellaneous Distributions

NPV Distribution

Figure 20 displays the NPV distribution.

The NPV Minimum is $2,793,397.08 and the Maximum is $26,6632,769.18. The NPV *Mean* is $10,434,370.84 and the *Standard Deviation* is $3,078,495.88. There is a 5% probability that the NPV will be below $6.12 MM, a 90% probability will be in the range of $6.12 MM – $15.97 MM; and a 5% probability that it will be above $15.97 MM as shown on the graph.

Figure 20. NPV distribution

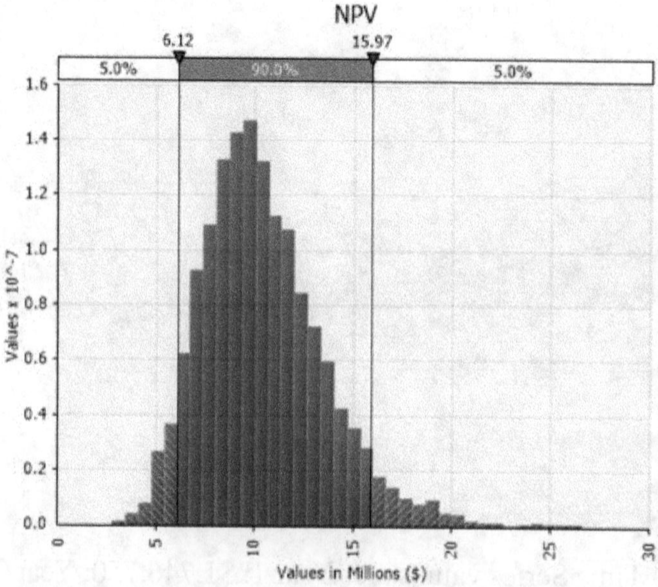

Statistics	NPV
Cell	C30
Minimum	$2,793,397.08
Maximum	$26,632,769.18
Mean	$10,438,370.84
90% CI	± $71,624.45
Mode	$9,599,629.43
Median	$10,038,970.41
Std Dev	$3,078,495.88
Skewness	0.7950
Kurtosis	4.1706
Values	5000
Errors	0
Filtered	0
Left X	$6,123,744.06
Left P	5.0%
Right X	$15,967,089.40
Right P	95.0%
Dif. X	$9,843,345.34
Dif. P	90.0%

Sensitivity Analysis

Sensitivity analysis provides for identifying and quantifying the main contributors to variability and risk based on the probability distribution.

The <u>Inputs Ranked by Effect on Output Mean</u> are given in Figure 21. The graph illustrates that the effect of the top variable Year 1 oil production (STB), on the NPV is a change in the range of $6,124,102.55 to $16,296,681.27. The ranges are respectively left and right from the Baseline of $10,438,370.84, which is marked on the graph. Also, Other variables are less influential as their associated effect has much smaller figures.

Figure 21. NPV inputs ranked by effect on output mean

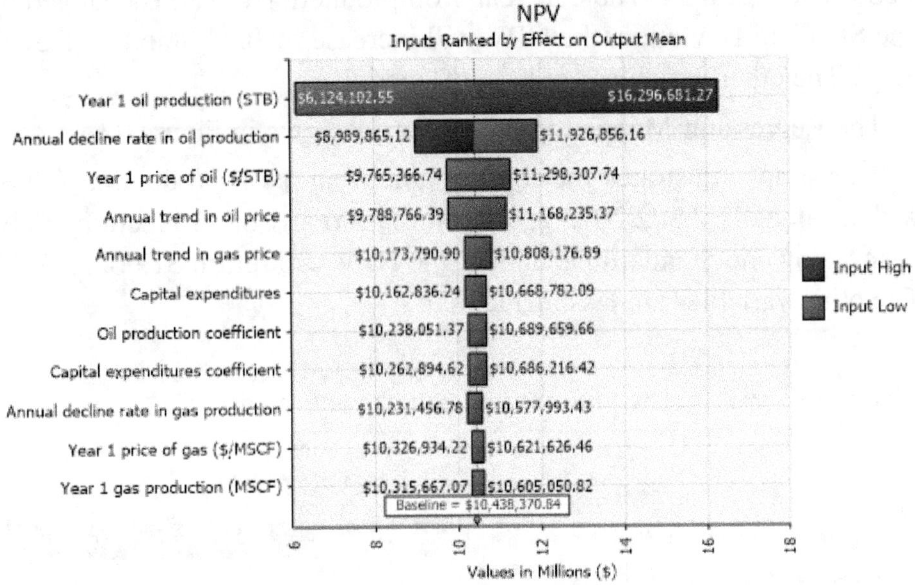

The Regression Coefficients graph is shown in Figure 22.

Figure 22. NPV regression coefficients

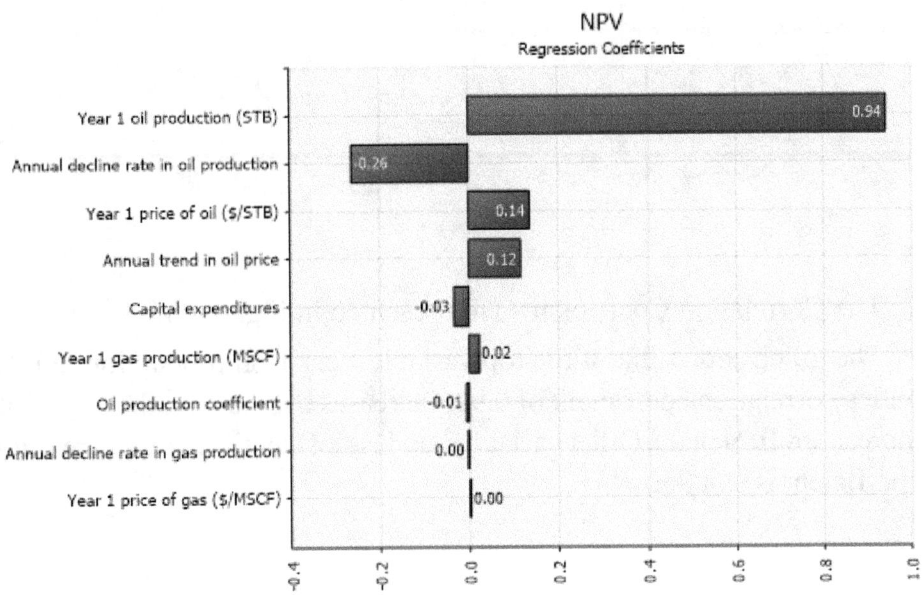

This graph illustrates the top variable Year 1 oil production (STB) with a coefficient of 0.94. Thus, if Year 1 oil production (STB) is changed by one Standard Deviation, the NPV will increase by 0.94 Standard Deviations. The other variables are less influential.

The Regression-Mapped-Values graph is shown in Figure 23.

This graph illustrates the top variable Year 1 oil production (STB) with a value of $2,902,207.92. Therefore, if Year 1 oil production (STB) changes by one Standard Deviation, the NPV will return $2,902,207.92. The other variables are less influential.

Figure 23. NPV regression mapped values coefficients

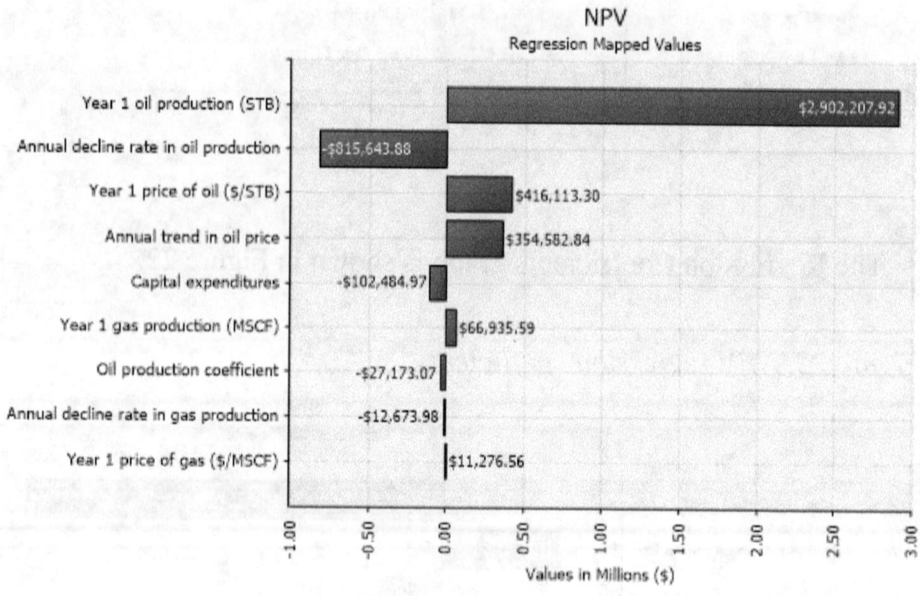

The Correlation Coefficients are presented in Figure 24.

The graph shows that if the top variable Year 1 oil production (STB), with a correlation coefficient of 0.94, increases by one unit, the NPV will increase by 0.94 units. Other variables are less influential as the correlation coefficient is smaller.

Figure 24. NPV correlation coefficients

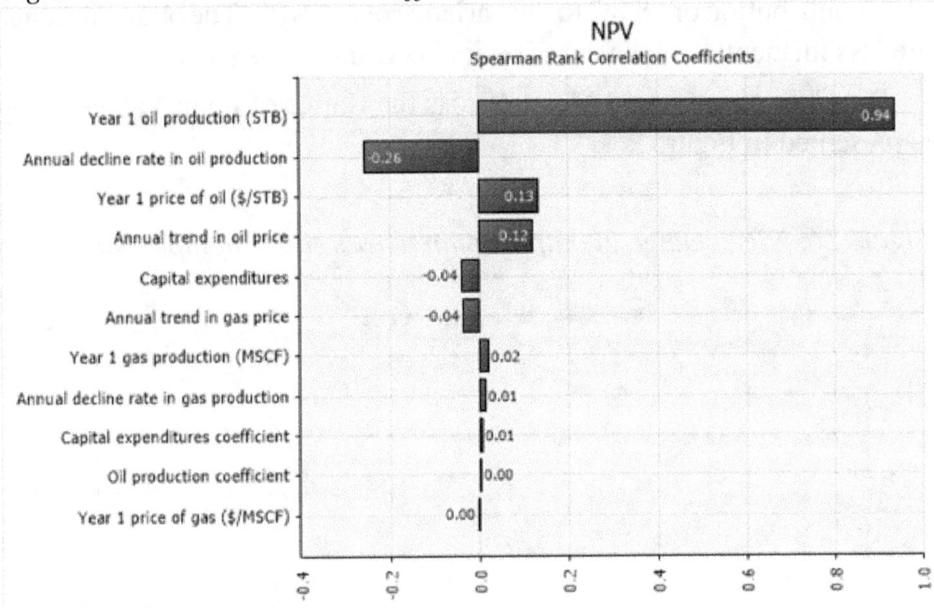

The Contribution to Variance graph is presented in Figure 25.

Figure 25. NPV contribution to variance

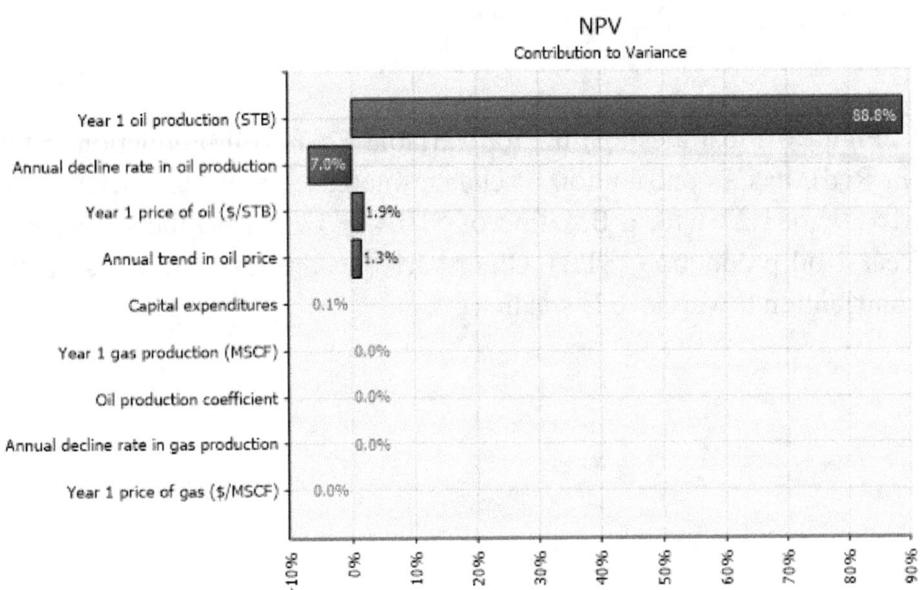

Figure 25 illustrates that the top variable Year 1 oil production (STB) has a contribution of 88.8% to the variance of the NPV. The other variables are less influential as the contribution to variances is smaller.

The Change in Output Mean Across the Range of Input Values graph is presented in Figure 26.

Figure 26. NPV change in output mean across range of input values

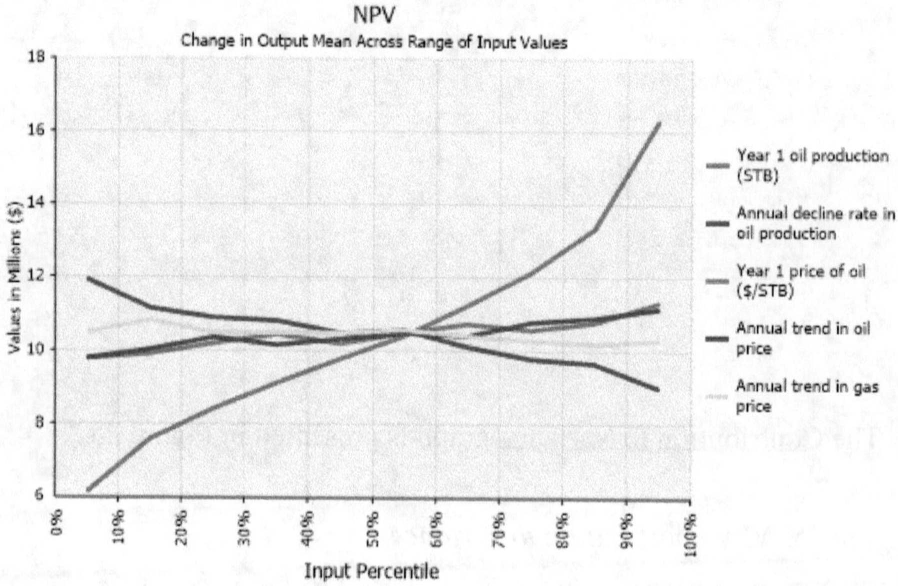

Figure 7 illustrates that the top variable Year 1 oil production (STB) (in Red), has a contribution of change increase from $6,124,102.55 to $16,296,681.27 with a Baseline of $10,438,370.84, to the variance of Year 1 oil production (STB). Other variables are less influential as the contribution to variance is smaller.

CONCLUSION

Oil and Gas Forecast

Initial Oil and Gas Forecast Model with Uncertainty

The oil and gas industry needs to make forecasts of production, revenues, and expenses for a multi-year period in the face of much uncertainty. The model shown here creates forecasts for 10 years, assuming all the inputs in the blue cells are known. The bottom line, an NPV of about $10.4 million, is a best guess, but with all the uncertainty that exists, it is hardly believable. A later version of the model that incorporates uncertainty provides much better insights.

Note: STB stands for *stock tank barrel*, and MSCF stands for *thousand standard cubic feet.*

Oil and Gas Forecast Basic @RISK Model

This model introduces essential improvements to the model in the file Initial Oil & Gas Forecast Model with Uncertainty. Each of the blue input cells is now modeled with the probability distribution shown to its right. These distributions would be assessed by oil/gas experts, possibly with the help of historical data.

There are several modeling assumptions. First, the values in rows 9, 10, 13, 14, 17, and 18 are generated once and then used each year. In particular, the decline in oil production and the decline in gas production are assumed to be *constant* from year to year. Second, the model assumes constant *trends* in oil and gas prices, the percentages in cells C13 and C14. But it also assumes some noise in the yearly prices around these trends, as indicated in the formulas in rows 24 and 25 for years 2 and beyond. Third, on the advice of an oil/gas analyst, the annual operating expenses vary around 3% of the initial capital expenditures plus $3 per barrel of oil. Using these as best guesses, actual coefficients are generated in rows 17 and 18, and they are used in row 28.

All the output sections have been colored red to indicate that these are designated @RISK outputs. However, except for the NPV cell, each output is the entire row of values. This lets you see time series graphs for each row, a few of which are shown.

Note: STB stands for *stock tank barrel*, and MSCF stands for *thousand standard cubic feet.*

Oil and Gas Forecast Sensitivity Analysis

This model is identical to the model in the file *Oil, Gas Forecast 1 - Basic @RISK Model*. However, the purpose now is to see which of the uncertain inputs the NPV output is most sensitive to, and it illustrates one of the options in @RISK sensitivity analysis. Besides the obvious inputs in blue, noise inputs for gas and oil prices are embedded in the formulas in rows 24 and 25. However, it might be better to ignore these noise inputs for the sensitivity analysis and focus only on the inputs in blue. To do this, a simulation setting must be changed, and a property function must be appended to the inputs in blue. Specifically:

1. Click the Simulation Settings button and under the Sampling tab, select the "Inputs Marked with Collect" option in the "Collect Distribution Samples" dropdown list.
2. Add the property function RiskCollect() to each of the inputs in the blue cells. For example, the formula in cell C6 becomes =RiskTriang(F6, G6, H6, RiskCollect()).

The resulting tornado chart, showing only the "collect" inputs, appears. NPV is most sensitive to the year 1 oil production and the annual decline in oil production. The last five inputs have such a small effect on NPV that it hardly seems necessary to treat them as uncertain. The reason oil dominates gas in this chart is price. The production numbers for oil and gas are of roughly the same magnitude, but the price of oil is *much* larger than the price of gas. Therefore, NPV is much more sensitive to the oil inputs.

REFERENCES

Belyadi, H.2016). *Hydraulic Fracturing in Unconventional Reservoirs: Theories, Operations, and Economic Analysis*. Golf Professional Publishing.

E, Y. (2021). *Day-to-day oil & gas trading and shipping delivery inside the oil & gas market (updated version)*. CreateSpace Independent Publisher.

May, M. (2017). Investing in Oil and Gas *(Sixth Edition): A Handbook for Direct Investing in Oil and Gas Well Drilling Ventures*. CreateSpace Independent Publishing Platform.

Poston, S., & Poe, B. D. (2020). Analysis of Production Decline Curves, Society of Petroleum Engineers. Society of Petroleum Engineers.

Sun, H. (2015). *Advanced Production Decline Analysis and Application.* Golf Professional Publishing.

Chapter 3
Correlation Between Porosity and Water Saturation

ABSTRACT

In oil/gas exploration, two important characteristics of rocks are porosity (percentage of "open space") and water saturation (fraction of water in the pore space). Empirical observations have indicated that these two characteristics tend to be negatively correlated. The model developed here uses simulation and structural properties to "derive" this negative correlation. The fixed and random inputs lead to the formulas for porosity and water saturation (through another output, formation factor). Two random models are tested. The first uses uniformly distributed input values, whereas the second uses triangular distributions. Applying this finding, a typical volumetric analysis for oil reserves would contain the product phi(1-Sw), where "phi" is porosity and "Sw" is water saturation. When modeling this (using the outputs from the current simulation as inputs for a model of oil reserves), the negative correlation should be considered.*

DOI: 10.4018/979-8-3373-0959-0.ch003

INTRODUCTION

Correlation

Correlation, in the finance and investment industries, is a statistic that measures the degree to which two securities move to each other. Correlations are used in advanced portfolio management, computed as the correlation coefficient, which has a value that must fall between -1.0 and +1.0.

- Correlation is a statistic that measures the degree to which two variables move to each other.
- In finance, the correlation can measure the movement of a stock with that of a benchmark index, such as the S&P 500.
- Correlation is closely tied to diversification, the concept that certain types of risk can be mitigated by investing in assets that are not correlated.
- Correlation measures association but doesn't show if x causes y or vice versa—or if the association is caused by a third factor.
- Correlation may be easiest to identify using a scatterplot, especially if the variables have a non-linear yet still strong correlation.

Correlation shows the strength of a relationship between two variables and is expressed numerically by the correlation coefficient. The correlation coefficient's values range between -1.0 and 1.0.

A perfect positive correlation means that the correlation coefficient is exactly 1. This implies that as one security moves, either up or down, the other security moves in lockstep, in the same direction. A perfect negative correlation means that two assets move in opposite directions, while a zero correlation implies no linear relationship at all.

For example, large-cap mutual funds generally have a high positive correlation to the Standard and Poor's (S&P) 500 Index or nearly one. Small-cap stocks tend to have a positive correlation to the S&P, but it's not as high or approximately 0.8.

However, put option prices and their underlying stock prices will tend to have a negative correlation. A put option gives the owner the right but not the obligation to sell a specific amount of an underlying security at a pre-determined price within a specified time frame.

Put option contracts become more profitable when the underlying stock price decreases. In other words, as the stock price increases, the put option prices go down, which is a direct and high-magnitude negative correlation.

There are several methods of calculating correlation. The most common method, the Pearson product-moment correlation, is discussed further in this article. The Pearson product-moment correlation measures the linear relationship between two variables. It can be used for any data set that has a finite covariance matrix. Here are the steps to calculate the correlation.

1. Gather data for your "x-variable" and "y variable.
2. Find the mean for the x-variable and find the mean for the y-variable.
3. Subtract the mean of the x-variable from each value of the x-variable. Repeat this step for the y-variable.
4. Multiply each difference between the x-variable mean and x-variable value by the corresponding difference related to the y-variable.
5. Square each of these differences and add the results.
6. Determine the square root of the value obtained in Step 5.
7. Divide the value in Step 4 by the value obtained in Step 6.

In investing, correlation is most important to a diversified portfolio. Investors who wish to mitigate risk can do so by investing in non-correlated assets. For example, consider an investor who owns airline stock. If the airline industry is found to have a low correlation to the social media industry, the investor may choose to invest in a social media stock understanding that a negative impact on one industry may not impact the other.

This is often the approach when considering investing across asset classes. Stocks, bonds, precious metals, real estate, cryptocurrency, commodities, and other types of investments each have different relationships to each other. While some may be heavily correlated, others may act as a hedge to diversify risk if they are not correlated.

The risk that can be diversified away is called unsystematic risk. This type of risk is specific to a company, industry, or asset class. Investing in different assets can reduce your portfolio's correlation and reduce your exposure to unsystematic risk.

Correlation is often dictated and related to other statistical considerations. It is common to see correlation cited when statistics are used to analyse variables.

In statistics, a P-value is used to indicate whether the findings are statistically significant. It is possible to determine that two variables are correlated, but there may not be enough supporting evidence to state this as a strong claim. A high p-value indicates there is enough evidence to meaningfully conclude that the population correlation coefficient is different from zero.

The easiest way to visualize whether two variables are correlated is to graphically depict them using a scatterplot. Each point on a scatterplot represents one sample item. The x-axis of the scatterplot represents one of the variables being tested, while the y-axis of the scatter plot represents the other.

The correlation coefficient of the two variables is depicted graphically often as a linear line mapped to show the relationship of the two variables. If the two variables are positively correlated, an increasing linear line may be drawn on the scatterplot. If two variables are negatively correlated, a decreasing linear line may be drawn. The stronger the relationship of the data points, the closer each data point will be to this line.

Scatterplots may be more useful when analysing more complex data that might have changing relationships. For example, two variables may be positively correlated to a certain point, then their relationship becomes negatively correlated. This non-linear relationship may be more difficult to identify using formulas but can be easier to spot when graphed on a scatterplot.

Last, scatterplots can easily depict correlation when they incorporate density shading. A density shade or density ellipse is a shaded area on a scatterplot that visually shows the densest region of data points on a scatterplot. The density ellipses will often mirror the direction of a linear correlation line if variables are related. Otherwise, density ellipses that are more circular with no defined direction indicate a lower correlation.

Another inherent difficulty in statistics is determining whether relationships between two variables are caused by those variables. Consider the following statement:

"Most basketball players are tall. Therefore, if you play basketball, you will become tall."

The statement above is not true. Individuals who are tall and understand this advantage may gravitate to basketball because their natural physical abilities best suit them for the sport. However, because height and activity in basketball may be positively correlated, statisticians and data scientists must be aware that a strong relationship between two variables may or may not be caused due to any one of the variables.

Like other aspects of statistical analysis, correlation can be misinterpreted. Small sample sizes may yield unreliable results, even if it appears as though the correlation between two variables is strong. Alternatively, a small sample size may yield uncorrelated findings when the two variables are linked.

Correlation is often skewed when an outlier is present. Correlation only shows how one variable is connected to another and may not identify how a single instance or outcome can impact the correlation coefficient.

Correlation may also be misinterpreted if the relationship between two variables is nonlinear. It is much easier to identify two variables with a positive or negative correlation. However, two variables may still be correlated with a more complex relationship.

Correlation is a statistical term describing the degree to which two variables move in coordination with one another. If the two variables move in the same direction, then those variables are said to have a positive correlation. If they move in opposite directions, then they have a negative correlation.

Correlations play an important role in finance because they are used to forecast future trends and to manage the risks within a portfolio. These days, the correlations between assets can be easily calculated using various software programs and online services. Correlations, along with other statistical concepts, play an important role in the creation and pricing of derivatives and other complex financial instruments.

Correlation is a widely used concept in modern finance. For example, a trader might use historical correlations to predict whether a company's shares will rise or fall in response to a change in interest rates or commodity prices. Similarly, a portfolio manager might aim to reduce their risk by ensuring that the individual assets within their portfolio are not overly correlated with one another.

Investors may prefer the level of correlation within their portfolio. In general, most investors will prefer to have a lower correlation as this mitigates risk in their portfolios of different assets or securities being impacted by similar market conditions. However, risk-seeking investors or investors wanting to put their money into a very specific type of sector or company may be willing to have a higher correlation within their portfolio in exchange for greater potential returns.

LITERATURE

Piersol et al. (2021): This work has been selected by scholars as being culturally important and is part of the knowledge base of civilisation as we know it. This work is in the public domain in the United States of America, and possibly other nations. Within the United States, you may freely copy and distribute this work, as no entity (individual or corporate) has a copyright on the body of the work. Scholars believe, and we concur, that this work is important enough to be preserved, reproduced, and made generally available to the public. To ensure a quality reading experience, this work has been proofread and republished using a format that seamlessly blends the original graphical elements with text in an easy-to-read typeface. We appreciate your support of the preservation process and thank you for being an important part of keeping this knowledge alive and relevant. Budhu (2015): An accessible, clear, concise, and contemporary course in geotechnical engineering, this key text: i) Strikes a balance between theory and practical applications for an introductory course in soil mechanics; ii) Keeps mechanics to a minimum for the students to appreciate the background, assumptions and limitations of the theories;

iii) Discusses implications of the key ideas to provide students with an understanding of the context for their application; iv) Gives a modern explanation of soil behaviour is presented particularly in soil settlement and soil strength; and v) Offers substantial on-line resources to support teaching and learning.

Selley (1978): Academic Journal Offprint from: - Quartal Journal Geological Society, 135, Part 1, 1978. 13pp, 16figs, Printed Card Cover, VGC. Hawkins (1978): Academic Journal Offprint from: - Quartal Journal Geological Society, 135, Part 1, 1978. 17pp, 10figs, 3 b/wpls, Printed Card Cover, VGC. **ELABORATION**

Simulation's Calculations (Define)

The Inputs are presented in Table 1:

Table 1. Inputs

	Uniform	Triangle
True formation resistivity	=@RiskUniform(F4,H4)	=@RiskTriang(F4,G4,H4)
Connate water resistivity	=@RiskUniform(F5,H5)	=@RiskTriang(F5,G5,H5)
Archie saturation exponent	2	2
Archie coefficient	0.62	0.62
Archie cementation exponent	=@RiskUniform(F8,H8)	=@RiskTriang(F8,G8,H8)
Bulk density	=@RiskUniform(F9,H9)	=@RiskTriang(F9,G9,H9)
Rock matrix density	=@RiskUniform(F10,H10)	=@RiskTriang(F10,G10,H10)
Reservoir fluid density	0.9	0.9

The input Parameters are presented in Table 2:

Table 2. Parameters

	Minimum	Most likely	Maximum
True formation resistivity	19	20	21
Connate water resistivity	0.055	0.065	0.075
Archie cementation exponent	2	2.15	2.3
Bulk density	2.36	2.37	2.38
Rock matrix density	2.58	2.605	2.63

The Term in volumetric analysis is presented in Table 3:

Table 3. Term in volumetric analysis

=@RiskNormal(0.138,0.0058,RiskCorrmat(J6:K7,1))*(1-@RiskNormal(0.379,0.031,RiskCorrmat(J6:K7,2)))

The Correlation matrix is shown in Table 4:

Table 4. Term in volumetric analysis

Correlation matrix	
1	
-0.53	1

The Outputs are presented in Table 5:

Table 5. Outputs

Outputs		
Porosity	=@RiskOutput("Porosity_Unif") + (C9-C10)/(C11-C10)	=@RiskOutput("Porosity_Triang") + (D9-D10)/(D11-D10)
Formation factor	=C7*C14^(-C8)	=D7*D14^(-D8)
Water saturation	=@RiskOutput("WaterSat_Unif") + (C15*C5/C4)^(1/C6)	=@RiskOutput("WaterSat_Triang") + (D15*D5/D4)^(1/D6)

The Standard deviations are given in Table 6:

Table 6. Outputs

Outputs		
Porosity	=@RiskStdDev(C14)	=@RiskStdDev(D14)
Water saturation	=@RiskStdDev(C16)	=@RiskStdDev(D16)

Simulation: Risk Evaluation and Sensitivity Analysis

Porosity Uniform Analysis and Evaluation

Figure 1 displays the Porosity Uniform distribution. The Porosity Uniform Minimum is 11.9580% and the Maximum is 15.5685%. The Maximum Porosity Uniform *Mean* is 13.7768% and the *Standard Deviation* is 0.8014%, which is good. There is a 5% probability that the Maximum Porosity Uniform will be below 12.485%, a 90% probability will be 15.082%; and a 5% probability that it will be above 15.082% as shown on the graph.

Figure 1. Porosity uniform distribution

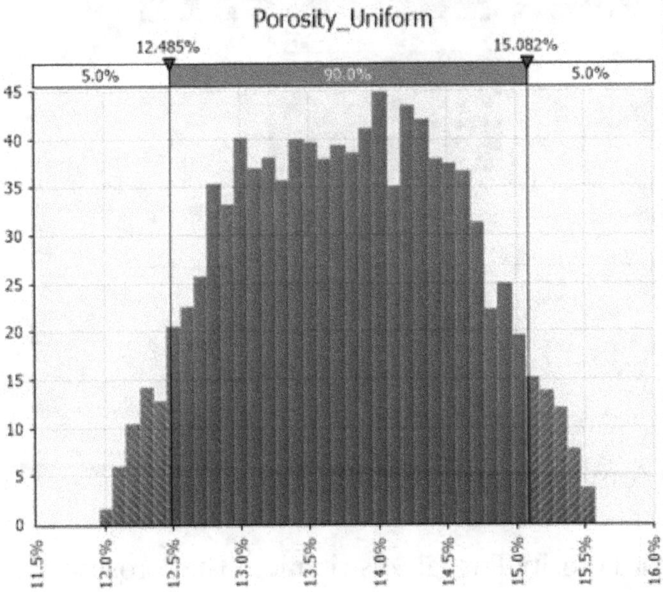

Statistics	Porosity_Uniform
Cell	C14
Minimum	11.9580%
Maximum	15.5685%
Mean	13.7768%
90% CI	± 0.0186%
Mode	14.2655%
Median	13.7877%
Std Dev	0.8014%
Skewness	0.0047
Kurtosis	2.1470
Values	5000
Errors	0
Filtered	0
Left X	12.485%
Left P	5.0%
Right X	15.082%
Right P	95.0%
Dif. X	2.5973%
Dif. P	90.0%

Sensitivity Analysis

Sensitivity analysis provides for identifying and quantifying the main contributors to variability and risk based on the probability distribution.

The Inputs Ranked by Effect on Output Mean are given in Figure 2.

The graph illustrates that the effect of the top variable Rock matrix density Uniform, on the Porosity Uniform is a change in the range of 12.65% to 14.920%, which are respectively left and right from the Baseline of 13.7768%, which is marked on the graph. Other variables are less influential as their associated effect has smaller arrays.

Figure 2. Porosity uniform inputs ranked by effect on output mean

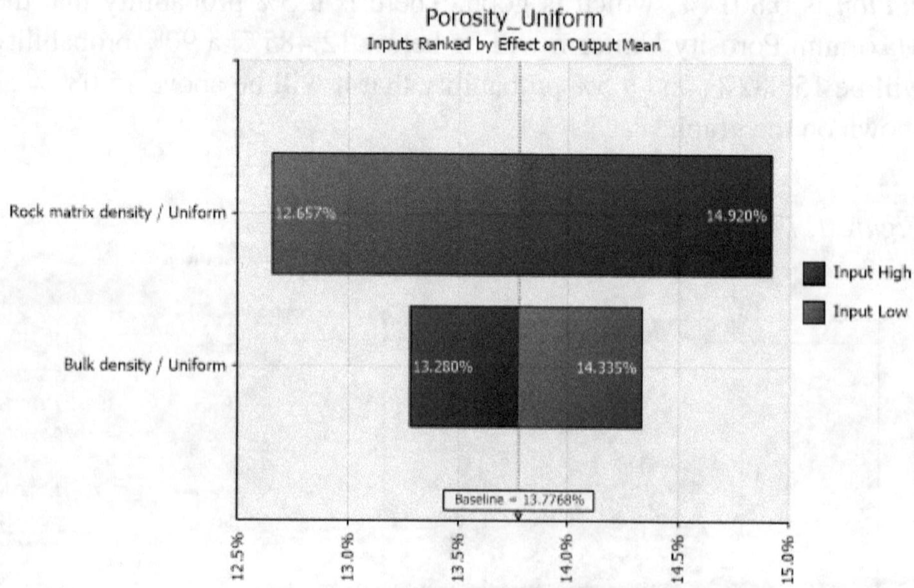

Porosity Triangle Analysis and Evaluation

Figure 3 displays the Porosity Triangle distribution. The Porosity Triangle Minimum is 12.0824% and the Maximum is 15.4350%. The Porosity Triangle *Mean* is 13.7799% and the *Standard Deviation* is 0.5744%. There is a 5% probability that the Porosity Triangle will be below 12.820%, a 90% probability that it will be 14.742%; and a 5% probability that it will be above 14.742% as shown on the graph.

Figure 3. Porosity triangle distribution

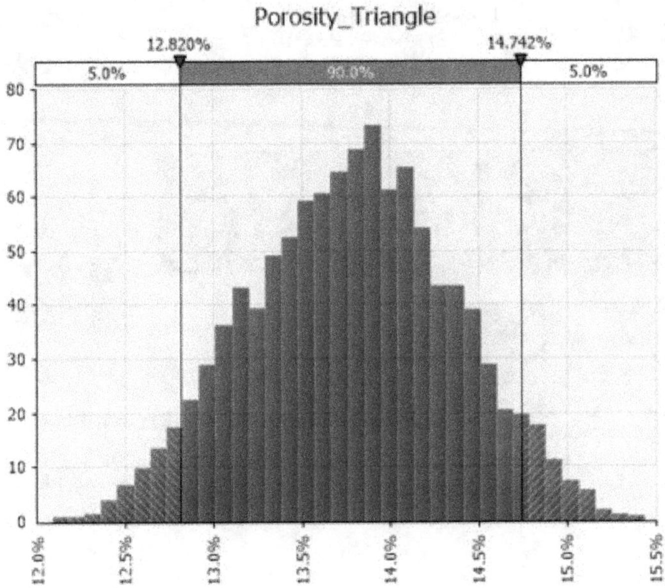

Statistics	Porosity_Triangle
Cell	D14
Minimum	12.0824%
Maximum	15.4350%
Mean	13.7799%
90% CI	± 0.0134%
Mode	14.0537%
Median	13.7982%
Std Dev	0.5744%
Skewness	-0.0299
Kurtosis	2.6112
Values	5000
Errors	0
Filtered	0
Left X	12.820%
Left P	5.0%
Right X	14.742%
Right P	95.0%
Dif. X	1.9219%
Dif. P	90.0%

Sensitivity Analysis

Sensitivity analysis provides for identifying and quantifying the main contributors to variability and risk based on the probability distribution.

The Inputs Ranked by Effect on Output Mean are given in Figure 4.

The graph illustrates that the effect of the top variable Rock matrix density Uniform, on the Porosity Triangle is a change in the range of 12.879% to 14.689%, which are respectively left and right from the Baseline of 13.7799%, which is marked on the graph. Other variables are less influential as their associated effect has smaller arrays.

Figure 4. Porosity triangle inputs ranked by effect on output mean

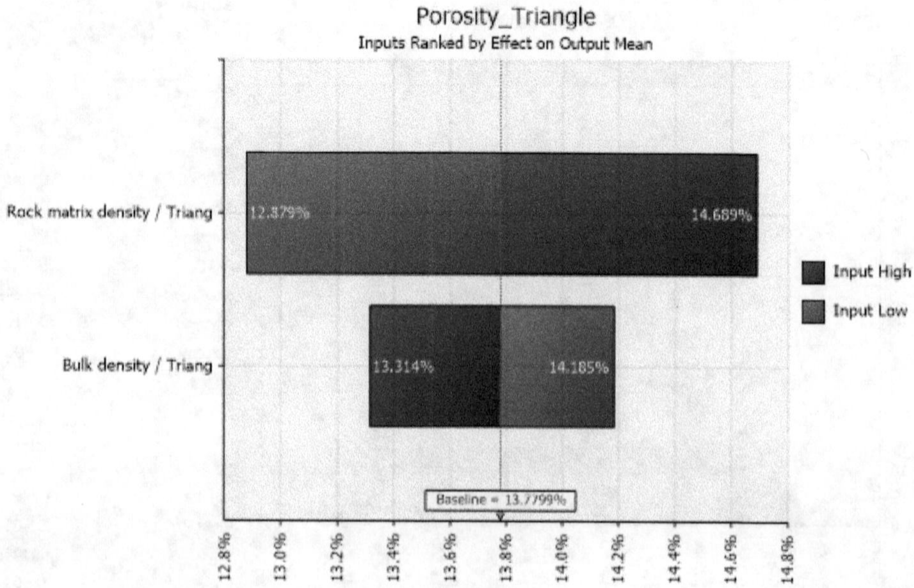

Water Saturation Uniform Analysis and Evaluation

Figure 5 displays the Water Saturation Uniform distribution.

The Water Saturation Uniform Minimum is 26.571% and the Maximum is 52.955%. The Maximum Water Saturation Uniform *Mean* is 38.061% and the *Standard Deviation* is 4.441%, which is good. There is a 5% probability that the Maximum Water Saturation will be 31.30%, a 90% probability will be 46.07%; and a 5% probability that it will be above 46.07% as shown on the graph.

Figure 5. Water saturation uniform distribution

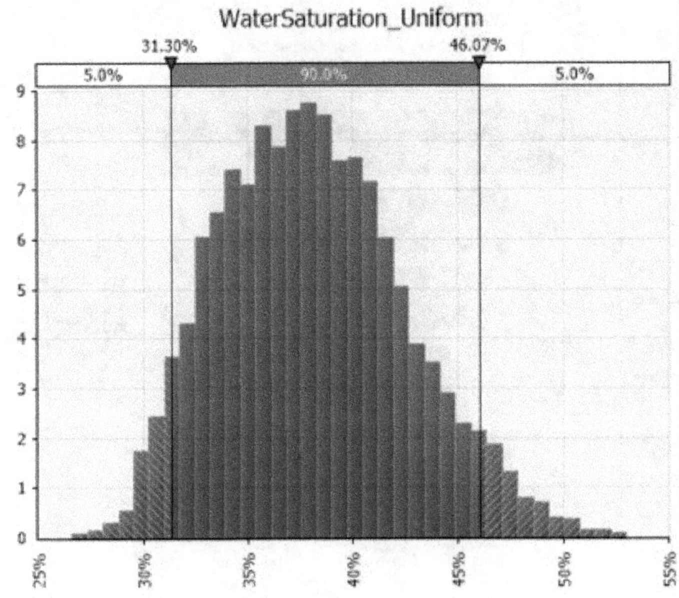

Statistics	WaterSaturation_U...
Cell	C16
Minimum	26.571%
Maximum	52.955%
Mean	38.061%
90% CI	± 0.103%
Mode	37.445%
Median	37.818%
Std Dev	4.441%
Skewness	0.3347
Kurtosis	2.7593
Values	5000
Errors	0
Filtered	0
Left X	31.30%
Left P	5.0%
Right X	46.07%
Right P	95.0%
Dif. X	14.767%
Dif. P	90.0%

Sensitivity Analysis

Sensitivity analysis provides for identifying and quantifying the main contributors to variability and risk based on the probability distribution.

The Inputs Ranked by Effect on Output Mean are given in Figure 6.

The graph illustrates that the effect of the top variable Archie cementation exponent Uniform, on the Water Saturation Uniform is a change in the range of 33.163% to 43.372%, which are respectively left and right from the Baseline of 38.061%, which is marked on the graph. Other variables are less influential as their associated effect has smaller arrays.

Figure 6. Water saturation uniform inputs ranked by effect on output mean

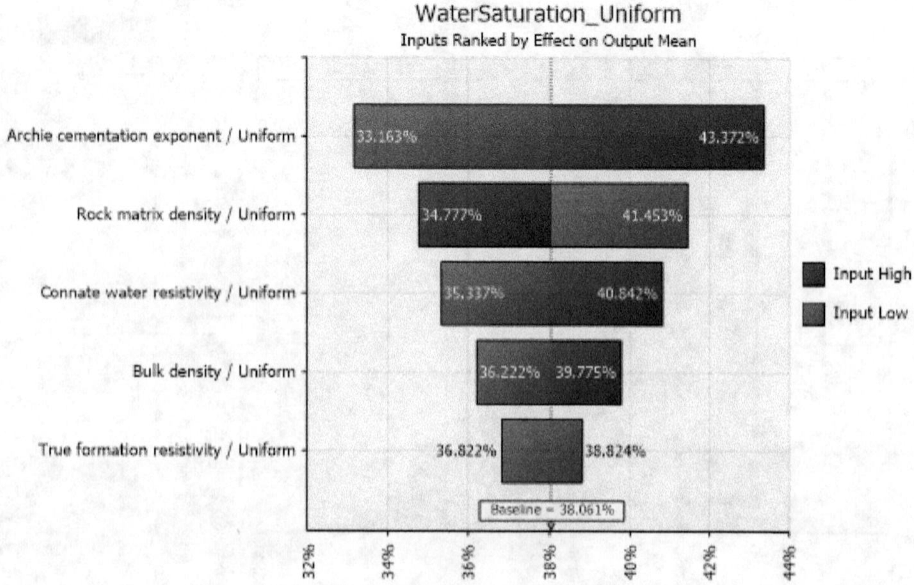

Water Saturation Triangle Analysis and Evaluation

Figure 7 displays the Water Saturation Triangle distribution.

The Water Saturation Triangle Minimum is 29.332% and the Maximum is 51.470%. The Porosity Triangle *Mean* is 37.926% and the *Standard Deviation* is 3.127%. There is a 5% probability that the Water Saturation Triangle will be below 33.10%, a 90% probability that it will be 43.41%; and a 5% probability that it will be above 4.341% as shown on the graph.

Figure 7. Water saturation triangle distribution

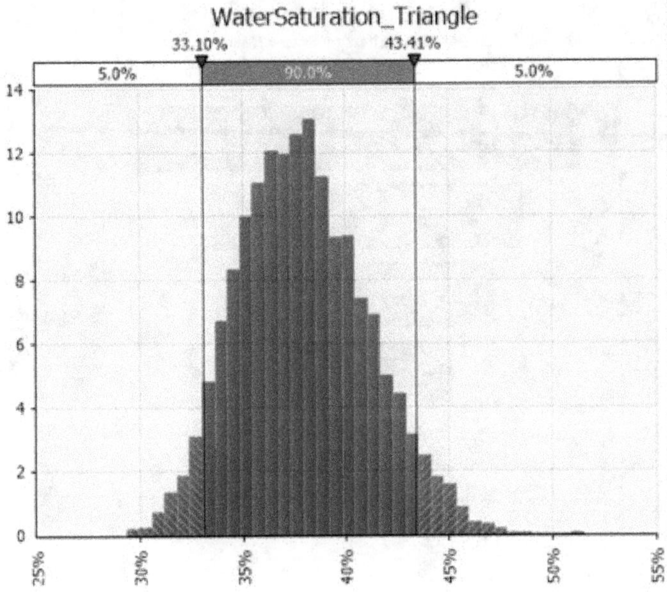

Statistics	WaterSaturation_T...
Cell	D16
Minimum	29.332%
Maximum	51.479%
Mean	37.926%
90% CI	± 0.0727%
Mode	37.723%
Median	37.750%
Std Dev	3.127%
Skewness	0.2763
Kurtosis	2.8693
Values	5000
Errors	0
Filtered	0
Left X	33.10%
Left P	5.0%
Right X	43.41%
Right P	95.0%
Dif. X	10.308%
Dif. P	90.0%

Sensitivity Analysis

Sensitivity analysis provides for identifying and quantifying the main contributors to variability and risk based on the probability distribution.

The Inputs Ranked by Effect on Output Mean are given in Figure 8.

The graph illustrates that the effect of the top variable Archie cementation exponent Triangle, on the Water Saturation Triangle is a change in the range of 34.054% to 41.959%, which are respectively left and right from the Baseline of 37.9256%, which is marked on the graph. Other variables are less influential as their associated effect has smaller arrays.

Figure 8. Water saturation triangle inputs ranked by effect on output mean

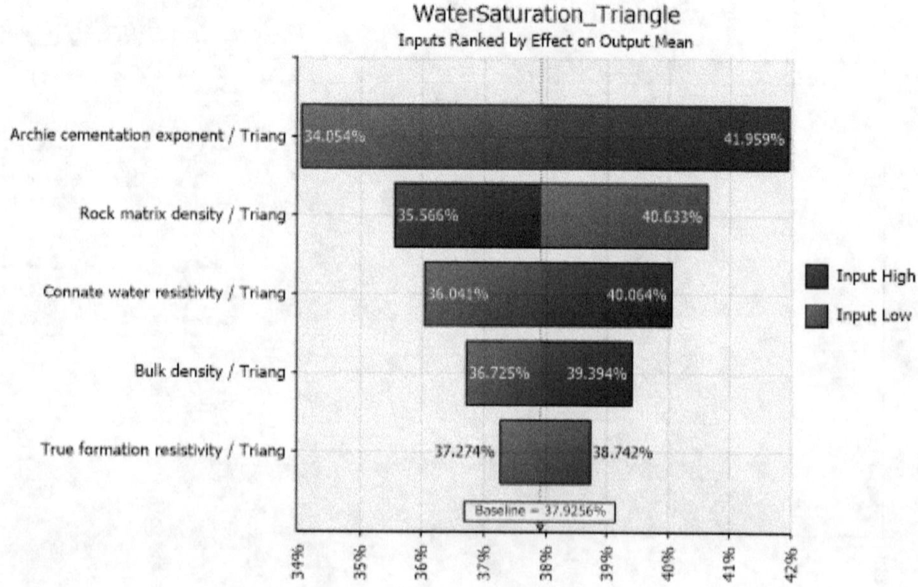

Porosity Uniform versus Water Saturation Uniform

The Porosity Uniform versus Water Saturation Uniform is presented in Figure 9.

The Porosity Uniform versus Water Saturation Uniform X-Axis *Mean* is 38.0632% and the Standard Deviation is 4.4199%.

The Porosity Uniform versus Water Saturation Uniform Y-Axis Mean is 13.7768% and the Standard Deviation is 0.79694%.

The Pearson Correlation is -0.5475 and the Rank Correlation is -0.5180.

Figure 9. Porosity uniform versus water saturation uniform

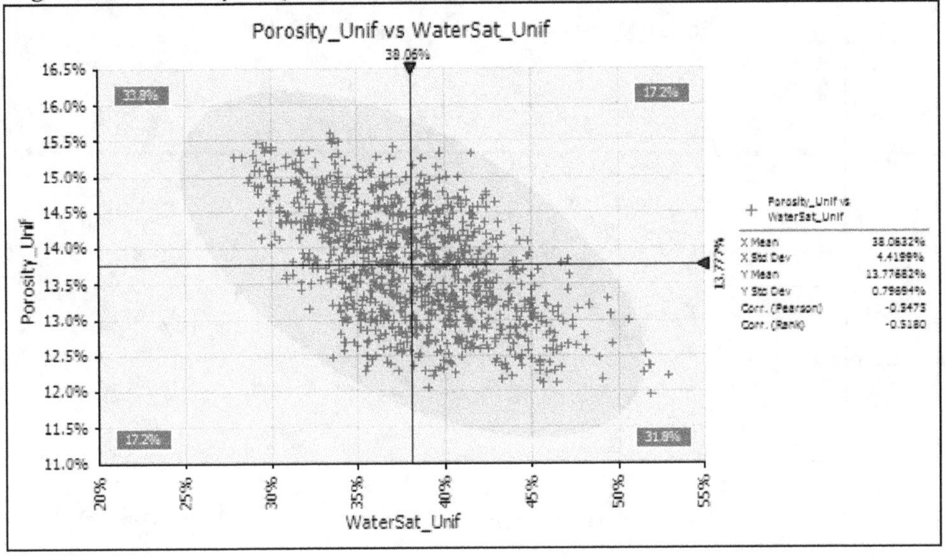

Porosity Triangle versus Water Saturation Triangle

The Porosity Triangle versus the Water Saturation Triangle is presented in Figure 10.

The Porosity Triangle versus Water Saturation Triangle X-Axis Mean is 37.9260% and the Standard Deviation is 3.1297%.

The Porosity Triangle versus Water Saturation Triangle Y-Axis *Mean* is 13.77983% and the Standard Deviation is 0.57636%.

The Pearson Correlation is -0.5337 and the Rank Correlation is -0.5106.

Figure 10. Porosity triangle versus water saturation triangle

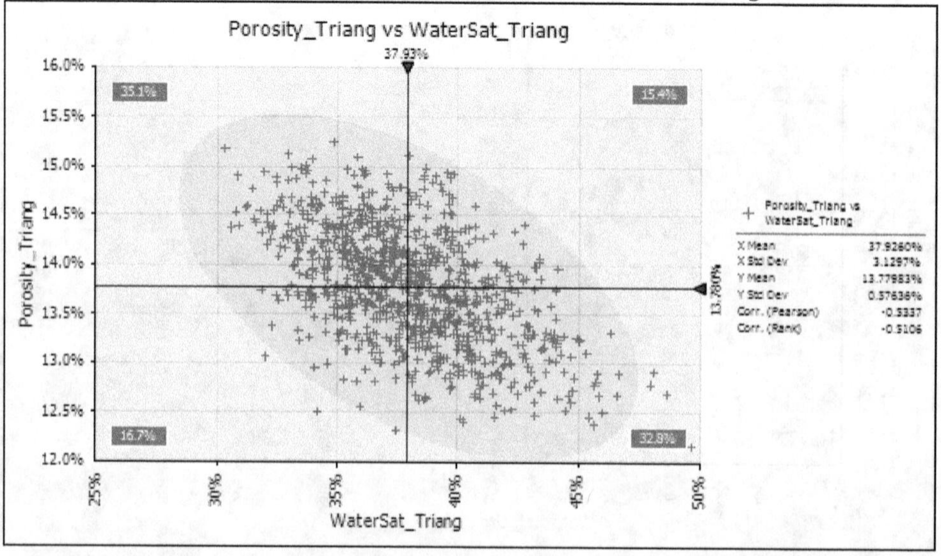

CONCLUSION

Correlation Between Porosity and Water Saturation

In oil/gas exploration, two important characteristics of rocks are porosity (percentage of "open space") and water saturation (fraction of water in the pore space). Empirical observations have indicated that these two characteristics tend to be negatively correlated. The model developed here uses simulation and structural properties to "derive" this negative correlation. The inputs in rows 4-11, some fixed and some random, lead to the formulas for porosity and water saturation (through another output, formation factor) in rows 14-16. Two random models are tested. The first uses uniformly distributed input values, whereas the second uses triangular distributions.

When you run the simulation, you can browse either output -- show its histogram -- and then request a scatterplot of this output versus its counterpart. The corresponding scatterplots are shown on the next sheet, and the negative correlation of slightly more than -0.5 is clear. As expected, outputs that are based on uniform distributions have larger standard deviations than those based on triangular distributions, but the negative correlation is about the same for both.

Applying this finding, a typical volumetric analysis for oil reserves would contain the product phi*(1-Sw), where phi is porosity and Sw is water saturation. When modeling this (using the outputs from the current simulation as inputs for a model of oil reserves), the negative correlation should be considered, as indicated in cell J3, for example.

REFERENCES

Budhu, M. (2015). Soil Mechanics Fundamentals. Wiley-Blackwell.

Hawkins, R. (1978). Relationship between diagenesis, porosity reduction, and oil emplacement in late Carboniferous sandstone reservoirs, Bothamsall Oilfield, E Midlands. *Quartal Journal Geological Society, 135*(Part 1).

Piersol. (2021). Porosity, Total Liquid Saturation, and Permeability of Illinois Oil Sands; Report of Investigations No. 67. Hassell Street Press.

Selley, R. (1978). *Porosity gradients in North Sea oil-bearing sandstones*. *Quartal Journal Geological Society, 135*(Part 1). DOI: 10.1144/gsjgs.135.1.0119

Chapter 4
Exponential Decline

ABSTRACT

The Decline Curve analysis of the oil and gas wells model examines the production forecasting for oil and gas wells, i.e., the exponential decline curve. The standard equation, q = qie-at (3.3), can be used with random variables for both qi (the initial production rate, sometimes called IP) and a (the constant decline rate). Here the model has an additional parameter, t (time), which makes the output (Rate, STB/YR) more complicated than the volumetric reserves output. The distributions of numbers for output and forecasts or graphs are needed. The worksheet has two input cells, IP and Decline, and a column of outputs for the Rate of production in STB/YR over 15 years. After the simulation, a summary graph is generated. This graph shows uncertainty over the 15 years. Two colors signify 1) the 5th and 95th percentiles and 2) the 25th and 75th percentiles, thus representing a 90% confidence interval.

INTRODUCTION

Exponential Decline

The decline curve is a method for estimating reserves and predicting the rate of oil or gas production. It typically shows the pace at which production is expected to decline over the lifetime of an energy asset.

DOI: 10.4018/979-8-3373-0959-0.ch004

- The decline curve is a method for estimating reserves and predicting the rate of oil or gas production.
- The decline curve is a method used to determine the estimated ultimate recovery (EUR) for an oil or gas reserve.
- Primarily based on good conditions, three types of decline curves can apply to the future trend: exponential, hyperbolic, and harmonic.

Knowing the decline curve can help a producer estimate the number of oil reserves that can come from a well over its lifetime, the present and future value of a well, and the rate at which assets should depreciate on a company's books. In aggregate, the decline curve can also help determine the rate of production for a total reservoir or even multiple reservoirs.

The decline curve is a method used to determine the estimated ultimate recovery (EUR) for an oil or gas reserve. This calculation rests on a set of equations that U.S. geologist J.J. Arps developed in 1945. It is of the utmost importance that drilling projects meet an acceptable EUR threshold for a project to be considered viable and profitable.

In theory, the decline curve can apply to most wells in the industry. Underlying the decline curve equations is an expectation that well-production typically follows a three-part pattern.

1. In the initial phase production phase, the flow of oil or gas remains relatively steady, as pressure stays nearly constant.
2. Next is a transient period in which the flow of oil or gas declines rapidly, as the quantity of recoverable assets and pressure in the wellbore decreases.
3. Lastly, assets deplete to a level at which they approach the well's defined boundaries.

Arps decline curve equations most often apply to the boundary-defined production phase.

Calculating the decline curve involves a curve-fitting exercise to interpolate the future rate of production based on past production levels. Therefore, a somewhat lengthy period of time-series data is needed to estimate the projected trend. Also, the decline-curve equations assume that multiple variables involved in production and operations stay constant during the lifetime of a good asset. Primarily based on good conditions, three types of decline curves can apply to the future trend: exponential, hyperbolic, and harmonic.

Analysing the decline curve can be a more straightforward way to estimate production levels relative to more-complex simulations. However, using the decline curve also can be less accurate than simulations.

Using the decline curve has several shortcomings, including that it can underestimate oil reserves, underestimate production rates, and overestimate reservoir performance. Because it relies on past data, the decline curve does not consider the labour, equipment, and technology changes that could affect production rates. It also cannot account for the likelihood of geologic changes that more-complex models may be able to include to a degree. However, the Arps equations are still in use today.

LITERATURE

Sun (2015): In recent years, production decline-curve analysis has become the most widely used tool in the industry for oil and gas reservoir production analysis. However, most curve analysis is done by computer today, promoting a "black box" approach to engineering and leaving engineers with little background in the fundamentals of decline analysis. Advanced Production Decline Analysis and Application starts from the basic concept of advanced production decline analysis and thoroughly discusses several decline methods, such as Arps, Fetkovich, Blasingame, Agarwal-Gardner, NPI, transient, long linear flow, and FMB. A practical systematic introduction to each method helps the reservoir engineer understand the physical and mathematical models, solve the type curves and match up analysis, analyse the processes and examples, and reconstruct all the examples by hand, giving way to mastering the fundamentals behind the software. An appendix explains the nomenclature and major equations, and as a bonus, online computer programs are available for download. Poston & Poe (2020): Long ago, engineers recognized the characteristic decline of oil and gas well performance and attempted to predict its course by fitting equations to the production history. This book covers the production characteristics and associated interpretation analyses of petroleum reservoirs in a complete, thorough, and consistent manner. Production decline-curve analyses are the most widely used tool in the industry for oil and gas reservoir production analyses. This book will serve as an authoritative reference on modern production decline-curve analyses, including details of some recent advances in the technology. Decline curves are probably the most widely used and least understood production-forecasting technique currently in use in the industry. Analysis of decline curves provides an unsophisticated reservoir-evaluation tool, but profound economic decisions often rest on the outcome of the prediction. A simplistic view of decline-curve analysis can lead to wide misuse, often caused by misunderstandings. There has been no single reference book on the meaning of production decline curves, their application, and their use and misuse. The authors have endeavoured to provide such a reference. Belyadi et al. (2016): Hydraulic Fracturing in Unconventional Reservoirs: Theories, Operations, and Economic Analysis introduces the basic characteristics and theories surrounding hydraulic fracturing and the main process of fracturing in shale, including the main workflow, the details in case analysis, and the fundamental differences between theory, study, and practical operation. The book takes the complex nature of hydraulic fracturing in unconventional reservoirs and applies a practical approach that can be used as a workflow for designing fracture treatments in various shale basins across the world. Providing the audience with theories, best practices, operation and execution, and economic analysis of hydraulic fracturing in unconventional reservoirs, this reference guides the engineer and manager through broad topics including an introduction to unconventional reservoirs, advanced shale reservoir characterization, and shale gas in place calculation as well as expanding to basic theories of hydraulic fracturing and advanced topics in shale reservoir stimulation. Rounding out with coverage of the environmental aspects and practice problems on design and economic analysis, the book delivers the critical link needed between academia and industry for all aspects of hydraulic fracturing operations. **ELABORATION**

Simulation's Calculations (Define)

The IP and Decline are given in Table 1:

Table 1. IP and decline

IP	=@RiskTriang(50,100,300)
Decline	=@RiskTriang(0.08,0.12,0.16)

The Time Year and Rate STB per Year are given in Table 2:

Table 2. Time year and rate STB per year

Year	Rate, STB/YR
0	=@RiskOutput(A7,$B$6,1)+$B$3*EXP(-$B$4*A7)
1	=@RiskOutput(A8,$B$6,1)+$B$3*EXP(-$B$4*A8)
2	=@RiskOutput(A9,$B$6,1)+$B$3*EXP(-$B$4*A9)
3	=@RiskOutput(A10,$B$6,1)+$B$3*EXP(-$B$4*A10)
4	=@RiskOutput(A11,$B$6,1)+$B$3*EXP(-$B$4*A11)
5	=@RiskOutput(A12,$B$6,1)+$B$3*EXP(-$B$4*A12)
6	=@RiskOutput(A13,$B$6,1)+$B$3*EXP(-$B$4*A13)
7	=@RiskOutput(A14,$B$6,1)+$B$3*EXP(-$B$4*A14)
8	=@RiskOutput(A15,$B$6,1)+$B$3*EXP(-$B$4*A15)
9	=@RiskOutput(A16,$B$6,1)+$B$3*EXP(-$B$4*A16)
10	=@RiskOutput(A17,$B$6,1)+$B$3*EXP(-$B$4*A17)
11	=@RiskOutput(A18,$B$6,1)+$B$3*EXP(-$B$4*A18)
12	=@RiskOutput(A19,$B$6,1)+$B$3*EXP(-$B$4*A19)
13	=@RiskOutput(A20,$B$6,1)+$B$3*EXP(-$B$4*A20)
14	=@RiskOutput(A21,$B$6,1)+$B$3*EXP(-$B$4*A21)
15	=@RiskOutput(A22,$B$6,1)+$B$3*EXP(-$B$4*A22)

The Average Rate STB per Year is given in Table 3:

Table 3. Average rate STB per year

Average Rate STB/YR	=@RiskOutput("Average Rate STB/YR")+SUM(B7:B22)/16

Simulation: Risk Evaluation and Sensitivity Analysis

Average Rate STB per Year (i.e., STB/YR) Analysis and Evaluation

Figure 1 displays the Average Rate of STB per Year (STB/YR).

Figure 1. Average rate STB/YR distribution

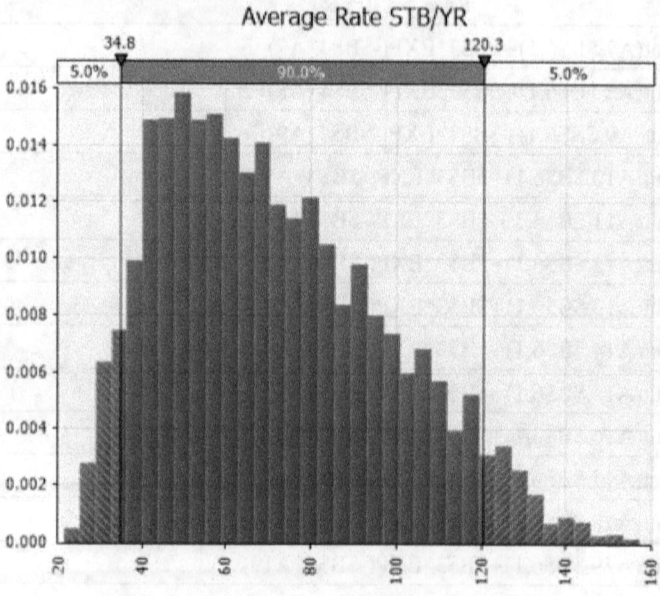

Statistics	Average Rate STB/YR
Cell	B23
Minimum	21.33
Maximum	157.21
Mean	71.20
90% CI	±0.616
Mode	49.68
Median	67.23
Std Dev	26.46
Skewness	0.5412
Kurtosis	2.5940
Values	5000
Errors	0
Filtered	0
Left X	34.8
Left P	5.0%
Right X	120.3
Right P	95.0%
Dif. X	85.54
Dif. P	90.0%

The Average Rate STB/YR Minimum is 21.33 STB, and the Maximum is 157.21 STB. The *Mean* is 71.20 STB, and the *Standard Deviation* is 26.46 STB, which is very high. There is a 5% probability that the Average Rate STB/YR will be below 34.8 STB; a 90% probability that it will be in the range of 34.8 STB – 120.3 STB; and a 5% probability that it will be above 120.3 STB.

Sensitivity Analysis

Sensitivity analysis provides for identifying and quantifying the main contributors to variability and risk based on the probability distribution.

The Inputs Ranked by Effect on Output Mean are given in Figure 2.

The graph illustrates that the effect of variable IP, on the Average Rate STB/YR is a change in the range of 34.764 STB to 119.78 STB, which are respectively left and right from the Baseline of 71.201 STB, which is marked on the graph. The other variable is less influential.

Figure 2. Average rate STB/YR inputs ranked by effect on output mean

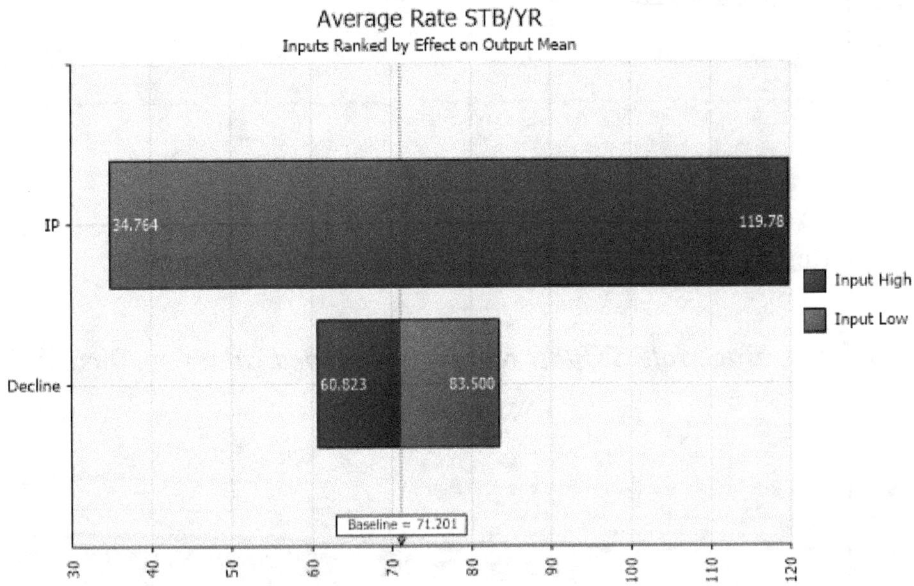

The Regression Coefficients graph is shown in Figure 3.

This graph illustrates the variable IP with a coefficient of 0.97. Therefore, if IP increases by one Standard Deviation, the Average Rate STB/YR will increase by 0.97 Standard Deviations. The other variable is less influential.

Figure 3. Average rate STB/YR regression coefficients

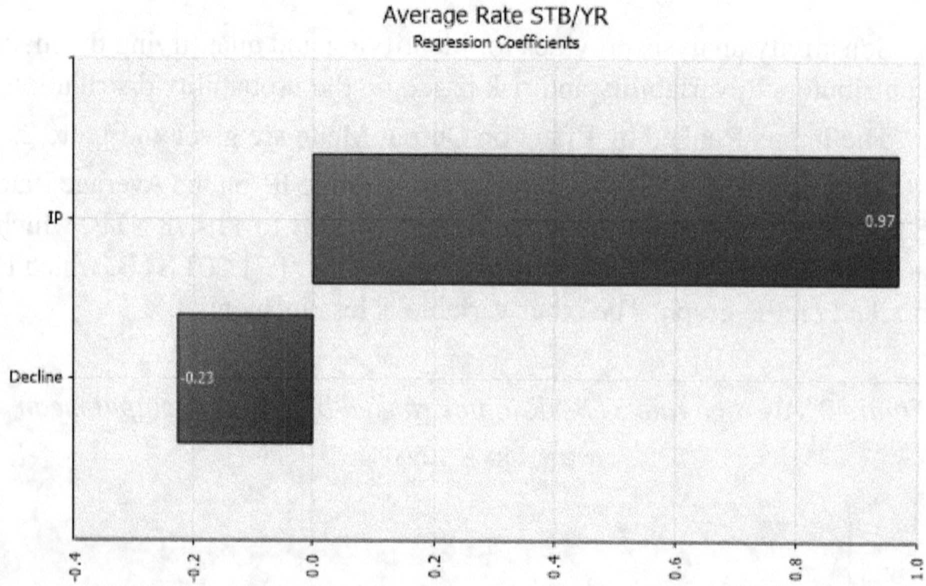

The Regression-Mapped-Values graph is shown in Figure 4.

Figure 4. Average rate STB/YR regression mapped values coefficients

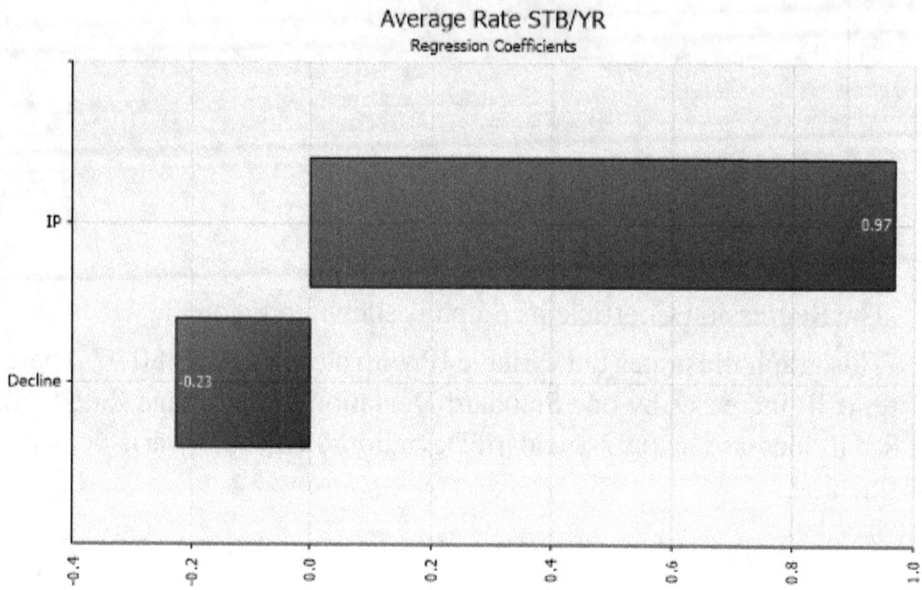

This graph illustrates the variable IP with a value of 25.593. Therefore, if IP changes by one Standard Deviation, the Average Rate STB will return 25.593. The other variable is less influential.

The Correlation Coefficients are presented in Figure 5.

Figure 5. Average rate STB/YR correlation coefficients

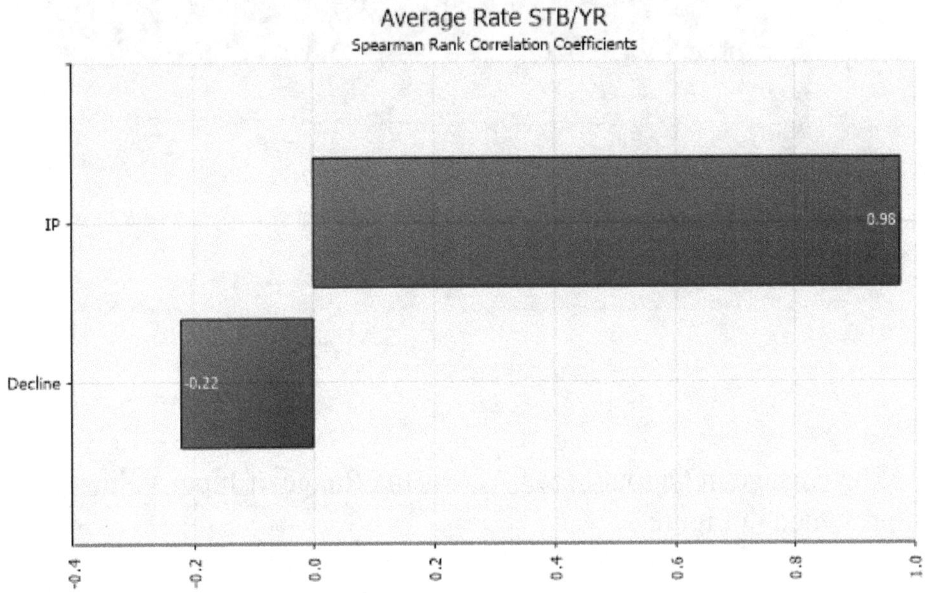

The graph shows that if the top variable IP, with a correlation coefficient of 0.98, increases by one unit, the Average Rate STB/YR will increase by 0.98 units. Other variables are less influential as the correlation coefficient is smaller.

The Contribution to Variance graph is presented in Figure 6.

Figure 6 illustrates that the top variable IP has a contribution of 94.2% to the variance of the Average Rate STB/YR. Another variable is less influential as the contribution to variance is smaller.

Figure 6. Average rate STB/YR contribution to variance

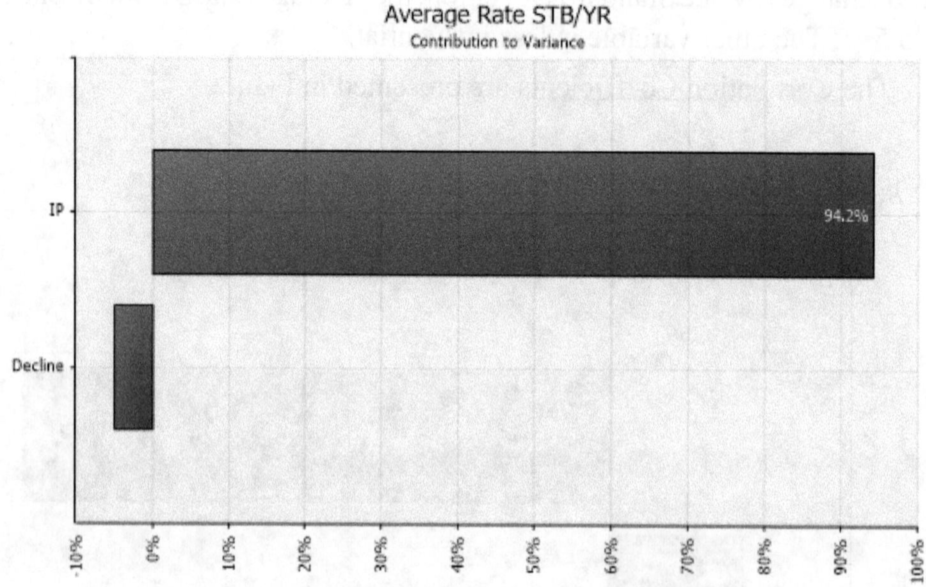

The <u>Change in Output Mean Across the Range of Input Values</u> graph is presented in Figure 7.

Figure 7. Average rate STB/YR change in output mean across range of input values

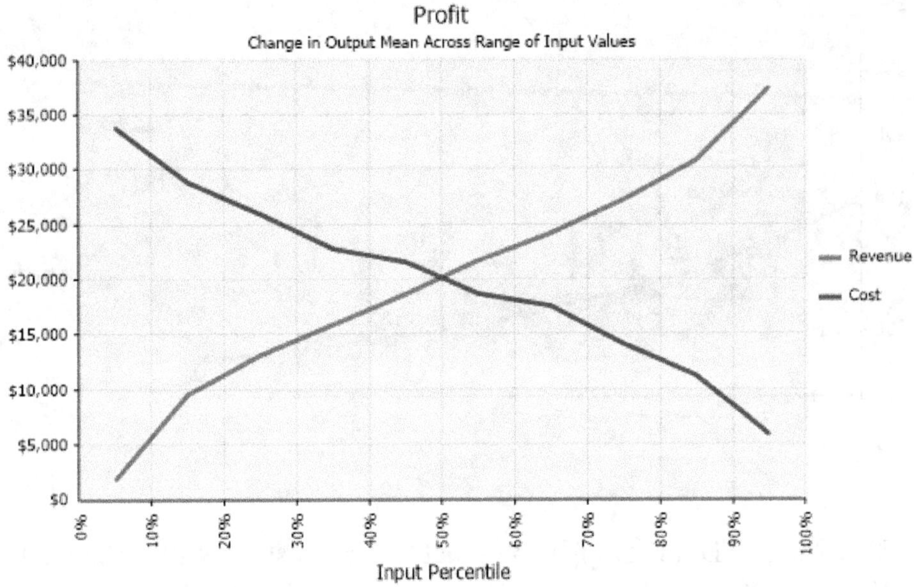

Figure 7 illustrates that the top variable Revenue (in Red), has a contribution of change increase from 34.764 STB to 119.78 STB with a Baseline of 71.201 STB, to the variance of Average Rate STB/YR. Other variables are less influential as the contribution to variance is smaller.

Rate, STB/YR Analysis

Figure 8 presents the Rate, STB/YR graph.

Figure 8. Growth rate / 2 versus growth rate / 2

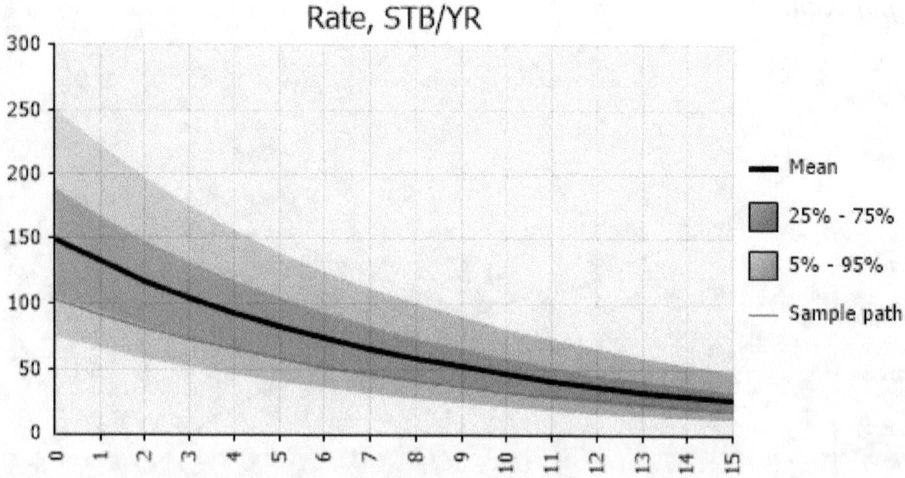

The Rate, STB/YR graph shows that the *Mean* starts with 150.00 STB in Year zero (0) and then gradually decreases to 24.79 STB as shown in Table 4.

Table 4. Rate, STB/YR

Time, YR	Rate, STB/YR
0	150.00
1	133.04
2	117.99
3	104.65
4	92.82
5	82.32
6	73.01
7	64.76
8	57.43
9	50.94
10	45.18
11	40.07

continued on following page

Table 4. Continued

Time, YR	Rate, STB/YR
12	35.54
13	31.52
14	27.96
15	24.79

CONCLUSION

Decline Curve Analysis of Oil and Gas Wells

This model examines the familiar production forecasting model for oil and gas wells, the exponential decline curve.

The standard equation, q = qie-at (3.3), can be used with random variables for both qi (the initial production rate, sometimes called IP) and a (the constant decline rate). Here the model has an additional parameter, t (time), which makes the output (Rate, STB/YR) more complicated than the volumetric reserves output.

No longer do we just want a distribution of numbers for output. Instead, we want a distribution of forecasts or graphs. The worksheet has two input cells, IP and Decline, and a column of outputs for the Rate of production in STB/YR over 15 years.

After the simulation, you can generate a summary graph like that shown in the model. This graph shows uncertainty over the 15 years. The light gray region represents the 5th and 95th percentiles. The dark gray region represents the 25th and 75th percentiles. Thus, this shaded area represents a 90% confidence interval.

REFERENCES

Belyadi, H.2016). *Hydraulic Fracturing in Unconventional Reservoirs: Theories, Operations, and Economic Analysis*. Golf Professional Publishing.

Poston, S., & Poe, B. D. (2020). Analysis of Production Decline Curves, Society of Petroleum Engineers. Society of Petroleum Engineers.

Sun, H. (2015). *Advanced Production Decline Analysis and Application*. Golf Professional Publishing.

Chapter 5
Forecasting Exponential Decline

ABSTRACT

Production and Economic Forecast Using Exponential Decline forecasts production, revenues, and present value based on exponential decline. The exponential decline pattern for oil production is represented using the formula q = qie-at, where qi is the annual production for the first year and a is the (fixed) annual percentage decline rate. Uncertain input factors include 1) Yearly production (YrlProd), represented by Lognormal distribution; 2) Decline rate (Declrate), represented by Lognormal distribution; 3) GOR (constant Gas-Oil-Ratio), represented by Triangle distribution; 4) Price of gas, represented by Normal distribution; 5) Price of oil, represented by Normal distribution; and 6) Rate of increase of oil and gas prices, which are represented by Normal distributions embedded in the Revenue formulas. For each year, a new sample is drawn from a new Normal distribution, modelling variation from year to year. Outputs are defined as 1) Total NPV and 2) Oil-Gros, or production, for each year.

DOI: 10.4018/979-8-3373-0959-0.ch005

INTRODUCTION

Decline Curve

The decline curve is a method for estimating reserves and predicting the rate of oil or gas production. It typically shows the pace at which production is expected to decline over the lifetime of an energy asset. Peak oil refers to the hypothetical point at which global crude oil production will hit its maximum rate, after which production will start to decline. This concept is derived from geophysicist Marion King Hubbert's "peak theory," which states that oil production follows a bell-shaped curve.

In the traditional vision of peak oil, the production decline accelerates as the cost of extracting new reserves grows. This would put pressure on existing reserves that are drawing down over time. If new reserves are not brought online more rapidly than the existing reserves drawdown, then peak oil has been reached. Peak oil has been declared several times, but each deceleration has proved premature because of new extraction technologies like hydraulic fracturing and better surveying techniques.

- Peak oil is a hypothetical scenario where oil production hits a maximum rate and begins to decline.
- When peak oil is reached, the discovery of new reserves cannot keep pace with the decline in existing reserves.
- Although declared several times, peak oil has not happened thanks to new technology that helped sustain oil production, keeping global supplies flowing.
- Peak oil might also happen due to declining demand, which would result from more efficient technologies and alternative energy sources.
- Studies of climate change suggest that a decline in oil consumption in favour of alternative energy sources will be necessary to avert catastrophic climate change.

Because oil is a non-replenishing resource, there is a limit to how much the world can extract and refine. However, the scenario of total depletion is just one version of peak oil. In theory, peak oil can be brought on by the production squeeze—the drawdown as new reserves get more expensive to extract. It can also be caused by a production decline when oil alternatives become more cost-effective, pricing oil out of the market and making it unprofitable to explore new reserves.

The Organization of Petroleum Exporting Countries (OPEC) brought peak oil to the forefront in 1973 when it orchestrated an oil embargo that exposed the United States' vulnerability to a drop in oil supplies. Since then, peak oil on the supply side, either from total drawdown or difficulty of extraction, has been a major concern for energy-dependent nations. But this same fear spurred investment in exploration and technology, which has continually pushed peak oil's projected date into the future.

Every time prices increase based on peak oil forecasts; the higher prices incentivize new investments in technology that postpone the peak. Of course, there is still a ceiling to oil extraction, but that may not be reached due to peak oil demand.

Peak oil demand refers to a scenario in which production falls due to lower consumption, rather than scarcity of resources. This is especially likely if green technology and alternative energy become more cost-effective than extracting oil. In 2016, OPEC (the one-time bogeyman of peak oil supply) started to discuss peak oil demand as a possibility within a decade.

One possible indication of peak oil occurred in 2020 when U.S. crude oil production fell by more than 8%, the largest recorded year-on-year drop. The drop was largely attributed to low oil prices, due to reduced consumption during the COVID-19 pandemic. So peak oil is once again appearing on the horizon—just not for the reasons expected in the 1970s.

There have been many predictions about when and if the world's oil production would peak. In 1962, Hubbert predicted that global oil production would peak near the year 2000 at a rate of 12.5 billion barrels per year. Twelve years later, he estimated that the world would hit peak oil if the current trends continued. Both his theories proved incorrect.

Some analysts and industry officials have predicted peak oil before 2030, but making these forecasts isn't always because of the difficulty in estimating the actual size of the world's unexplored oil reserves.

Climate scientists have warned that oil is a major source of carbon dioxide, a driver of global climate change. A successful effort to curb global warming would likely require a reduction in oil consumption.

Some of the most obvious consequences of hitting peak oil supply are directly related to the economy. A sudden drop in oil supplies will lead to a sharp spike in prices, with a ripple effect in oil-dependent industries. Major sectors like agriculture could see a steep decline, due to the scarcity of oil-based fertilizers and fuel. The ripple effect could continue to shipping, transportation, and even the food and manufacturing industries. In a worst-case scenario, large areas of the world could experience famine because of higher food prices.

Peak oil would also have a sizeable effect on the climate, by reducing the carbon footprints of oil-dependent industries. Fossil fuels such as oil, coal, and natural gas are major sources of atmospheric carbon dioxide and a leading factor in anthropogenic climate change. A 2021 report by the Intergovernmental Panel on Climate Change (IPCC) warned that global temperatures have already risen by around 1.07 degrees Celsius due to human activity. Without "deep reductions" in carbon dioxide and other greenhouse gas emissions, global temperatures will likely increase by over 2 degrees Celsius before 2100.

Exponential Decline

The decline curve is a method for estimating reserves and predicting the rate of oil or gas production. It typically shows the pace at which production is expected to decline over the lifetime of an energy asset.

- The decline curve is a method for estimating reserves and predicting the rate of oil or gas production.
- The decline curve is a method used to determine the estimated ultimate recovery (EUR) for an oil or gas reserve.
- Primarily based on good conditions, three types of decline curves can apply to the future trend: exponential, hyperbolic, and harmonic.

Knowing the decline curve can help a producer estimate the number of oil reserves that can come from a well over its lifetime, the present and future value of a well, and the rate at which assets should depreciate on a company's books. In aggregate, the decline curve can also help determine the rate of production for a total reservoir or even multiple reservoirs.

The decline curve is a method used to determine the estimated ultimate recovery (EUR) for an oil or gas reserve. This calculation rests on a set of equations that U.S. geologist J.J. Arps developed in 1945. It is of the utmost importance that drilling projects meet an acceptable EUR threshold for a project to be considered viable and profitable.

In theory, the decline curve can apply to most wells in the industry. Underlying the decline curve equations is an expectation that well-production typically follows a three-part pattern.

1. In the initial phase production phase, the flow of oil or gas remains relatively steady, as pressure stays nearly constant.
2. Next is a transient period in which the flow of oil or gas declines rapidly, as the quantity of recoverable assets and pressure in the wellbore decreases.
3. Lastly, assets deplete to a level at which they approach the well's defined boundaries.

Arps decline curve equations most often apply to the boundary-defined production phase.

Calculating the decline curve involves a curve-fitting exercise to interpolate the future rate of production based on past production levels. Therefore, a somewhat lengthy period of time-series data is needed to estimate the projected trend. Also, the decline-curve equations assume that multiple variables involved in production and operations stay constant during the lifetime of a good asset. Primarily based on good conditions, three types of decline curves can apply to the future trend: exponential, hyperbolic, and harmonic.

Analysing the decline curve can be a more straightforward way to estimate production levels relative to more-complex simulations. However, using the decline curve also can be less accurate than simulations.

Using the decline curve has several shortcomings, including that it can underestimate oil reserves, underestimate production rates, and overestimate reservoir performance. Because it relies on past data, the decline curve does not consider the labour, equipment, and technology changes that could affect production rates. It also cannot account for the likelihood of geologic changes that more-complex models may be able to include to a degree. However, the Arps equations are still in use today.

LITERATURE

Sun (2015): In recent years, production decline-curve analysis has become the most widely used tool in the industry for oil and gas reservoir production analysis. However, most curve analysis is done by computer today, promoting a "black box" approach to engineering and leaving engineers with little background in the fundamentals of decline analysis. Advanced Production Decline Analysis and Application starts from the basic concept of advanced production decline analysis and thoroughly discusses several decline methods, such as Arps, Fetkovich, Blasingame, Agarwal-Gardner, NPI, transient, long linear flow, and FMB. A practical systematic introduction to each method helps the reservoir engineer understand the physical and mathematical models, solve the type curves and match up analysis, analyse the processes and examples, and reconstruct all the examples by hand, giving way to mastering the fundamentals behind the software. An appendix explains the nomenclature and major equations, and as a bonus, online computer programs are available for download. Poston & Poe (2020): Long ago, engineers recognized the characteristic decline of oil and gas well performance and attempted to predict its course by fitting equations to the production history. This book covers the production characteristics and associated interpretation analyses of petroleum reservoirs in a complete, thorough, and consistent manner. Production decline-curve analyses are the most widely used tool in the industry for oil and gas reservoir production analyses. This book will serve as an authoritative reference on modern production decline-curve analyses, including details of some recent advances in the technology. Decline curves are probably the most widely used and least understood production-forecasting technique currently in use in the industry. Analysis of decline curves provides an unsophisticated reservoir-evaluation tool, but profound economic decisions often rest on the outcome of the prediction. A simplistic view of decline-curve analysis can lead to wide misuse, often caused by misunderstandings. There has been no single reference book on the meaning of production decline curves, their application, and their use and misuse. The authors have endeavoured to provide such a reference. Belyadi et al. (2016): Hydraulic Fracturing in Unconventional Reservoirs: Theories, Operations, and Economic Analysis introduces the basic characteristics and theories surrounding hydraulic fracturing and the main process of fracturing in shale, including the main workflow, the details in case analysis, and the fundamental differences between theory, study, and practical operation. The book takes the complex nature of hydraulic fracturing in unconventional reservoirs and applies a practical approach that can be used as a workflow for designing fracture treatments in various shale basins across the world. Providing the audience with theories, best practices, operation and execution, and economic analysis of hydraulic fracturing in unconventional reservoirs, this reference guides the engineer and manager through broad topics including an introduction to unconventional reservoirs, advanced shale reservoir characterization, and shale gas in place calculation as well as expanding to basic theories of hydraulic fracturing and advanced topics in shale reservoir stimulation. Rounding out with coverage of the environmental aspects and practice problems on design and economic analysis, the book delivers the critical link needed between academia and industry for all aspects of hydraulic fracturing operations. **ELABORATION**

The scenario presented in this chapter is hypothetical, using published data by Palisade™ Corporation. Production and Economic Forecast (DMAIC Define)

The model Input Description is presented in Table 1:

Table 1. Input description

Lease	**SaltDome**
Code	A1224
Location	NWNE
Operator	ABC Oil
Engineer	JAM
Date	=DATE(2000,4,1)

The model Input Parameters are given in Table 2:

Table 2. Input parameters

YrlProd	=@RiskLognorm(32000,8000)	STB/yr
Decorate	=@RiskLognorm(0.12,0.04)	fraction
G-O-R	=@RiskTriang(500,750,1500)	SCF/STB
PriceGas	=@RiskNormal(1.2,0.1)	$/Mscf
PriceOil	=@RiskNormal(20,2)	$.STB
Discount	=@RiskSimtable({0.12,0.14})	fraction

The model Production Forecast is given in Table 3:

Table 3. Production forecast

Year	**OilGros**	**GasGros**
	STB	**Mcf**
2008	=@RiskOutput(,"OilGros",1)+YRLPROD*EXP(-DECLRATE*(A18-$A$18))	=B18*GOR/1000
2009	=@RiskOutput(,"OilGros",1)+YRLPROD*EXP(-DECLRATE*(A19-$A$18))	=B19*GOR/1000
2010	=@RiskOutput(,"OilGros",1)+YRLPROD*EXP(-DECLRATE*(A20-$A$18))	=B20*GOR/1000
2011	=@RiskOutput(,"OilGros",1)+YRLPROD*EXP(-DECLRATE*(A21-$A$18))	=B21*GOR/1000
2012	=@RiskOutput(,"OilGros",1)+YRLPROD*EXP(-DECLRATE*(A22-$A$18))	=B22*GOR/1000
2013	=@RiskOutput(,"OilGros",1)+YRLPROD*EXP(-DECLRATE*(A23-$A$18))	=B23*GOR/1000
2014	=@RiskOutput(,"OilGros",1)+YRLPROD*EXP(-DECLRATE*(A24-$A$18))	=B224*GOR/1000
2015	=@RiskOutput(,"OilGros",1)+YRLPROD*EXP(-DECLRATE*(A25-$A$18))	=B25*GOR/1000
2016	=@RiskOutput(,"OilGros",1)+YRLPROD*EXP(-DECLRATE*(A26-$A$18))	=B26*GOR/1000
2017	=@RiskOutput(,"OilGros",1)+YRLPROD*EXP(-DECLRATE*(A27-$A$18))	=B27*GOR/1000

The model Economic Forecast is given in Table 4:

Table 4. Economic forecast

Revenue	OpExp	NetCash	PresVal	Year
=B18*PRICEOIL*(1+@ RiskNormal(1,0.01))^(A18-$A$18)+C18* PRICEGAS*(1+@RiskNormal(1, 0.01))^(A18-$A$18)	=@ RiskTriang (1000000, 1200000, 1400000)	=D18-E18	=F18/(1+ DISCOUNT)^(A18-$A$18)	2008
=B19*PRICEOIL*(1+@ RiskNormal(1,0.01))^(A19-$A$18)+C19* PRICEGAS*(1+@RiskNormal(1, 0.01))^(A19-$A$18)	=10000	=D19-E19	=F18/(1+ DISCOUNT)^(A18-$A$18)	2009
=B20*PRICEOIL*(1+@ RiskNormal(1,0.01))^(A20-$A$18)+C20* PRICEGAS*(1+@RiskNormal(1, 0.01))^(A20-$A$18)	=10000	=D20-E20	=F18/(1+ DISCOUNT)^(A18-$A$18)	2010
=B21*PRICEOIL*(1+@ RiskNormal(1,0.01))^(A21-$A$18)+C21* PRICEGAS*(1+@RiskNormal(1, 0.01))^(A21-$A$18)	=10000	=D21-E21	=F18/(1+ DISCOUNT)^(A18-$A$18)	2011
=B22*PRICEOIL*(1+@ RiskNormal(1,0.01))^(A22-$A$18)+C22* PRICEGAS*(1+@RiskNormal(1, 0.01))^(A22-$A$18)	=10000	=D22-E22	=F18/(1+ DISCOUNT)^(A18-$A$18)	2012
=B23*PRICEOIL*(1+@ RiskNormal(1,0.01))^(A23-$A$18)+C23* PRICEGAS*(1+@RiskNormal(1, 0.01))^(A23-$A$18)	=10000	=D23-E23	=F18/(1+ DISCOUNT)^(A18-$A$18)	2013
=B24*PRICEOIL*(1+@ RiskNormal(1,0.01))^(A24-$A$18)+C24* PRICEGAS*(1+@RiskNormal(1, 0.01))^(A24-$A$18)	=10000	=D24-E24	=F18/(1+ DISCOUNT)^(A18-$A$18)	2014
=B25*PRICEOIL*(1+@ RiskNormal(1,0.01))^(A25-$A$18)+C25* PRICEGAS*(1+@RiskNormal(1, 0.01))^(A25-$A$18)	=10000	=D25-E25	=F18/(1+ DISCOUNT)^(A18-$A$18)	2015
=B26*PRICEOIL*(1+@ RiskNormal(1,0.01))^(A26-$A$18)+C26* PRICEGAS*(1+@RiskNormal(1, 0.01))^(A26-$A$18)	10000	=D26-E26	=F18/(1+ DISCOUNT)^(A18-$A$18)	2016
=B27*PRICEOIL*(1+@ RiskNormal(1,0.01))^(A27-$A$18)+C27* PRICEGAS*(1+@RiskNormal(1, 0.01))^(A27-$A$18)	10000	=D27-E27	=F18/(1+ DISCOUNT)^(A18-$A$18)	2017

The model Total is given in Table 5:

Table 5. Total

=SUM(B18:B27)	=SUM(C18:C27)	=SUM(D18:D27)	=SUM(E18:E27)	=SUM(F18:F27)

The model Total NPV is given in Table 6:

Table 6. Total NPV

Total NPV:
=@RiskOutput("Total NPV")+SUM(G18:G27)

Simulation 1: Risk Evaluation and Sensitivity Analysis

Total Net Present Value (NPV) Analysis and Evaluation

Figure 1 displays the Total Net Present Value (NPV) distribution.

Figure 1. Total Net Present Value (NPV) distribution

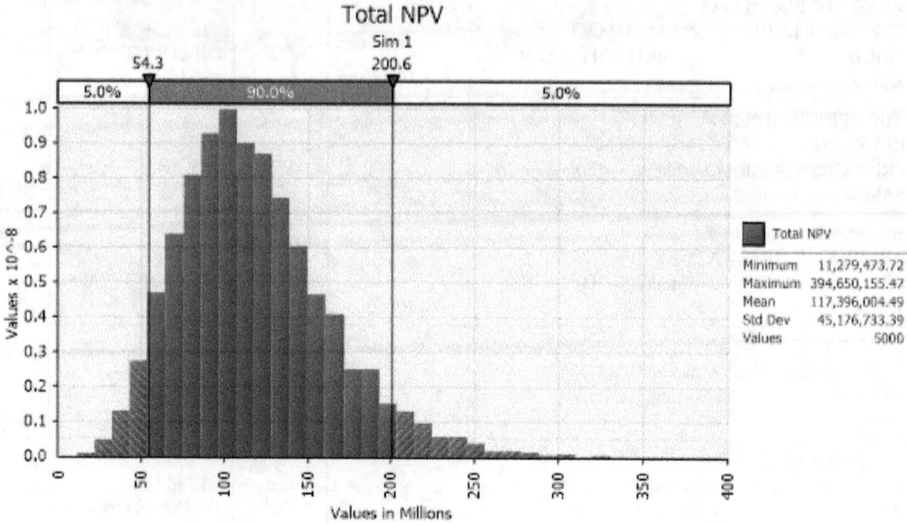

The Net Present Value (NPV) Minimum is $11,279,473.72 and Maximum is $394,650,155.47. The NPV *Mean* is $117,396,004.49 and the Standard Deviation is $45,176,733.39, which is very high. There is a 5% probability that the return will be below $54.3 MM; a 90% probability that it will be in the range of $54.3 MM – $200.6 MM; and a 5% probability that it will be above $200.6 MM.

Sensitivity Analysis

Sensitivity analysis provides for identifying and quantifying the main contributors to variability and risk based on the probability distribution.

The Inputs Ranked by Effect on Output Mean are given in Figure 2.

The graph illustrates that the effect of variable DECLRATE, on the Total NPV is a change in the range of $62,065,296.20 to $167,561,584.65, which are respectively left and right from the Baseline of $117,396,004.49, which is marked on the graph. The other variables are less influential.

Figure 2. Total NPV inputs ranked by effect on output mean

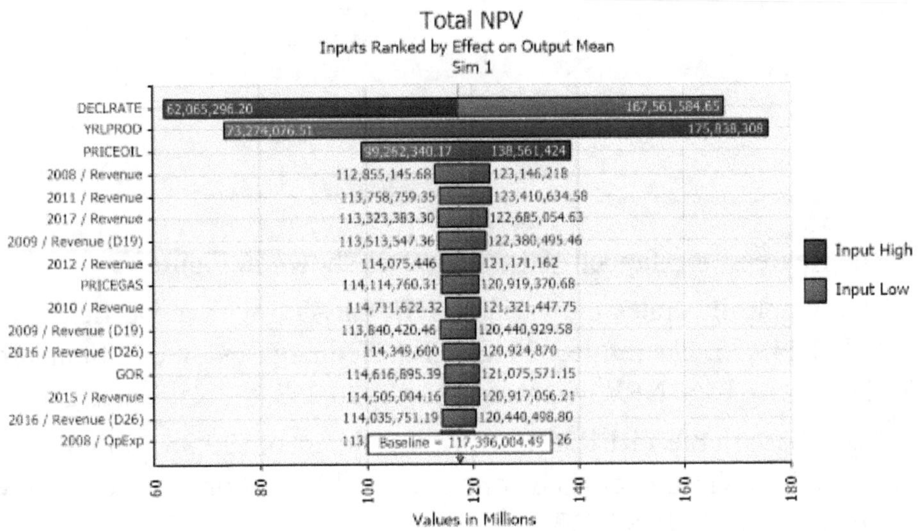

The Regression Coefficients graph is shown in Figure 3.

This graph illustrates the DECLRATE variable with a coefficient of -0.67. Therefore, if DECLRATE increases by one Standard Deviation, the Total NPV will increase by -0.67 Standard Deviations, i.e., negative.

Also, the variable YRLRATE with a coefficient of 0.65. Therefore, if YRLRATE increases by one Standard Deviation, the Total NPV will increase by 0.65 Standard Deviations

The other variables are less influential.

Figure 3. Total NPV regression coefficients

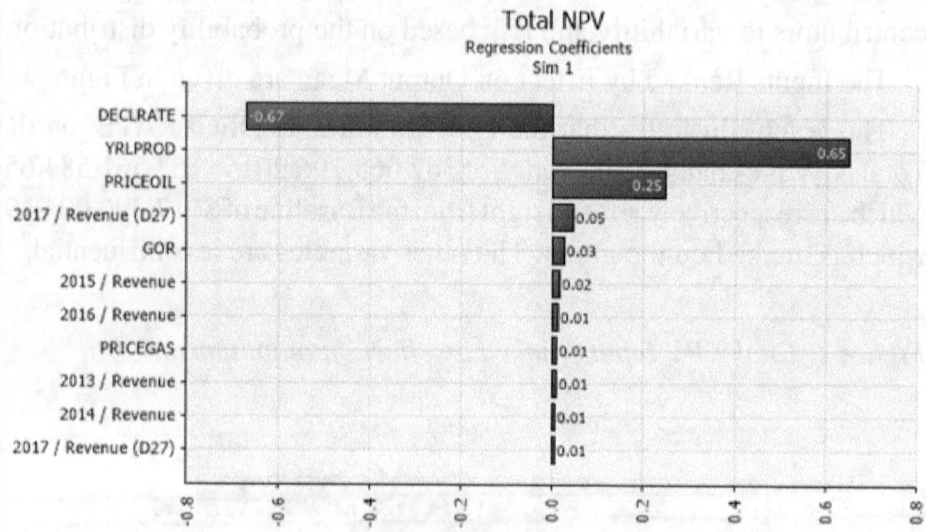

The Regression Mapped Values graph is shown in Figure 4.

This graph illustrates the variable DECLRATE with a coefficient of -$30,263,248.25. Therefore, if DECLRATE increases by one Standard Deviation, the Total NPV will increase by -$30,263,248.25, i.e., negative.

Also, the variable YRLRATE with a coefficient of $29,387,530. Therefore, if YRLRATE increases by one Standard Deviation, the Total NPV will increase by $29,387,530.

The other variables are less influential.

Figure 4. Total NPV regression mapped values coefficients

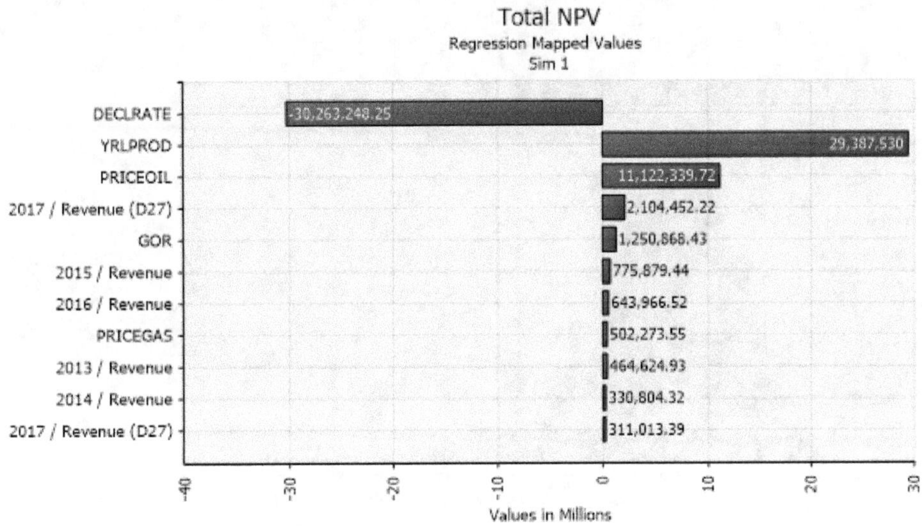

Simulation 2: Risk Evaluation and Sensitivity Analysis

Total Net Present Value (NPV) Analysis and Evaluation

Figure 5 displays the Total Net Present Value (NPV) distribution.

The Net Present Value (NPV) Minimum is $10,014,545.43 and Maximum is $344,793,787. The NPV *Mean* is $102,856,735.84 and the Standard Deviation is $39,470,910.12, which is very high. There is a 5% probability that the return will be below $47.6 MM; a 90% probability that it will be in the range of $47.6 MM – $175.7 MM; and a 5% probability that it will be above $175.7 MM.

Figure 5. Total Net Present Value (NPV) distribution

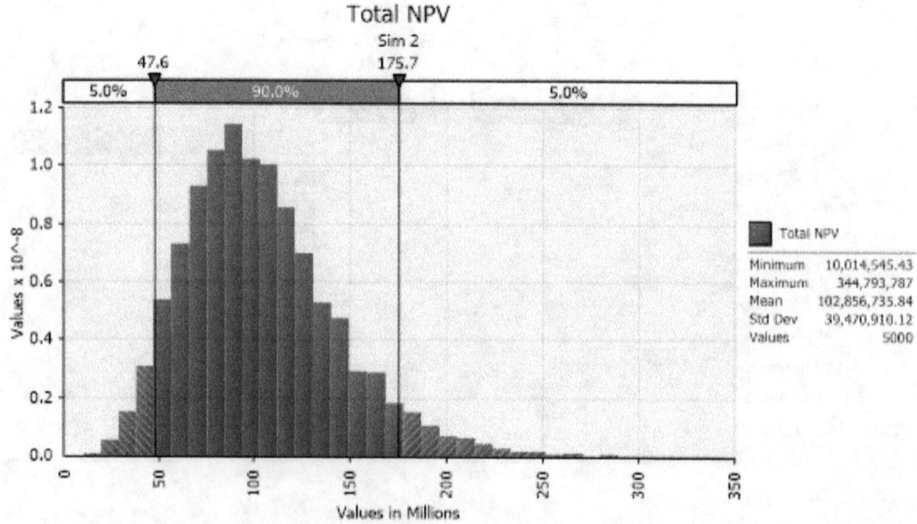

Sensitivity Analysis

Sensitivity analysis provides for identifying and quantifying the main contributors to variability and risk based on the probability distribution.

The Inputs Ranked by Effect on Output Mean are given in Figure 6.

The graph illustrates that the effect of variable DECLRATE, on the Total NPV is a change in the range of $54,661,357.77 to $146,453,396.80, which are respectively left and right from the Baseline of $102,856,735.84, which is marked on the graph. The other variables are less influential.

Figure 6. Total NPV inputs ranked by effect on output mean

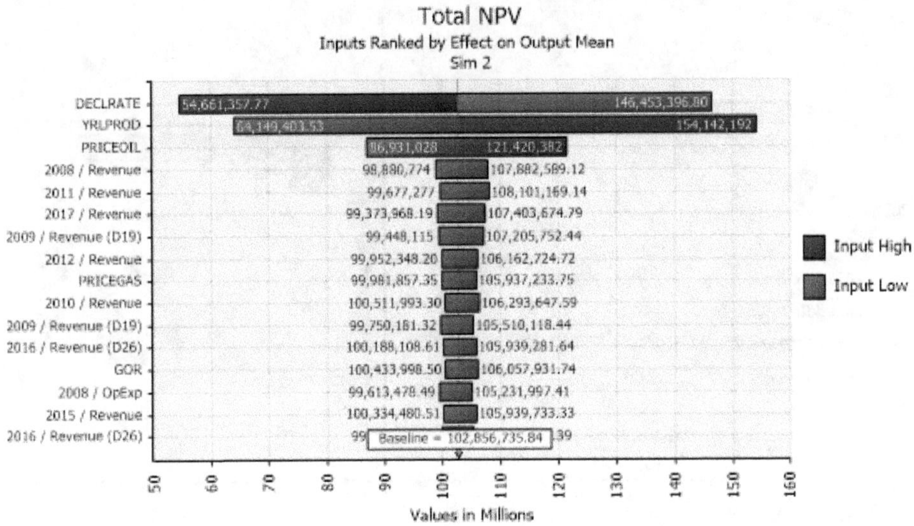

The Regression Coefficients graph is shown in Figure 7.

This graph illustrates the variable DECLRATE with a coefficient of -0.67. Therefore, if DECLRATE increases by one Standard Deviation, the Total NPV will increase by -0.67 Standard Deviations, i.e., negative.

Also, the variable YRLRATE with a coefficient of 0.65. Therefore, if YRLRATE increases by one Standard Deviation, the Total NPV will increase by 0.65 Standard Deviations.

The other variables are less influential.

Figure 7. Total NPV regression coefficients

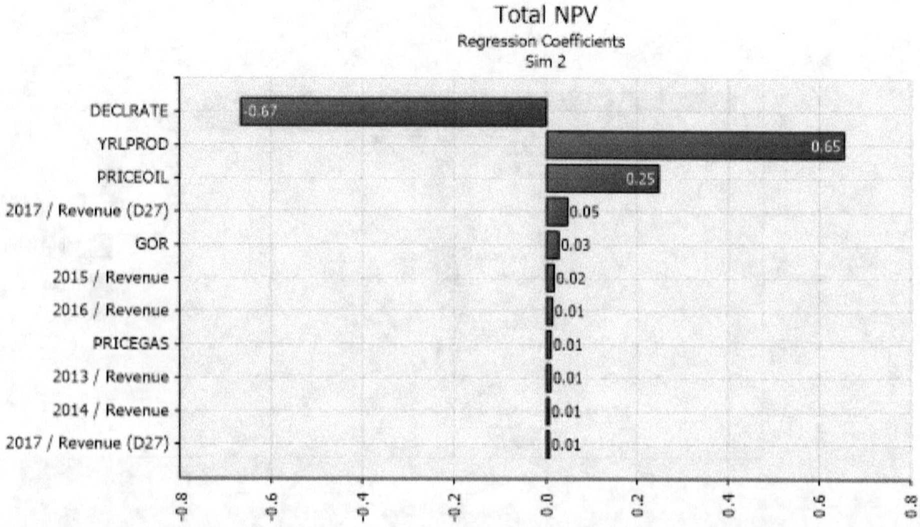

The Regression Mapped Values graph is shown in Figure 8.

Figure 8. Total NPV regression mapped values coefficients

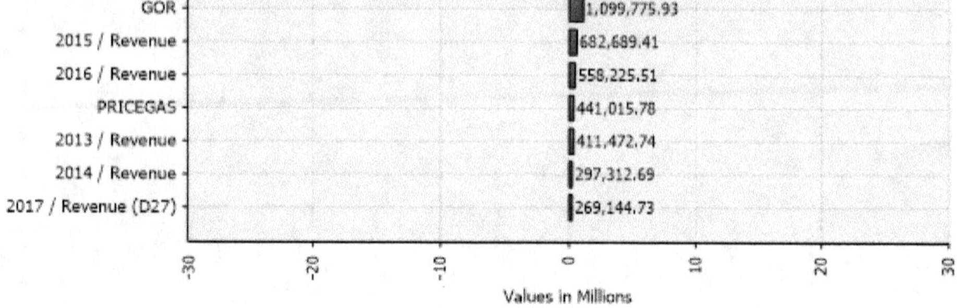

This graph illustrates the variable DECLRATE with a coefficient of -$26,339,639.62. Therefore, if DECLRATE increases by one Standard Deviation, the Total NPV will increase by -$26,339,639.62, i.e., negative.

Also, the variable YRLRATE with a coefficient of $25,787,044.96. Therefore, if YRLRATE increases by one Standard Deviation, the Total NPV will increase by $25,787,044.96.

The other variables are less influential.

Change in Oil-Gros Over Time Analysis

Figure 9 presents the Change in the Oil-Gros Sim#1 graph.

Figure 9. Oil-gros Sim#1

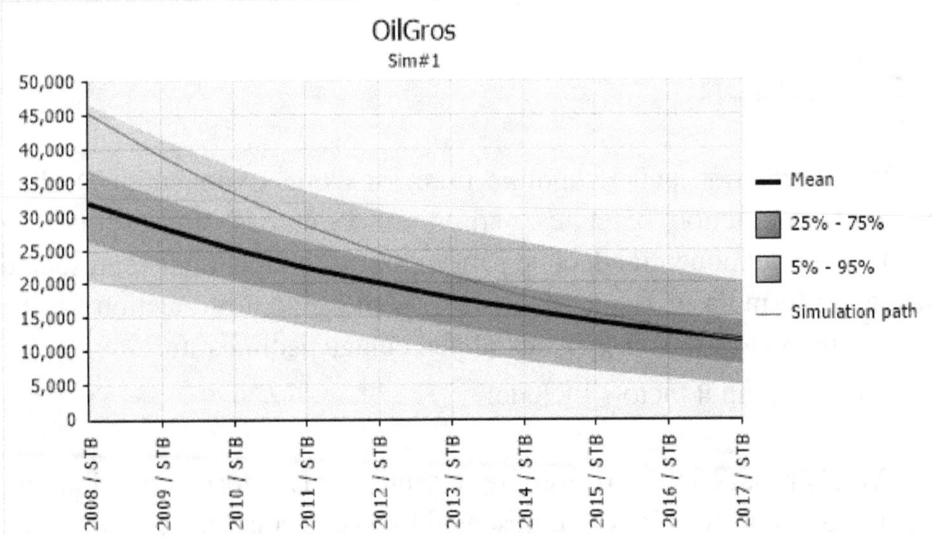

The Oil-Gros Sim#1 graph shows that the *Mean* started with 32,000 STB in the Year 2008 and then gradually decreased to 10,867 STB as shown in Table 7.

Table 7. Oil-gros Sim#1

Year	Oil-Gros Sim#1
2008	32000
2009	28381
2010	25172
2011	22326
2012	19801
2013	17562
2014	15576
2015	13815
2016	12253
2017	10867

CONCLUSION

The Production and Economic Forecast using Exponential Decline forecasts production, revenues, and present value based on exponential decline. The exponential decline pattern for oil production is represented using the formula: q = qie-at, where qi is the annual production for the first year and a is the (fixed) annual percentage decline rate.

Uncertain input factors include:

i) Yearly production (YrlProd), represented by Lognormal distribution.
ii) Decline rate (Declrate), represented by Lognormal distribution.
iii) GOR (constant Gas-Oil-Ratio), represented by Triangle distribution.
iv) Price of gas, represented by Normal distribution.
v) Price of oil, represented by Normal distribution; and
vi) Rate of increase of oil and gas prices, which are represented by Normal distributions embedded in the Revenue formulas. For each year, a new sample is drawn from a new Normal distribution, modelling variation from year to year.

Outputs are defined as:

i) Total NPV; and
ii) OilGros, or production, for each year.

You can generate a summary graph to see the change in OilGros over time. Finally, a SimTable function has been used in the Discount Rate input that is used to calculate Total NPV. This contains two possible values for Discount Rate – 12% and 14% - enabling you to run two back-to-back simulations to compare the effect of different discount rates on your Total NPV

REFERENCES

Belyadi, H.2016). *Hydraulic Fracturing in Unconventional Reservoirs: Theories, Operations, and Economic Analysis*. Golf Professional Publishing.

Poston, S., & Poe, B. D. (2020). Analysis of Production Decline Curves, Society of Petroleum Engineers. Society of Petroleum Engineers.

Sun, H. (2015). *Advanced Production Decline Analysis and Application*. Golf Professional Publishing.

Chapter 6
Oil Depletion Allowance

ABSTRACT

The Oil Depletion Allowance projects the income for an oil company that made a $10 million investment in land that is estimated to have approximately 625,000 barrels of oil. The drilling will be done over the next 5 years. The model is the oil depletion allowance, which can be deducted from net income for tax purposes. In each year, the depletion allowance is the larger of two quantities: (1) $16 per barrel of oil recovered, where this $16 is calculated as the unit investment cost per barrel ($10 million divided by the estimated 625,000 Barrel reserve), and (2) 22% of gross revenue up to a maximum of 35% of net income. The tornado chart shown on the last sheet indicates that the mean NPV is most sensitive to the number of barrels recovered in year 1, but all the uncertain inputs have a fairly large effect on mean NPV.

INTRODUCTION

Oil Depletion

Depletion is an accrual accounting technique used to allocate the cost of extracting natural resources such as timber, minerals, and oil from the earth.

Like depreciation and amortisation, depletion is a non-cash expense that lowers the cost value of an asset incrementally through scheduled charges to income. Where depletion differs is that it refers to the gradual

DOI: 10.4018/979-8-3373-0959-0.ch006

exhaustion of natural resource reserves, as opposed to the wearing out of depreciable assets or the aging life of intangibles.

Depletion for accounting and financial reporting purposes is meant to assist in accurately identifying the value of the assets on the balance sheet and recording expenses in the appropriate period on the income statement.

When the costs associated with natural resource extraction have been capitalised, the expenses are systematically allocated across different periods based on the resources extracted. The costs are held on the balance sheet until expense recognition occurs.

- Depletion is an accrual accounting method used to allocate the cost of extracting natural resources such as timber, minerals, and oil from the earth.
- When the costs associated with natural resource extraction have been capitalized, the expenses are systematically allocated across different periods based on the resources extracted.
- There are two basic forms of depletion allowance: percentage depletion and cost depletion.

To calculate what expenses, need to be spread out for the use of natural resources, each different phase of production must be taken into consideration. The depletion base is the capitalized costs depleted across multiple accounting periods. Four main factors affect the depletion base:

- *Acquisition*: Costs associated with purchasing or leasing the property rights to land that the company believes has natural resources.
- *Exploration*: Expenses linked to digging under the land that was leased or bought.
- *Development*: The costs necessary to prepare the land for natural resource extraction, such as tunnelling or developing wells.
- *Restoration*: Expenses associated with restoring the land to its original condition after completion.

One method of calculating depletion expense is the percentage depletion method. It assigns a fixed percentage to gross revenue—sales minus costs—to allocate expenses. For example, if $10 million of oil is extracted and the fixed percentage is 15%, $1.5 million of capitalized costs to extract the natural resource are depleted.

The percentage depletion method requires a lot of estimates and is, therefore, not a heavily relied upon or accepted method of depletion.

The second method of calculating depletion is the cost depletion method. Cost depletion is calculated by taking the property's basis, total recoverable reserves, and number of units sold into account. The property's basis is distributed among the total number of recoverable units. As natural resources are extracted, they are counted and taken out from the property's basis.

The Internal Revenue Service (IRS) requires the cost method to be used with timber.1 It requires the method that yields the highest deduction to be used with mineral property, which it defines as oil and gas wells, mines, and other natural deposits, including geothermal deposits.2

Because the percentage depletion looks at the property's gross income and taxable income limit, as opposed to the amount of the natural resource extracted, it is not an acceptable reporting method for certain natural resources.

LITERATURE

Heinberg (2006): Since oil is the primary fuel of global industrial civilization, its imminent depletion is a problem that will have a profound impact on every aspect of modern life. Without international agreement on how to manage the decline of this vital resource, the world faces unprecedented risk of conflict and collapse. "The Oil Depletion Protocol" describes a unique accord whereby nations would voluntarily reduce their oil production and oil imports according to a consistent, sensible formula. This would enable energy transition to be planned and supported over the long term, providing a context of stable energy prices and peaceful cooperation. The protocol will be presented at international gatherings, initiating the process of country-by-country negotiation and adoption and mobilizing public support. To this end, this book: provides an overview of the data concerning Peak Oil and its timing; briefly explains the protocol and its implications for the reader and decision-makers in government and industry around the world; deals with frequently asked questions and objections; and, looks forward to how the protocol can be adopted and how municipalities and ordinary citizens can facilitate the process. Timely and critically important, "The Oil Depletion Protocol" is a must-read for policymakers and for all who seek to avert a Peak Oil disaster. Campbell (2013): Campbell's Atlas of Oil and Gas Depletion, Second Edition, is the product of a half-century of critical analysis and updating of data on the status of oil and gas depletion by country, region, and the world. Separate analyses of conventional and non-conventional oil and gas, which are depleting at different rates and costs, show when these critical energy sources peak and decline. The Atlas also summarizes the history and political circumstances of each country to assess the impact on oil and gas production and reserves. It contrasts the First Half of the Oil Age, which saw the rapid expansion of the world economy, allowing the population to grow six-fold, with the Second Half, which will witness a general contraction as these easy, high-density energy supplies dwindle. The transition threatens to be a time of great economic, financial, and political tensions. The Atlas, which has been compiled and updated by prominent geologist, former oil company executive, and oil analyst Colin Campbell since the 1960s, addresses the need for a reliable and comprehensive database on a subject essential to governments, industry, academia, and the population as we attempt to adapt to these critically changing circumstances. Campbell (2003): Oil and Gas are finite fossil fuels from the geological past that are inevitably subject to depletion. Eventually, we must run out, but what matters more is the inevitable peak of production when growth gives way to decline. The wider implications of this historic discontinuity are colossal. Understanding depletion is not difficult, but public data on production and reserves are very unreliable. This book attempts to present more realistic estimates and definitions than are available elsewhere. Colin Campbell, author of the highly acclaimed The Coming Oil Crisis, is a leading member of the growing number of experts whose models of depletion show that the world will reach a peak within about ten years. After the peak comes increasing scarcity, as production can no longer meet demand. The implications for Mankind are huge, opening an entirely new world.

ELABORATION

Input Data and Calculations (Define) Input Data and Calculations Table 1 presents Input Data and Calculations:

Table 1. Data and calculations

Initial investment	$10,000,000
Year 1 barrels	=@RiskTriang (E3, F3, G3)
% Decrease in barrels	=@RiskTriang (E4, F4, G4)
Year 1 oil price	=@RiskTriang (E5, F5, G5)
% Change in oil price	=@RiskTriang (E6, F6, G6)
Year 1 cost %	=@RiskTriang (E7, F7, G7)
% Change in cost %	=@RiskTriang (E8, F8, G8)
Depletion option 1	$16
Depletion option 2	22%
Tax rate	42%
Discount rate	15%

Table 2 displays the Risk Triangle Parameters:

Table 2. Risk triangle parameters

Minimum	Most likely	Maximum
130,000	155,000	165,000
11%	14%	20%
$75	$80	$85
-7%	1%	6%
35%	40%	45%
-5%	0%	5%

Five Years Calculations

Table 3 displays the calculations for five years:

Table 3. Five years calculations

Year	1	2	3	4	5
Barrels produced	=C3	=C15*(1-$C$4)	=D15*(1-$C$4)	=E15*(1-$C$4)	=F15*(1-$C$4)
Price per barrel	=C5	=C16*(1+$C$6)	=D16*(1+$C$6)	=E16*(1+$C$6)	=F16*(1+$C$6)
Gross revenue	=C16*C15	=D16*D15	=E16*E15	=F16*F15	=G16*G15
Operating cost %	=C7	=C18*(1+$C$8)	=D18*(1+$C$8)	=E18*(1+$C$8)	=F18*(1+$C$8)
Net income	=C17*(1-C18)	=D17*(1-D18)	=E17*(1-E18)	=F17*(1-F18)	=G17*(1-C18)
Depletion allowance	=MAX($C$9*C15,MIN ($C$10*C17,$E$10*C19))	=MAX($C$9*D15,MIN ($C$10*D17,$E$10*D19))	=MAX($C$9*E15,MIN ($C$10*E17,$E$10*E9))	=MAX($C$9*F15,MIN ($C$10*F17,$E$10*F19))	=MAX($C$9*G15,MIN ($C$10*G17,$E$10*G19))
Taxable income	=C19-C20	=D19-D20	=E19-E20	=F19-F20	=G19-G20
Tax	=$C$11*C21	=$C$11*D21	=$C$11*E21	=$C$11*F21	=$C$11*G21
After-tax income	=C19-C22	=D19-D22	=E19-E22	=F19-F22	=G19-G22

The Simulation Output: Net Present Value (NPV) and Depletion exceeds Investment

Table 4 displays the NPV and Depletion exceeds Investment:

Table 4. NPV and depletion exceed investment

NPV	=@RiskOutput("NPV")+-C2+NPV(C12,C23:G23)
Depletion exceeds Investment	=@RiskOutput("High Depletion")+IF(SUM(C20:G20)>C2,1,0)

The Summary Measures: Net Present Value (NPV) and Depletion exceed Investment

Table 5 displays the Summary Measures: NPV and Depletion exceed Investment:

Table 5. Summary measures - NPV and depletion exceed investment

Summary measures	Mean	Standard Deviation	5th Percentile	95th Percentile
NPV	=@ RiskMean(C25)	=@ RiskStdDev(C25)	=@ RiskPercentile(C25,0.05)	=@ RiskPercentile(C25,0.95)
Depletion exceeds Investment	=@ RiskMean(C26)			

Simulation: Risk Evaluation and Sensitivity Analysis (Analyse)

Net Present Value (NPV)

Figure 1 displays the Net Present Value (NPV) distribution.

Figure 1. NPV distribution

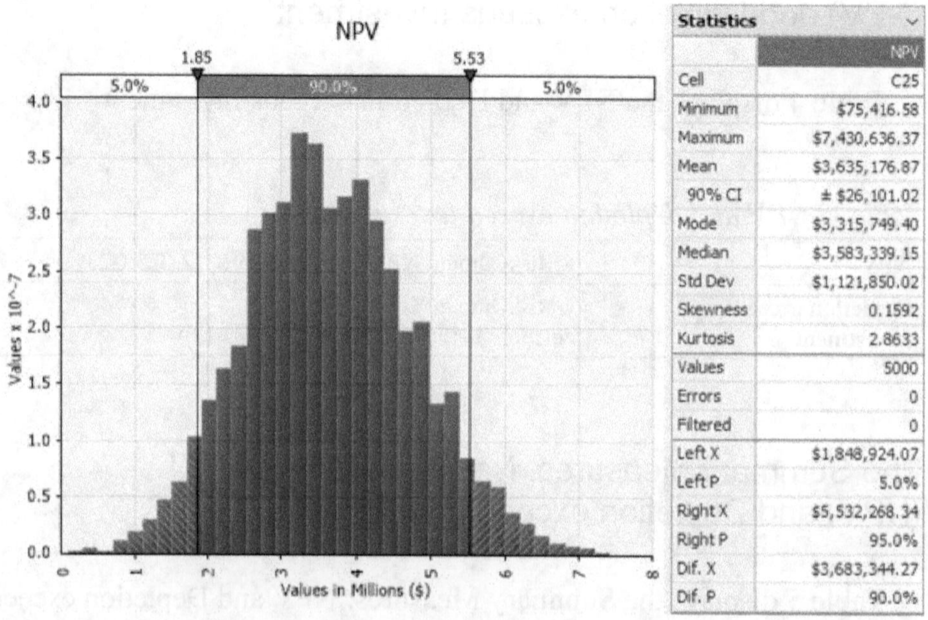

The NPV Minimum is $75,416.58 and the NPV Maximum is $7,430,636.37. The NPV *Mean* is $3,635,176.87 and the *Standard Deviation* is $1,121,850.02. There is a 5% probability that the NPV will be below $1.85 MM; a 90% probability that it will be in the range of $1.85 MM – $5.53 MM; and a 5% probability that it will be above $5.53 MM.

Sensitivity Analysis

Sensitivity analysis provides for identifying and quantifying the main contributors to variability and risk based on the probability distribution.

The Inputs Ranked by Effect on Output Mean are given in Figure 2.

The graph illustrates that the effect of variable Year 1 Barrels, on the NPV is a change in the range of $2,348,117.68 to $4,647,849.33, which are respectively left and right from the Baseline of $3,635,176.87, which is marked on the graph. The other scenarios are less influential.

Figure 2. NPV inputs ranked by effect on output mean

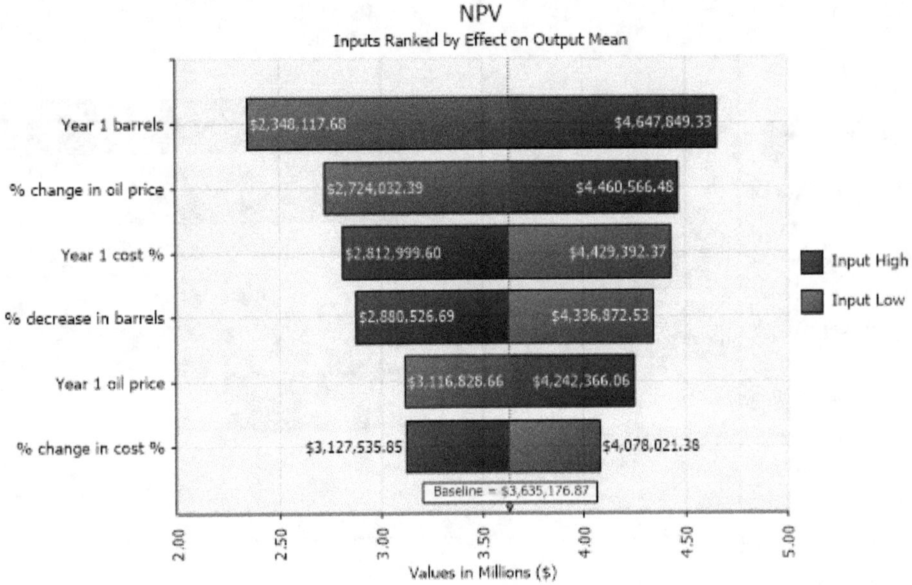

The Regression Coefficients graph is shown in Figure 3.

This graph illustrates the variable Year 1 Barrel with a coefficient of 0.60. Therefore, if Year 1 Barrels increase by one Standard Deviation, the NPV will increase by 0.60 Standard Deviations.

Also, the variable % Change in Oil Prices with a coefficient of 0.43. Therefore, if the % Change in Oil Prices increases by one Standard Deviation, the NPV will increase by 0.43 Standard Deviations.

The other variables are less influential.

Figure 3. NPV regression coefficients

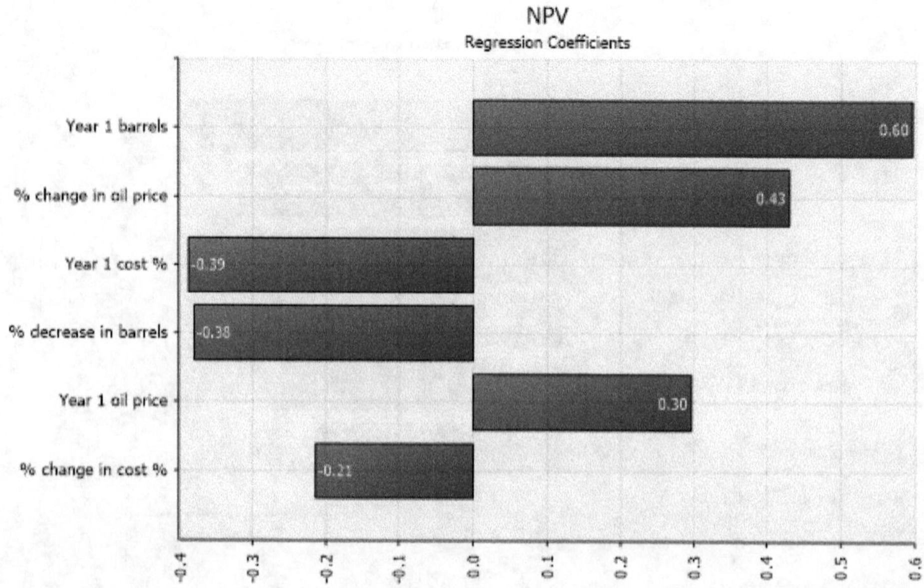

The Regression Mapped Values graph is shown in Figure 4.

This graph illustrates the variable Year 1 Barrel with a coefficient of $669,563.57. Therefore, if Year 1 Barrels increase by one Standard Deviation, the NPV will increase by $669,563.57, i.e., negative.

Also, the variable % Change in Oil Price with a coefficient of $481,891.75. Therefore, if the % Change in Oil Price increases by one Standard Deviation, the NPV will increase by $481,891.75.

The other variables are less influential.

Figure 4. NPV regression mapped values coefficients

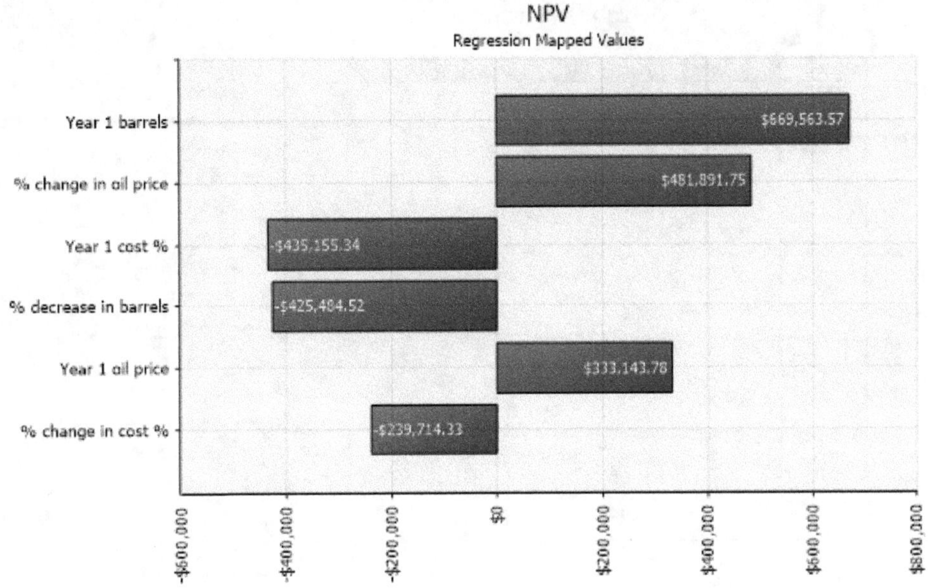

High Depletion Analysis and Evaluation

Figure 5 displays the High Depletion distribution.

The High Depletion Minimum is zero (0) and Maximum 1. The High Depletion *Mean* is 0.2202 and the Standard Deviation is 0.4144, which is very high. There is a 5% probability that the High Depletion will be below 0.000; a 90% probability that it will be in the range of 0.000 – 1.000; and a 5% probability that it will be above 1.000.

Figure 5. High depletion distribution

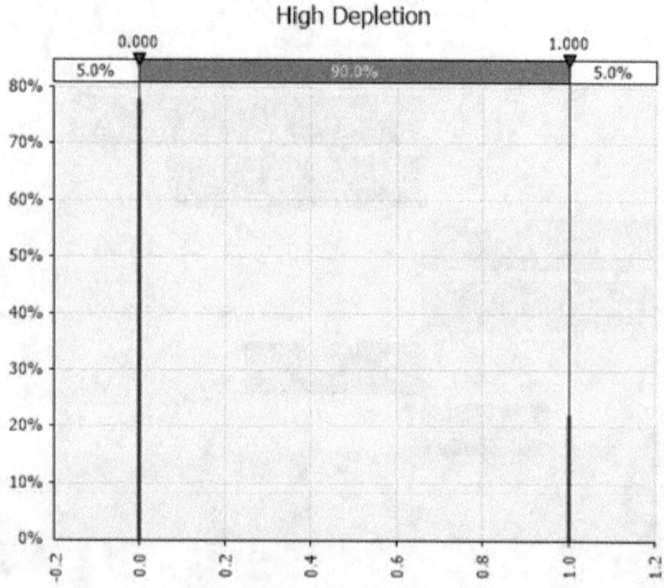

Statistics	High Depletion
Cell	C26
Minimum	0
Maximum	1
Mean	0.2202
90% CI	± 0.00964
Mode	0
Median	0
Std Dev	0.4144
Skewness	1.3509
Kurtosis	2.8247
Values	5000
Errors	0
Filtered	0
Left X	0.000
Left P	5.0%
Right X	1.000
Right P	95.0%
Dif. X	1
Dif. P	90.0%

Sensitivity Analysis

Sensitivity analysis provides for identifying and quantifying the main contributors to variability and risk based on the probability distribution.

The Inputs Ranked by Effect on Output Mean are given in Figure 6.

The graph illustrates that the effect of variable Year 1 Barrels, on the High Depletion is a change in the range of 0.0060000 to 0.54400, which are respectively left and right from the Baseline of 0.22020, which is marked on the graph. The other variables are less influential.

Figure 6. High depletion inputs ranked by effect on output mean

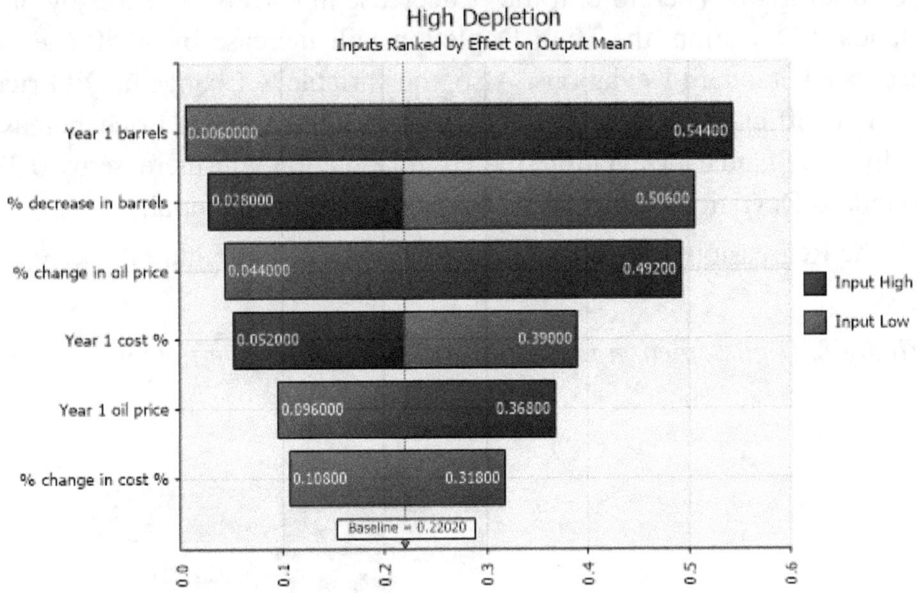

The Regression Coefficients graph is shown in Figure 7.

Figure 7. High depletion regression coefficients

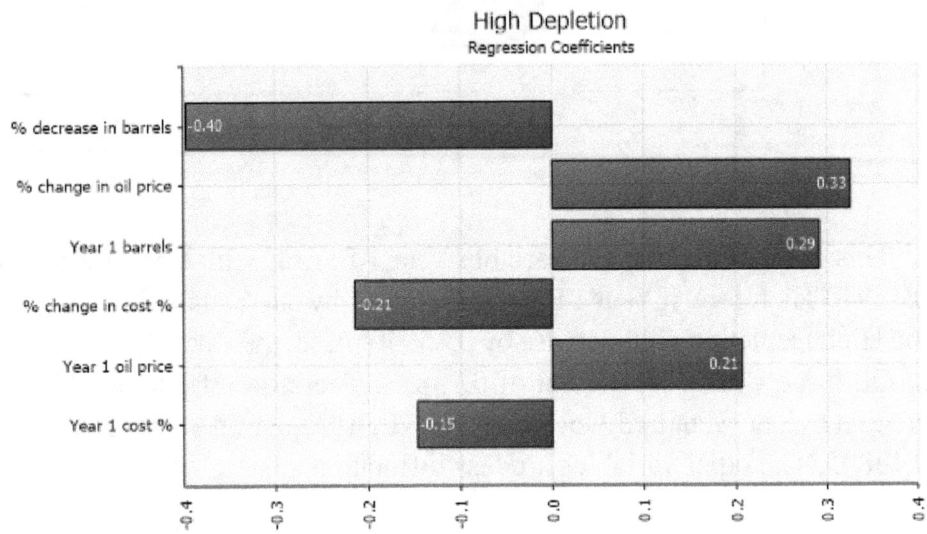

This graph illustrates the variable % Decrease in barrels with a coefficient of -0.40. Therefore, if the % decrease in barrels increases by one Standard Deviation, the High Depletion will increase by -0.40 (i.e., a decrease) Standard Deviations. Also, the variable % Change in Oil Price with a coefficient of 0.33. Therefore, if the % Change in Oil Price increases by one Standard Deviation, the High Depletion will increase by 0.33 Standard Deviations. The other variables are less influential.

The Regression Mapped Values graph is shown in Figure 8.

Figure 8. High depletion regression mapped values coefficients

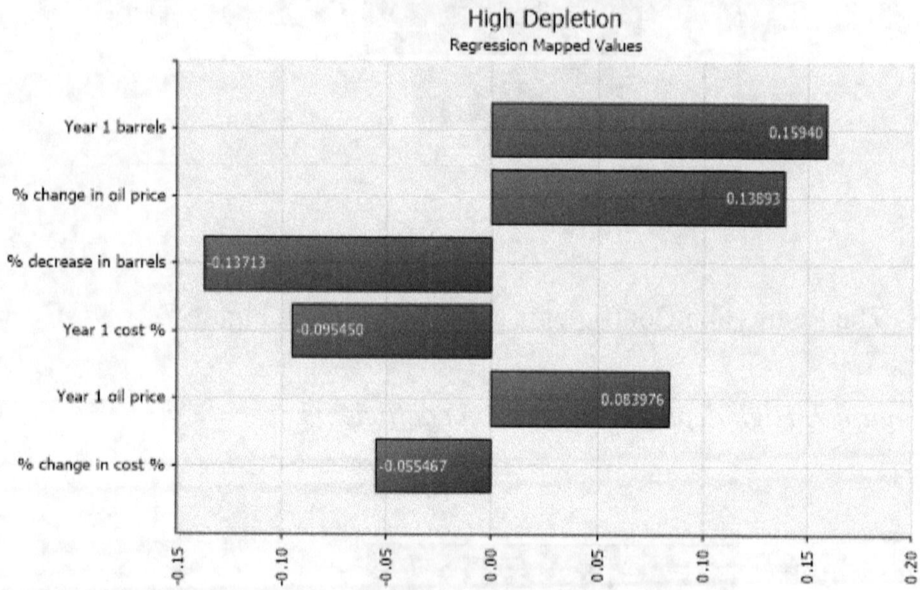

This graph illustrates the variable Year 1 Barrels with a coefficient of 0.15940 Therefore, if Year 1 Barrels increases by one Standard Deviation, the High Depletion will increase by 0.15940. Also, the variable % Change in Oil Price with a coefficient of 0.13893. Therefore, if YRLRATE increases by one Standard Deviation, the High Depletion will increase by 0.13893. The other variables are less influential.

CONCLUSION

Oil Depletion Allowance

This model was a straightforward projection of incomes for an oil company that has just made a $10 million investment in land that is estimated to have approximately 625,000 Barrels of oil. The drilling will be done over the next 5 years. An important aspect of the model is the oil depletion allowance, which can be deducted from net income for tax purposes. In each year, the depletion allowance is the larger of two quantities: (1) $16 per barrel of oil recovered, where this $16 is calculated as the unit investment cost per barrel ($10 million divided by the estimated 625,000 Barrel reserve), and (2) 22% of gross revenue up to a maximum of 35% of net income.

The tornado chart shown on the last sheet indicates that the mean NPV is most sensitive to the number of barrels recovered in year 1, but all of the uncertain inputs have a fairly large effect on mean NPV.

REFERENCES

Campbell, C. J. (2003). The Essence of Oil and Gas Depletion. Multi-Science Publishing Co.

Campbell, C. J. (2013). Campbell's Atlas of Oil and Gas Depletion. Springer. DOI: 10.1007/978-1-4614-3576-1

Heinberg, R. (2006). *The Oil Depletion Protocol: A Plan to Avert Oil Wars, Terrorism and Economic Collapse*. Clairview Books.

Chapter 7
Oil Pipeline Risk

ABSTRACT

Nine types of risks and nine routes in the Oil Pipeline Network are simulated. Each route has three characteristics: diameter, mean pressure, and distance. For each type of risk and each route, two quantities are simulated: the number of events where that risk type occurs and the typical magnitude of such a risk. These are then accumulated to find the severities of the risk types, by route and total over all routes. Sufficient historical data is available to estimate regression equations relating the frequency and Mean magnitude of each risk type to the characteristics of the routes. The resulting coefficients are presented in Parameters and Errors. With Simulating Risk Frequency or Mean Risk Magnitude, the error coefficient is multiplied by a standard normal random variable to provide extra variability. Risk Frequencies are Poisson distributed with Means from Regressions. Event Magnitudes are lognormally distributed with Means from Regressions and Standard Deviations.

INTRODUCTION

Oil Pipeline Risk

Oil prices have been steadily pulling back from six-month highs as trade worries intensify, with the U.S. threat to raise tariffs against Chinese goods appearing likely to become reality tonight. Both sides have been

DOI: 10.4018/979-8-3373-0959-0.ch007

hardening their stance, and if we see an all-out tariff war, oil could slide lower along with a global rout in equities and commodity currencies.

The trade spat is raising global growth concerns, which could put a dent in the demand side of the argument for higher oil prices. If talks do not completely fall apart, we could see oil markets quickly focus on the geopolitical risks from Iran, Russia, Venezuela, and Libya.

The OANDA order book indicator showed just before the U.S. close that the percentage of open positions held by OANDA's clients was 63.7% short and 36.3% long, while 0.6% of pending sell orders are at the 1.3510 level.

LITERATURE

Miesner & Leffler (2021): In this edition of Oil and Gas Pipelines in Nontechnical Language, Tom Miesner and Bill Leffler leverage the hundreds of courses they have taught in the past decade, along with the interaction with their audiences, clients, and opposing attorneys to present an understandable view of pipeline inception, planning, construction, start-up, and operation. Those experiences allowed them to expand but simplify the complexities of pipelines, including a revised chapter on equipment that provides a complete view of pipeline components. A separate chapter on control systems updates this technology. An expanded discussion of pipeline integrity including the concept of risk management demonstrates how important the subjects of safety, reliability, efficiency, and environmental performance have become.

Timashev & Bushinskaya (2016): The book contains solutions to fundamental problems that arise due to the logic of the development of specific branches of science, which are related to pipeline safety, but mainly are subordinate to the needs of pipeline transportation. The book deploys important but not yet solved aspects of reliability and safety assurance of pipeline systems, which are vital aspects not only for the oil and gas industry and, in general, fuel and energy industries, but also for virtually all contemporary industries and technologies. The volume will be useful to specialists and experts in the field of diagnostics/ inspection, monitoring, reliability, and safety of critical infrastructures. First and foremost, it will be useful to the decision-making persons—operators of different types of pipelines, pipeline diagnostics/inspection vendors, designers of in-line –inspection (ILI) tools, industrial and ecological safety specialists, as well as to researchers and graduate students.

Muhlbauer (2004): Here's the ideal tool if you're looking for a flexible, straightforward analysis system for your everyday design and operations decisions. This new third edition includes sections on stations, geographical information systems, "absolute" versus "relative" risks, and the latest regulatory developments. From design to day-to-day operations and maintenance, this unique volume covers every facet of pipeline risk management, arguably the most important, the most hotly debated, aspect of pipelining today. Now expanded and updated, this widely accepted standard reference guides you in managing the risks involved in pipeline operations. You'll also find ways to create a resource allocation model by linking risk with cost and customize the risk assessment technique to your specific requirements. The clear step-by-step instructions and more than 50 examples make it easy. This edition has been expanded to include offshore pipelines and distribution system pipelines as well as cross-country liquid and gas transmission pipelines.

ELABORATION

Oil Pipeline Risks (Define)

Parameters

Table 1 displays the Risk Type Index for identification:

Table 1. Risk type index for identification

Index	Risk Type
1	External corrosion
2	Internal corrosion
3	Damages by third parties
4	Flooding
5	Earthquakes, landslides
6	Operational stoppages
7	Unplanned maintenance
8	Design errors
9	Sabotage, vandalism

Table 2 displays the Frequency Coefficients:

Table 2. Frequency coefficients

Diameter	Pressure	Distance	Constant	Error	Index
0.0027	0.0005	0.0029	0.0018	0.0006	1
0.0065	0.0057	0.0024	0.0044	0.0068	2
0.0014	0.0010	0.0063	0.0032	0.0032	3
0.0054	0.0070	0.0025	0.0041	0.0074	4
0.0034	0.0068	0.0072	0.0058	0.0052	5
0.0032	0.0038	0.0045	0.0034	0.0002	6
0.0015	0.0074	0.0038	0.0002	0.0032	7
0.0019	0.0039	0.0005	0.0035	0.0027	8
0.0022	0.0058	0.0037	0.0056	0.0063	9

Table 3 displays the Magnitude Coefficients:

Table 3. Magnitude coefficients

Diameter	Pressure	Distance	Constant	Error	VAR	Index
0.0027	0.0005	0.0029	0.0018	0.0006	20%	1
0.0065	0.0057	0.0024	0.0044	0.0068	12%	2
0.0014	0.0010	0.0063	0.0032	0.0032	45%	3
0.0054	0.0070	0.0025	0.0041	0.0074	70%	4
0.0034	0.0068	0.0072	0.0058	0.0052	300%	5
0.0032	0.0038	0.0045	0.0034	0.0002	9%	6
0.0015	0.0074	0.0038	0.0002	0.0032	62%	7
0.0019	0.0039	0.0005	0.0035	0.0027	35%	8
0.0022	0.0058	0.0037	0.0056	0.0063	250%	9

Table 4 displays the Pipeline Route Inputs:

Table 4. Pipeline route inputs

Route	1	2	3	4	5	6	7	8	9
Diameter (mm)	350	350	300	300	150	300	300	250	250
Mean Pressure (PSI)	1100	1100	1200	1200	1440	1100	1100	1100	1100
Distance (miles)	92.1	131	9.7	67.2	123	40.7	42.7	41.5	53.8

Table 5 displays the Simulation of Event Frequencies (Poisson Distribution) for Event Type\Route 1, 2, etcetera, 9. It is very easy to understand this concept:

Table 5. Simulation of total event severities

Event type\Route	1	2	Etc.	9
External corrosion	=@ RiskCompound(C10,C22)	=@ RiskCompound(D10,D22)	Etc.	=@ RiskCompound(K10,K22)
Internal corrosion	=@ RiskCompound(C11,C23)	=@ RiskCompound(D11,D23)	Etc.	=@ RiskCompound(K11,K23)
Damages by third parties	=@ RiskCompound(C12,C24)	=@ RiskCompound(D12,D24)	Etc.	=@ RiskCompound(K12,K24)
Flooding	=@ RiskCompound(C13,C25)	=@ RiskCompound(D13,D25)	Etc.	=@ RiskCompound(K13,K25)

continued on following page

Table 5. Continued

Event type\Route	1	2	Etc.	9
Earthquakes, landslides	=@ RiskCompound(C14,C26)	=@ RiskCompound(D14,D26)	Etc.	=@ RiskCompound(K14,K25)
Operational stoppages	=@ RiskCompound(C15,C27)	=@ RiskCompound(D15,D27)	Etc.	=@ RiskCompound(K15,K27)
Unplanned maintenance	=@ RiskCompound(C16,C28)	=@ RiskCompound(D16,D28)	Etc.	=@ RiskCompound(K16,K28)
Design errors	=@ RiskCompound(C17,C29)	=@ RiskCompound(D17,D29)	Etc.	=@ RiskCompound(K17,K29)
Sabotage, vandalism	=@ RiskCompound(C18,C30)	=@ RiskCompound(D18,D30)	Etc.	=@ RiskCompound(K18,K30)

Table 6 displays the Simulation of the Totals and Grand Total Severity:

Table 6. Simulation of totals and grand total severity

Event type\Route	Totals
External corrosion	=@RiskOutput(,"Total SeverityTypes",1)+SUM(C34:K34)
Internal corrosion	=@RiskOutput(,"Total SeverityTypes",2)+SUM(C35:K35)
Damages by third parties	=@RiskOutput(,"Total SeverityTypes",3)+SUM(C36:K36)
Flooding	=@RiskOutput(,"Total SeverityTypes",4)+SUM(C37:K37)
Earthquakes, landslides	=@RiskOutput(,"Total SeverityTypes",5)+SUM(C38:K38)
Operational stoppages	=@RiskOutput(,"Total SeverityTypes",6)+SUM(C39:K39)
Unplanned maintenance	=@RiskOutput(,"Total SeverityTypes",7)+SUM(C40:K40)
Design errors	=@RiskOutput(,"Total SeverityTypes",8)+SUM(C41:K41)
Sabotage, vandalism	=@RiskOutput(,"Total SeverityTypes",9)+SUM(C42:K42)
Grand Total Severity	=@RiskOutput("Grand Total Severity")+SUM(L34:L42)

Simulation: Risk Evaluation and Sensitivity Analysis (Analyse)

Grand Total Severity Analysis

Figure 1 displays the Grand Total Severity Distribution.

Figure 1. Grand total severity distribution

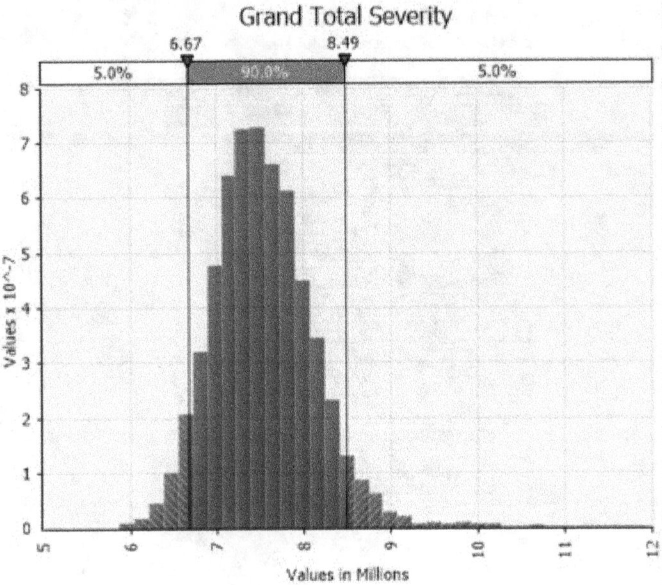

Statistics	Grand Total Severity
Cell	Model!L43
Minimum	5,874,061.96
Maximum	11,940,878.48
Mean	7,528,896
90% CI	± 13,473.20
Mode	7,623,617.54
Median	7,487,246.63
Std Dev	579,092.48
Skewness	0.7825
Kurtosis	5.6432
Values	5000
Errors	0
Filtered	0
Left X	6,673,087.70
Left P	5.0%
Right X	8,488,418.95
Right P	95.0%
Dif. X	1,815,331.25
Dif. P	90.0%

The Grand Total Severity *Mean* is $7,528,896 and the *Standard Deviation* is $579,092.48. There is a 5% probability that the Grand Total Severity will be below $6.67 MM; a 90% probability that it will be in the range of $6.67 MM – $8.49 MM; and a 5% probability that it will be above $8.49 MM.

Sensitivity Analysis

Sensitivity analysis provides for identifying and quantifying the main contributors to variability and risk based on the probability distribution.

The Inputs Ranked by Effect on Output Mean are given in Figure 2.

The graph illustrates that the effect of variable Earthquake's landslides / 5, on the Grand Total Severity is a change in the range of $7,386 to $7,895,530.95, which are respectively left and right from the Baseline of $7,528,896, which is marked on the graph. The other scenarios are less influential.

Figure 2. Grand total severity inputs ranked by effect on output mean

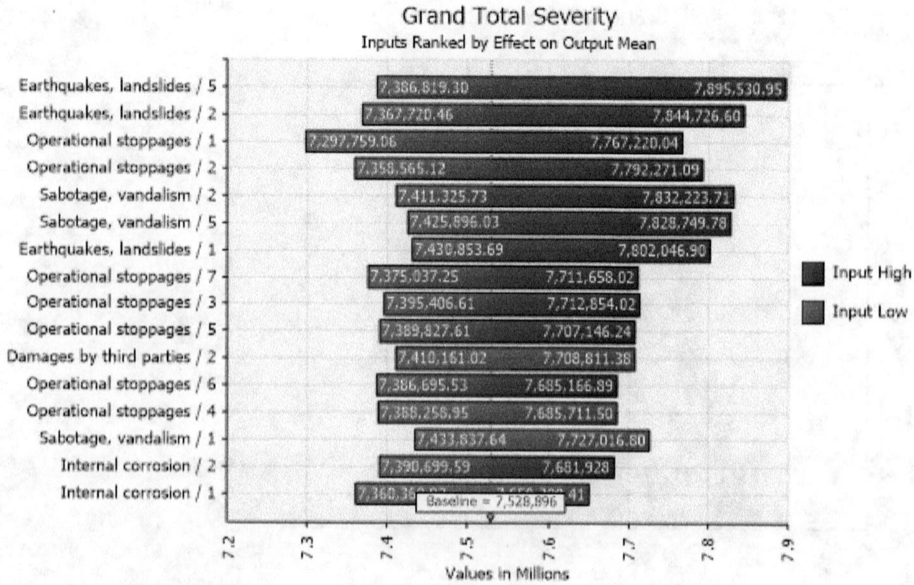

External Corrosion Totals Analysis

Figure 3 displays the External Corrosion Totals distribution. The External Corrosion Totals *Mean* is $166,010.02 and the *Standard Deviation* is $145,448. There is a 5% probability that the CSCO Average Price will be below $95,045; a 90% probability that it will be in the range of 95,045 – $245,502; and a 5% probability that it will be above $245,502.

Figure 3. External corrosion totals distribution

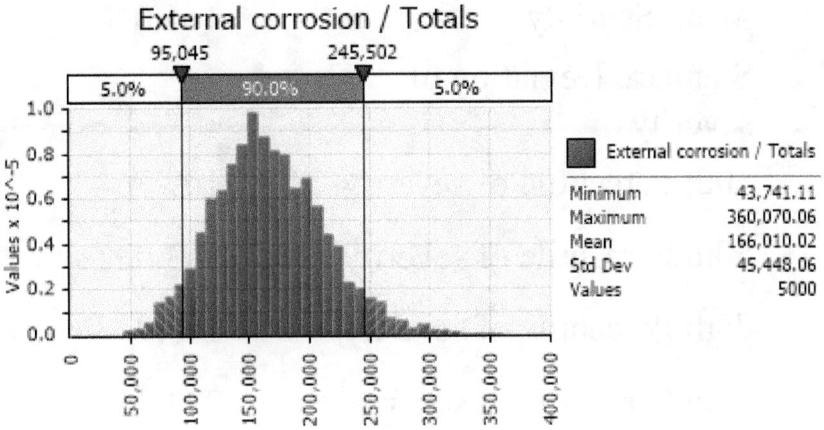

The External Corrosion Totals Data (In $) Severities are given in Figure 4. The graph illustrates that the *Mean* Severity is $166,010 with a Standard Deviation of severity is $45,448. The percentiles start with the 10th Percentile of severity at $109,764 and gradually increase to the 99th Percentile at $282,870.

Figure 4. External corrosion totals data severities

Mean Severity	166,010
Standard Deviation of severity	45,448
10th Percentile of severity	109,764
50th Percentile of severity	163,022
75th Percentile of severity	195,940
90th Percentile of severity	224,416
95th Percentile of severity	245,502
99th Percentile of severity	282,870

Internal Corrosion Totals Analysis

Figure 5 displays the Internal Corrosion Totals distribution. The Internal Corrosion Totals *Mean* is $1,514,510.27 and the *Standard Deviation* is $177,212.93. There is a 5% probability that the Internal Corrosion Totals will be below $1.233 MM; a 90% probability that it will be in the range of $1.233 MM – $1.809 MM; and a 5% probability that it will be above $1.809 MM.

Figure 5. Internal corrosion totals distribution

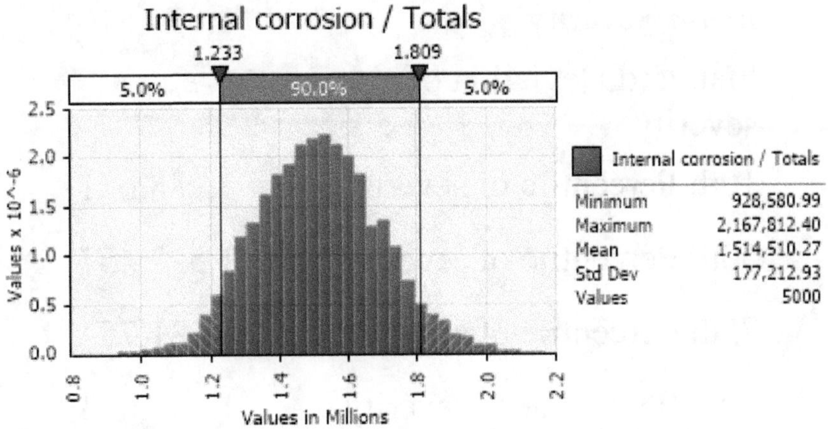

The Internal Corrosion Totals Data (In $) Severities are given in Figure 6. The graph illustrates that the *Mean* Severity is $1,514,510 with a Standard Deviation of severity is $177,213. The percentiles start with the 10th Percentile of severity $1,288,671 and gradually increase to the 99th Percentile of $1,946,361.

Figure 6. Internal corrosion totals data severities

Mean Severity	1,514,510
Standard Deviation of severity	177,213
10th Percentile of severity	1,288,671
50th Percentile of severity	1,512,457
75th Percentile of severity	1,631,754
90th Percentile of severity	1,742,693
95th Percentile of severity	1,808,823
99th Percentile of severity	1,946,361

Damage - Third Parties Totals Analysis

Figure 7 displays the Damage - third Parties Totals distribution. The Damage - third Parties Totals *Mean* is $586,133.42 and the *Standard Deviation* is $153,474.84. There is a 5% probability that the Damage - third Parties Totals will be below $0.347 MM; a 90% probability that it will be in the range of $0.347 MM – $0.849 MM; and a 5% probability that it will be above $0.849 MM.

Figure 7. Damage - third parties totals distribution

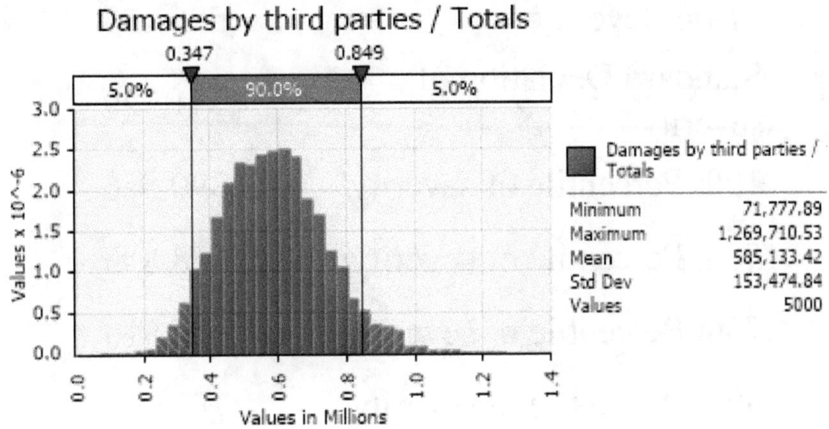

The Damage third Parties Totals Data (In $) Severities are given in Figure 8. The graph illustrates that the *Mean* Severity is $585,133 with a Standard Deviation of severity is $741,929. The percentiles are from the 10th Percentile of the severity of $390,576 and gradually increase to the 99th Percentile of $966,280.

Figure 8. Damage - third parties totals data severities

Mean Severity	585,133
Standard Deviation of severity	741,929
10th Percentile of severity	390,576
50th Percentile of severity	578,855
75th Percentile of severity	684,510
90th Percentile of severity	783,005
95th Percentile of severity	849,339
99th Percentile of severity	966,280

Flooding Totals Analysis

Figure 9 displays the Flooding - third Parties Totals distribution. The Flooding - third Parties Totals *Mean* is $741,928.86 and the *Standard Deviation* is $106,603.73. There is a 5% probability that the Flooding - third Parties Totals will be below $0.573 MM; a 90% probability that it will be in the range of $0.573 MM – $0.922 MM; and a 5% probability that it will be above $0.922 MM.

Figure 9. Flooding - third parties totals distribution

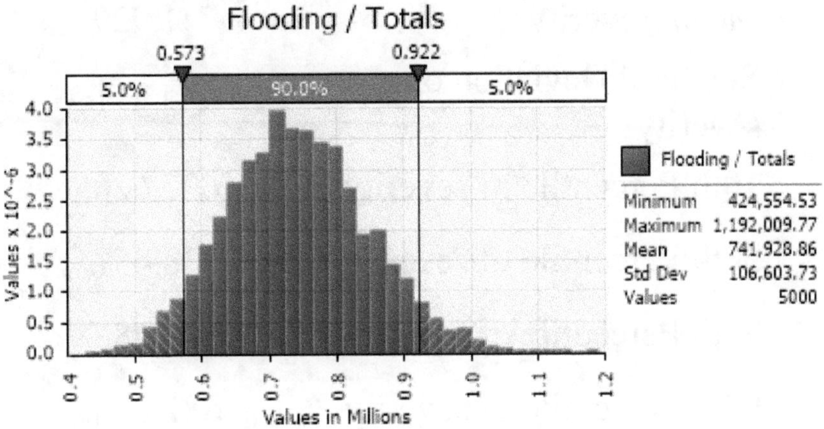

The Flooding Totals Data (In $) Severities are given in Figure 10. The graph illustrates that the *Mean* Severity is $741,929 with a Standard Deviation of severity is $832,321. The percentiles start with the 10th Percentile of severity $607,620 and gradually increase to the 99th Percentile of $1,002,027.

Figure 10. Flooding - third parties totals data severities

Mean Severity	741,929
Standard Deviation of severity	832,321
10th Percentile of severity	607,620
50th Percentile of severity	738,451
75th Percentile of severity	809,484
90th Percentile of severity	881,088
95th Percentile of severity	922,214
99th Percentile of severity	1,002,027

Earthquakes, Landslides Totals Analysis

Figure 11 displays the Earthquakes, Landslides - third Parties Totals distribution. The Earthquakes, Landslides - third Parties Totals *Mean* is \$832,321.35 and the *Standard Deviation* is \$319,211.18. There is a 5% probability that the Earthquakes, Landslides - third Parties Totals will be below \$0.473 MM; a 90% probability that it will be in the range of \$0.473 MM – \$1.366 MM; and a 5% probability that it will be above \$1.366 MM.

Figure 11. Earthquakes, landslides - third parties totals distribution

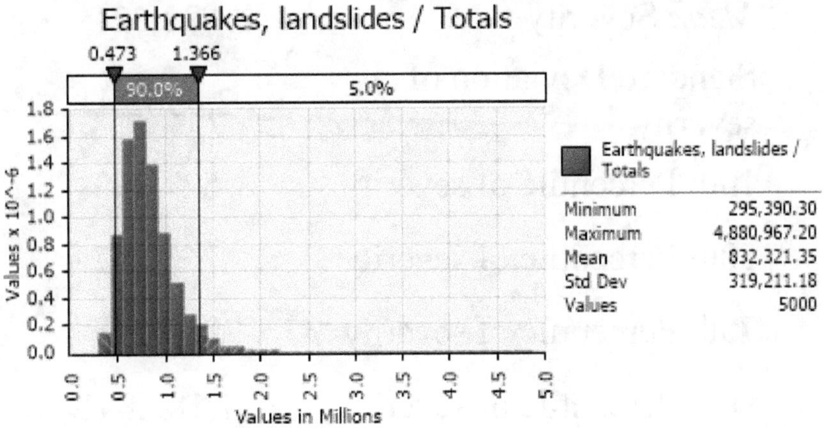

The Earthquakes, Landslides Totals Data (In $) Severities are given in Figure 12. The graph illustrates that the *Mean* Severity is $832,321 with a Standard Deviation of severity is $2,056,241. The percentiles start with the 10th Percentile of severity $527,693 and gradually increase to the 99th Percentile of $1,929,627.

Figure 12. Earthquakes & landslides - third parties totals data severities

Mean Severity	832,321
Standard Deviation of severity	2,056,241
10th Percentile of severity	527,693
50th Percentile of severity	773,297
75th Percentile of severity	956,245
90th Percentile of severity	1,182,831
95th Percentile of severity	1,366,234
99th Percentile of severity	1,929,627

Operational Stoppages Totals Analysis

Figure 13 displays the Operational Stoppages - third Parties Totals distribution. The Operational Stoppages - third Parties Totals *Mean* is \$2,056,240.66 and the *Standard Deviation* is \$293,755.50. There is a 5% probability that the Operational Stoppages - third Parties Totals will be below \$1.592 MM; a 90% probability that it will be in the range of \$1.592 MM – \$2.551 MM; and a 5% probability that it will be above \$2.551 MM.

Figure 13. Operational stoppages - third parties totals distribution

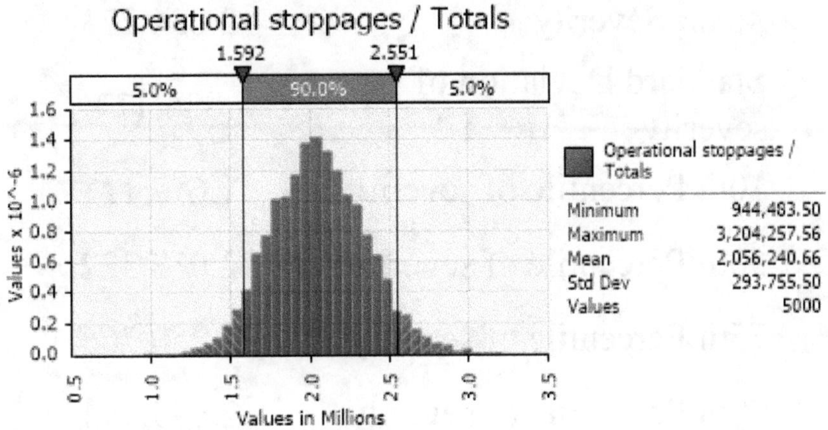

The Operational Stoppages Totals Data (In $) Severities are given in Figure 14. The graph illustrates that the *Mean* Severity is $2,054,773 with a Standard Deviation of severity is $836,477. The percentiles start with the 10th Percentile of the severity of $1,657,123 and gradually increase to the 99th Percentile of $2,725,400.

Figure 14. Earthquakes & landslides - third parties totals data severities

Mean Severity	2,054,773
Standard Deviation of severity	836,477
10th Percentile of severity	1,657,123
50th Percentile of severity	2,018,327
75th Percentile of severity	2,250,766
90th Percentile of severity	2,495,444
95th Percentile of severity	2,603,040
99th Percentile of severity	2,725,400

Unplanned Maintenance Totals Analysis

Figure 15 displays the Unplanned Maintenance - third Parties Totals distribution. The Unplanned Maintenance - third Parties Totals *Mean* is \$836,476.82 and the *Standard Deviation* is \$105,772.86. There is a 5% probability that the Unplanned Maintenance - third Parties Totals will be below \$0.653 MM; a 90% probability that it will be in the range of \$0.653 MM – \$1.006 MM; and a 5% probability that it will be above \$1.006 MM.

Figure 15. Unplanned maintenance - third parties totals distribution

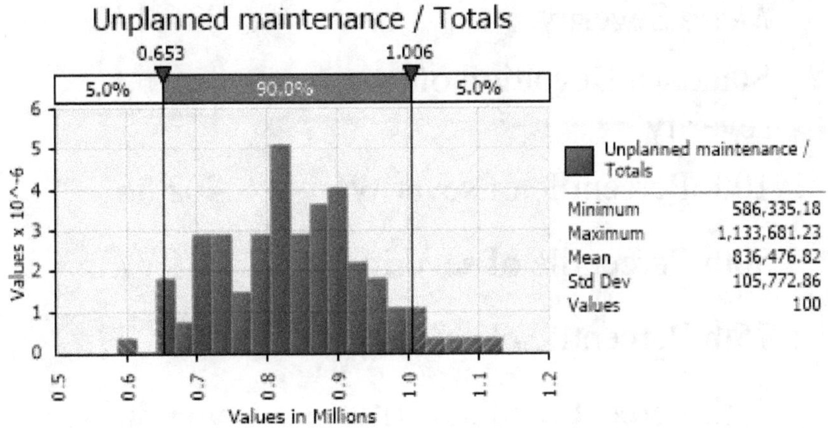

The Unplanned Maintenance Totals Data (In $) Severities are given in Figure 16. The graph illustrates that the *Mean* Severity is $836,477 with a Standard Deviation of severity is $122,687. The percentiles start with the 10th Percentile of the severity of $702,861 and gradually increase to the 99th Percentile of $1,098,430.

Figure 16. Unplanned maintenance - third parties totals data severities

Mean Severity	836,477
Standard Deviation of severity	122,687
10th Percentile of severity	702,861
50th Percentile of severity	831,773
75th Percentile of severity	895,779
90th Percentile of severity	963,807
95th Percentile of severity	1,005,768
99th Percentile of severity	1,098,430

Design Errors Totals Analysis

Figure 17 displays the Design Errors - third Parties Totals distribution. The Design Errors - third Parties Totals *Mean* is $122,686.63 and the *Standard Deviation* is $18,687.64. There is a 5% probability that the Design Errors - third Parties Totals will be below $94,502; a 90% probability that it will be in the range of $94,502 – $154,533; and a 5% probability that it will be above $154,533.

Figure 17. Design errors - third parties totals distribution

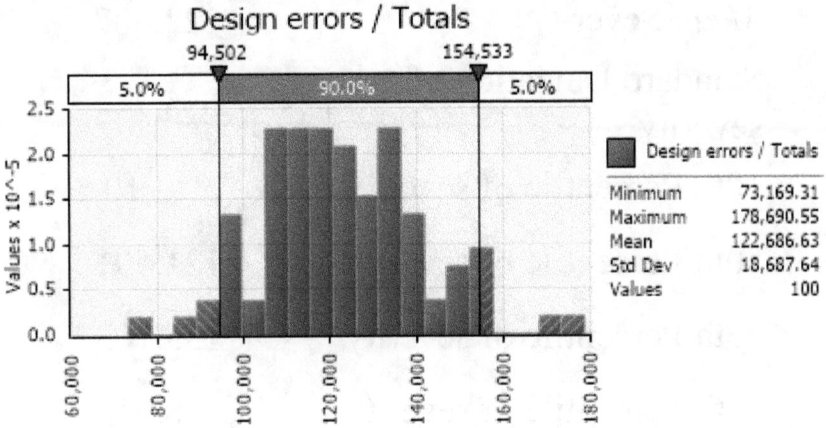

The Design Errors Totals Data (In $) Severities are given in Figure 18. The graph illustrates that the *Mean* Severity is $122,687 with a Standard Deviation of severity is $675,744. The percentiles start with the 10th Percentile of severity at $97,910 and gradually increase to the 99th Percentile at $173,283.

Figure 18. Design errors - third parties totals data severities

Mean Severity	122,687
Standard Deviation of severity	675,744
10th Percentile of severity	97,910
50th Percentile of severity	121,501
75th Percentile of severity	135,103
90th Percentile of severity	148,010
95th Percentile of severity	154,533
99th Percentile of severity	173,283

Sabotage, Vandalism Totals Analysis

Figure 19. Sabotage, vandalism - third parties totals distribution

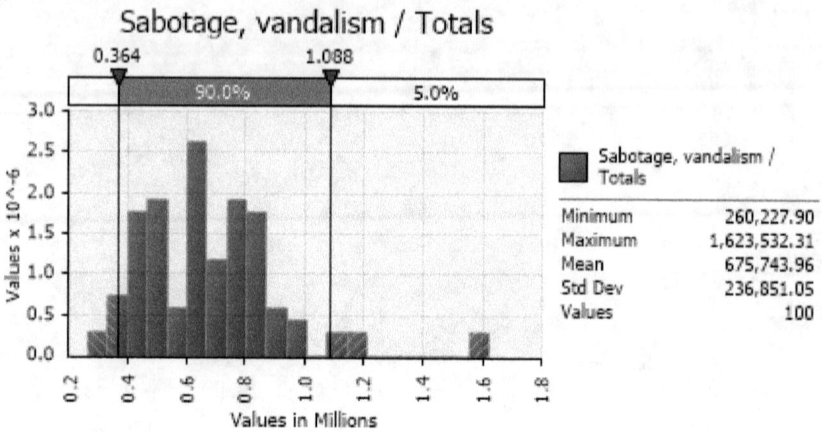

Figure 19 displays the Sabotage, Vandalism - third Parties Totals distribution. The Sabotage, Vandalism - third Parties total m*ean* is $675,743.96 and the *Standard Deviation* is $236,851.05. There is a 5% probability that the Sabotage, Vandalism - third Parties Totals will be below $0.364 MM; a 90% probability that it will be in the range of $0.364 MM – $1.088 MM; and a 5% probability that it will be above $1.088 MM.

The Sabotage and vandalism Totals Data (In $) Severities are given in Figure 20. The graph illustrates that the *Mean* Severity is $675,744 with a Standard Deviation of severity is $7,533,899. The percentiles start with the 10th Percentile of severity $406,549 and gradually increase to the 99th Percentile of $1,566,190.

Figure 20. Sabotage, vandalism - third parties totals data severities

Mean Severity	675,744
Standard Deviation of severity	7,533,899
10th Percentile of severity	406,549
50th Percentile of severity	654,151
75th Percentile of severity	798,784
90th Percentile of severity	922,352
95th Percentile of severity	1,088,444
99th Percentile of severity	1,566,190

Grand Total Risk Severity Totals Analysis

Figure 21. Grand total risk severity - third parties totals distribution

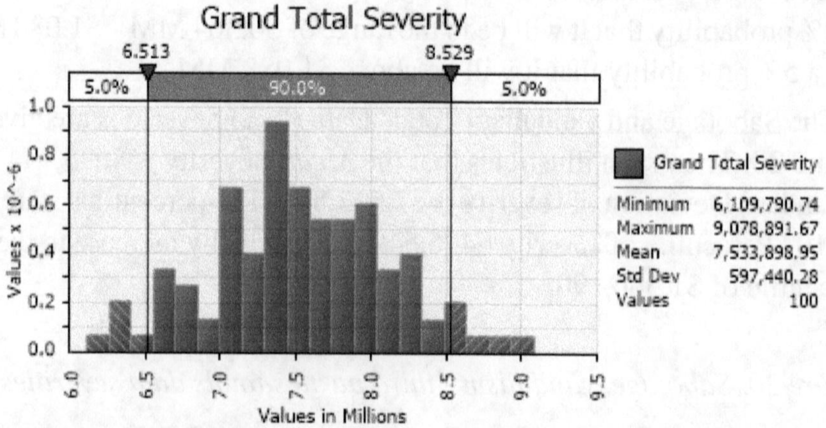

Figure 21 displays the Grand Total Risk Severity - the Third Party's total distribution. The Grand Total Risk Severity - third Parties Totals *Mean* is $7,533,898.95 and the *Standard Deviation* is $597,440.28. There is a 5% probability that the Grand Total Risk Severity - third Parties Totals will be below $6.513 MM; a 90% probability that it will be in the range of $6.513 MM – $8.529 MM; and a 5% probability that it will be above $8.529 MM.

The <u>Grand Total Risk Severity total data ($) Severities</u> are given in Figure 22. The graph illustrates that the *Mean* Severity is $7,533,899 with a Standard Deviation of severity is $7,533,899. The percentiles start with the 10th Percentile of severity at $6,668,586 and gradually increase to the 99th Percentile at $8,837,851.

Figure 22. Grand total risk severity - third parties totals data severities

Mean Severity	7,533,899
Standard Deviation of severity	7,533,899
10th Percentile of severity	6,668,586
50th Percentile of severity	7,496,252
75th Percentile of severity	8,007,535
90th Percentile of severity	8,258,278
95th Percentile of severity	8,528,506
99th Percentile of severity	8,837,851

CONCLUSION

Oil Pipeline Risks

This model simulates various risks in a network of oil pipelines. There are nine types of risks, and there are nine routes in the pipeline network. Each route has three characteristics, as listed in rows 4-6 of the Model sheet: diameter, mean pressure, and distance. For each type of risk and each route, two quantities are simulated: the number of events where that risk type occurs and the typical magnitude of such a risk. These are then accumulated to find the severities of the risk types, by route and total over all routes.

More specifically, the model assumes that sufficient historical data is available to estimate regression equations relating the frequency and mean magnitude of each risk type to the characteristics of the routes. The resulting coefficients appear in the Parameters sheet. Besides the usual constant and variable coefficients, there are also Error columns. When simulating either a risk frequency or a mean risk magnitude, this error coefficient is multiplied by a standard normal random variable to provide extra variability (so that the calculated parameters do not lie *exactly* on the regression lines). The risk frequencies are then assumed to be Poisson distributed with means from the regressions. The typical event magnitudes are assumed to be lognormally distributed with means from the regressions and standard deviations equal to given percentages of the means. These percentages are in the "Coeff of var" column in the Parameters sheet.

To accumulate the total severity for any risk type and route, one possibility is to multiply the frequency by the typical magnitude. However, this would assume that all events for that risk type/route combination have the *same* magnitude. A better way is to use the Risk-Compound function, as is done here. Then each of the events for that risk type/route combination has its own lognormally distributed magnitude.

The Results sheet is set up to display summary statistics and a histogram for each risk type and the total of all risk types. When you run the simulation, these results will "come alive."

REFERENCES

Miesner, T. O., & Leffler, W. L. (2021). *Oil & Gas Pipelines in Nontechnical Language*. PennWell.

Muhlbauer, W. K. (2004). *Oil & Gas Pipelines in Nontechnical Language*. Gulf Professional Publishing.

Timashev, S., & Bushinskaya, A. (2016). Oil & Gas Pipelines in Nontechnical Language. Springer.

Chapter 8
Oil Transportation With Weather Disruptions

ABSTRACT

An oil rig in the middle of the Gulf of Mexico serves as an inventory stocking point for several other platforms. Crude oil is generated daily. Some of it is shipped to the coast, some is sent through a pipeline, and the rest is stored at the rig. The potential crude output generated daily is Pert distributed. This output is constrained because of storage capacity. If the inventory after shipping and pipeline amounts are greater than the storage capacity, the crude output is decreased and the final inventory that day is equal to the storage capacity, implemented in the Inventory Calculations. There are two sources of uncertainty: whether severe weather starts on any given day, and if so, how long it lasts. The random weather behavior is implemented in the Weather Calculations using the parameters, using historical data. In particular, the probability of severe weather varies by month.

INTRODUCTION

Oil Transportation With Weather Disruptions

Short sellers targeting the Oil & Gas Storage & Transportation sector have made $6.58 billion in mark-to-market profits this year, said S3 Partners in a note published: i) Short sellers amassed $6.5 billion in profits betting

DOI: 10.4018/979-8-3373-0959-0.ch008

against oil & gas storage and transportation; ii) Only 6.5% of stocks in the sector did not generate a profit for shorts; and iii) Investors increased bets against stocks and USO ETF as crude fell.

Short sellers targeting the Oil & Gas Storage & Transportation sector have made $6.58 billion in mark-to-market profits this year, said S3 Partners in a note published Tuesday.

Investors betting against the sector hit "oil, black gold, Texas tea" in every stock except 6.5% which generated a relatively small loss of $2.07 million. The most profitable shorts were Energy Transfer LP, Enbridge, One-ok, Enterprise Products, and Pembina Pipeline. Short interest in the sector has averaged $13.76 billion in 2020. Before last week, short sellers were actively covering their positions to realize profits. They decided to reverse course and started short selling across a broad range of stocks in the sector over the last week, according to the note from the financial analytics firm.

> *"With oil production building and storage facilities closing in on full capacity, the Oil & Gas Storage & Transportation Sector is a potential epicentre of volatility over the short term. Short sellers are now in the unenviable position of trying to protect and realize 2020 mark-to-market profits versus deploying additional resources to a sector that may have room to run," wrote Ihor Dusaniwsky, Managing Director Predictive Analytics, S3 Partners. "Further oil price volatility in both the spot and futures market will create more opportunities in the sector."*

Short sellers also began circling the United States Oil Fund LP, the largest oil fund, after the prospects for crude looked bleak. After actively short covering into the weakening oil market from Jan. 1 to Feb. 27, S3 says they went into overdrive, tripling the USO shares shorted from Feb. 27 to April 21.

> *"Over the last month, shares shorted increased by +15.04 million shares, +29.52%, and over the last week an increase of +6.50 million shares, +10.93%. USO short interest is now $213 million, 75.82 million shares shorted, 15.47% short interest % of the float," wrote Dusaniwsky in a separate note published.*

On the other hand, investors at Robinhood are piling into USO. See the chart below from Robin-track, a website that tracks investments on the platform.

LITERATURE

Akaky (2005): Before the coming of the "dot com" era it was by no accident that the richest individuals in the world were involved with tankers. Probably the most famous ship owner in the world was Aristotle Socrates Onassis. But before one looks at tanker freights of which Onassis among others managed to secure a good return on capital it is crucial to recap and examine some of the factors that affected the tanker industry starting with the Second World War. The Transportation of Oil by Sea offers a fascinating introductory account of crude oil transportation and how international issues from World War II, pre-independence Zimbabwe, and the Iran-Iraq War have been influenced by considerations for oil production and transportation. Author Tony Akaki presents a diversity of geographical, political, environmental, and economic insights in one volume, offering a compelling look at this often-overlooked aspect of history.

Saxton (2023): A series of personal accounts by highly trained helicopter pilots, including those with distinguished careers in the military and commercial flying, who with divers, ensured that essential staff could operate in North Sea oil exploration and oil supply. They were the vital link in the process and operated in the most challenging circumstances, often in high levels of danger and sometimes with loss of life, for example, the Piper Alpha Disaster which made national news. The ferrying of essential personnel and supplies could involve rescues as well as routine flying missions. The narrative is often technical but written to ensure good understanding for lay readers and it will, of course, appeal to the many with flying experience in the forces, in commercial flying, and in government service. Above all, it is a series of graphic personal stories as recounted by individuals faced with extremes of climate, weather, technical, engineering, and aeronautical problems and often with human life at stake. The people who come to life with domestic and social concerns and interests are 'real' and believable. It is a history of the North Sea oil episode in UK political and economic history and in conjunction with international oil politics is of huge importance to Britain's economy. This is a period of progress to domestic oil independence by about 1984 and so a key period with subsequent importance even to the present. All aspects of the operations are covered within individual stories and include the broader questions of company policy, regulation, and trade union involvement.

Frittelli et al. (2014): North America is experiencing a boom in crude oil supply, primarily due to growing production in the Canadian oil sands and the recent expansion of shale oil production from the Bakken fields in North Dakota and Montana as well as the Eagle Ford and Permian Basins in Texas. Taken together, these new supplies are fundamentally changing the U.S. oil supply-demand balance. The United States now meets 66% of its crude oil demand from production in North America, displacing imports from overseas and positioning the United States to have excess oil and refined products supplies in some regions.

Saxton (2023): The rapid expansion of North American oil production has led to significant challenges in transporting crudes efficiently and safely to domestic markets—principally refineries—using the nation's legacy pipeline infrastructure. In the face of continued uncertainty about the prospects for additional pipeline capacity, and as a quicker, more flexible alternative to new pipeline projects, North American crude oil producers are increasingly turning to rail as a means of transporting crude supplies to U.S. markets. According to rail industry officials, U.S. freight railroads are estimated to have carried more than 400,000 carloads of crude oil in 2013 (roughly equivalent to 280 million barrels), compared to 9,500 carloads in 2008. Crude imports by rail from Canada have increased more than 20-fold since 2011. While oil by rail has demonstrated benefits to the efficient movement of oil from producing regions to market hubs, it has also raised significant concerns about transportation safety and potential impacts on the environment. The most recent data available indicate that railroads consistently spilled less crude oil per ton-mile transported than other modes of land transportation. Nonetheless, safety and environmental concerns have been underscored by a series of major accidents across North America involving crude oil transportation by rail—including a catastrophic fire that caused numerous fatalities and destroyed much of Lac Mégantic, Quebec, in 2013. Following that event, the U.S. Department of Transportation issued a safety alert warning that the type of crude oil being transported from the Bakken region may be more flammable than traditional heavy crude oil. Legislation introduced in Congress following the Lac Mégantic disaster would require railroads to have at least two crew members aboard all trains. In addition, policymakers are discussing regulatory changes involving tank car design, prevention of derailments, and selection of preferred routes for transporting oil by rail. Congress may evaluate these changes in the reauthorization of the Rail Safety Improvement Act of 2008.

United States Government Accountability Office (2014): Technology advancements such as horizontal drilling and hydraulic fracturing (pumping water, sand, and chemicals into wells to fracture underground rock formations and allow oil or gas to flow) have allowed companies to extract oil and gas from shale and other tight geological formations. As a result, oil and gas production has increased more than fivefold from 2007 through 2012. DOT oversees the safety of the U.S. transportation system. GAO was asked to review oil and gas transportation infrastructure issues. This report examines (1) overall challenges that increased oil and gas production may pose for transportation infrastructure, (2) specific pipeline safety risks and how the DOT is addressing them, and (3) specific rail safety risks and how the DOT is addressing them. GAO analysed federal transportation infrastructure and safety data generally from 2008 to 2012 or 2013 (as available), reviewed documents, and interviewed agency, industry, and safety stakeholders, as well as state and industry officials in states with large-scale shale oil and gas development.

ELABORATION

Oil Transportation with Weather Disruptions (Define) The Probabilities of Severe Weather Events by Month are given in Table 1:

Table 1. Probabilities of severe weather events by month

Month	Means	Coefficient of variation	Random (normal) seasonality index	Probability of severe weather	Seasonality factor	Seasonally adjusted probability
1	0.485	20.52%	=@RiskNormal(C4,D4*C4)	=E4/$E$16	=F4*12	=$H$16*G4
2	0.507	17.36%	=@RiskNormal(C5,D5*C5)	=E5/$E$16	=F5*12	=$H$16*G5
3	0.712	10.77%	=@RiskNormal(C6,D6*C6)	=E6/$E$16	=F6*12	=$H$16*G6
4	0.961	5.48%	=@RiskNormal(C7,D7*C7)	=E7/$E$16	=F7*12	=$H$16*G7
5	1.201	4.60%	=@RiskNormal(C8,D8*C8)	=E8/$E$16	=F8*12	=$H$16*G8
6	1.396	2.88%	=@RiskNormal(C9,D9*C9)	=E9/$E$16	=F9*12	=$H$16*G9
7	1.501	2.33%	=@RiskNormal(C10,D10*C10)	=E10/$E$16	=F10*12	=$H$16*G10
8	1.459	2.85%	=@RiskNormal(C11,D11*C11)	=E11/$E$16	=F11*12	=$H$16*G11
9	1.303	3.27%	=@RiskNormal(C12,D12*C12)	=E12/$E$16	=F12*12	=$H$16*G12
10	1.067	5.23%	=@RiskNormal(C13,D13*C13)	=E13/$E$16	=F13*12	=$H$16*G13
11	0.829	7.11%	=@RiskNormal(C14,D14*C14)	=E14/$E$16	=F14*12	=$H$16*G14
12	0.579	5.08%	=@RiskNormal(C15,D15*C15)	=E15/$E$16	=F15*12	=$H$16*G15
Sum	1.000		1.000	=SUM(F4:F15)	=AVERAGE(G4:G15)	7.36%

The Minimum and Maximum Days are presented in Table 2:

Table 2. Minimum and maximum days

Min Days	0
Max Days	10

The Historical Data are given in Table 3:

Table 3. Historical data

Days	1	2	3	4	5	6
Frequency	48	86	58	15	6	2

The Typical Length is in Table 4:

Table 4. Typical length

Typical Length	=ROUND(@RiskGeneral(C19,C20,C23:H23,C24:H24),0)

The Fixed Inputs are in Table 5:

Table 5. Fixed inputs

Initial crude inventory (Barrels)	30,000
Maximum storage capacity (Barrels)	40,000
Maximum daily pipeline capacity (Barrels/Day)	750

The Parameters Inputs are in Table 6:

Table 6. Parameters input

Daily (unconstrained) crude output (Pert) in Barrels	550	1,200	1,300
Ship capacity (Pert) in Barrels	1,100	1,700	2,000
Days between ship loadings (Truncated Poisson)	3.30	3	
Pipeline performance coefficient (Pert)	40%	88%	95%

The Inventory Outputs from Simulation in Table 7:

Table 7. Inventory outputs from simulation

Days output constrained	=@RiskOutput()+SUM(R12:R376)
Ship loading days	=@RiskOutput()+COUNTIF(O12:O376,”>0”)
Average amount shipped	=@RiskOutput()+SUM(O12:O376)/C4
Average thru pipeline	=@RiskOutput()+AVERAGE(P12:P376)
Average final inventory	=@RiskOutput()+AVERAGE(S12:S376)

The Severe Weather Outputs from Simulation Table 8:

Table 8. Severe weather outputs from simulation

Events	=@RiskOutput("Severe Weather Events")+SUM(F12:F376)
Days	=@RiskOutput("Severe Weather Days")+SUM(J12:J376)

Oil Transportation with Weather Disruptions (Analysis)

Days' Output Constrained Analysis

Figure 1 displays the Day output-constrained distribution.

Figure 1. Days' output-constrained distribution

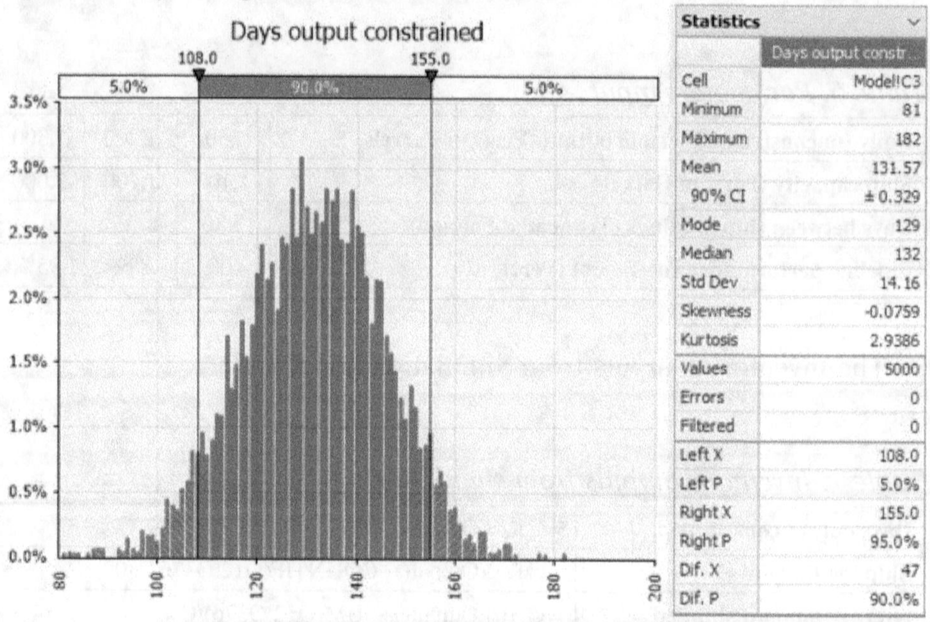

The Days output constrained *Mean* is 137.57 (i.e., 138 days) and the *Standard Deviation* is 14.16 (i.e., 14 days). There is a 5% probability that the day output will be below 108.0; a 90% probability that it will be in the range of 108.0 – 155.0; and a 5% probability that it will be above 155.0.

Sensitivity Analysis

Sensitivity analysis provides for identifying and quantifying the main contributors to variability and risk based on the probability distribution.

The Inputs Ranked by Effect on Output Mean are given in Figure 2.

Figure 2. Days' output constrained inputs ranked by effect on output mean

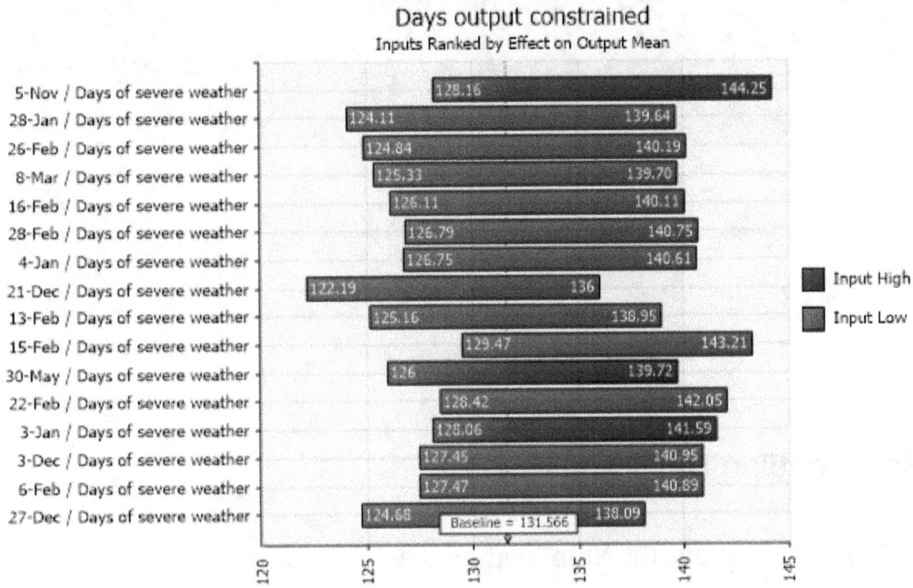

The graph illustrates that the effect of the variable 5-Nov / Days of severe weather, on the Days' output constrained is a change in the range of 128.16 (i.e.,128) to 144.25 (i.e., 144), respectively left and right from the Baseline of 131.566 (132), which is marked on the graph. The other outputs are less influential.

The Change in Output Mean Across the Range of Input Values graph presented in Figure 3 illustrates that the top variable 5-Nov / Days of severe weather (in Red), has a contribution of change increase from 128.16 (i.e.,128) to 144.25 (i.e., 144), respectively left and right from the Baseline of 131.566 (i.e., 132), to the variance of Days' output constrained. Other variables are less influential as the contribution to variance is smaller.

Figure 3. Days' output-constrained chart

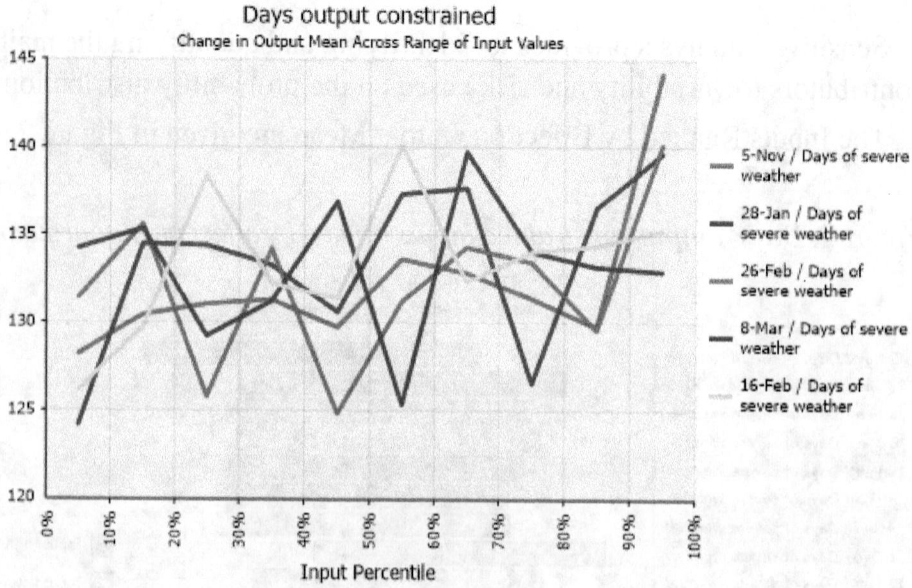

Ship Loading Days Analysis

Figure 4 displays the Ship loading days distribution.

Figure 4. Ship loading days distribution

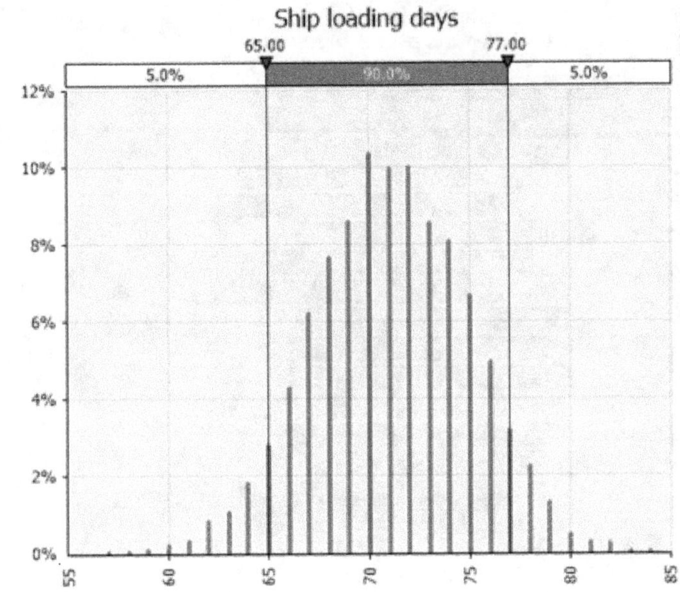

Statistics	Ship loading days
Cell	Model!C4
Minimum	57
Maximum	84
Mean	71.097
90% CI	± 0.0892
Mode	70
Median	71
Std Dev	3.832
Skewness	-0.0558
Kurtosis	2.9076
Values	5000
Errors	0
Filtered	0
Left X	65.00
Left P	5.0%
Right X	77.00
Right P	95.0%
Dif. X	12
Dif. P	90.0%

The Ship loading days *Mean* is 71.097 (i.e., 71 days) and the *Standard Deviation* is 3.832 (i.e., 4 days). There is a 5% probability that the Ship loading days output will be below 65.00; a 90% probability that it will be in the range of 65.00 – 77.00; and a 5% probability that it will be above 77.00.

Sensitivity Analysis

Sensitivity analysis provides for identifying and quantifying the main contributors to variability and risk based on the probability distribution.

The Inputs Ranked by Effect on Output Mean are given in Figure 5.

Figure 5. Ship loading days inputs ranked by effect on output mean

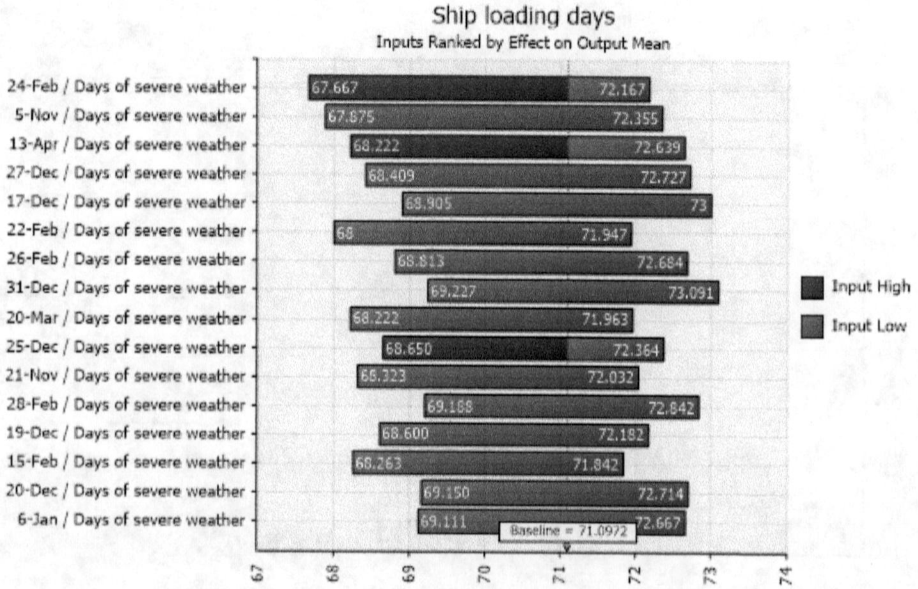

The graph illustrates that the effect of the variable 24-Feb / Days of severe weather, on the Ship loading days is a change in the range of 67.667 (i.e.,68) to 72.167 (i.e., 72), respectively left and right from the Baseline of 71.0972 (i.e., 71), which is marked on the graph. The other outputs are less influential.

The <u>Change in Output Mean Across the Range of Input Values</u> graph presented in Figure 6 illustrates that the top variable 24-Feb / Days of severe weather (in Red), has a contribution of change increase from 67.667 (i.e.,68) to 72.167 (i.e., 72), respectively left and right from the Baseline of 71.0972 (i.e., 71), to the variance of Ship loading days. Other variables are less influential as the contribution to variance is smaller.

Figure 6. Ship loading days chart

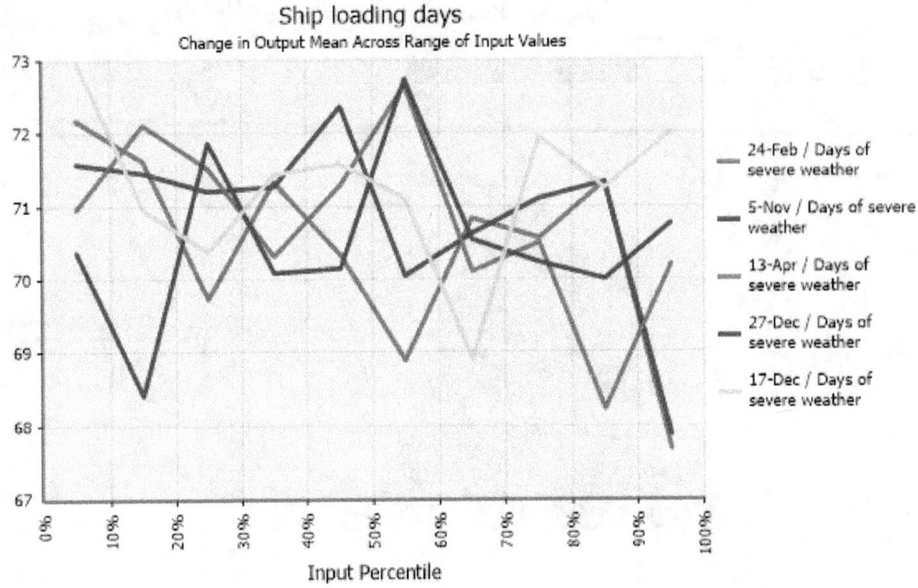

Average Amount Shipped Analysis

Figure 7 displays the Average amount shipped distribution. The Average amount shipped *Mean* is 1,650.34 (i.e., 1,650) and the *Standard Deviation* is 19.58 (i.e., 20). There is a 5% probability that the Average amount shipped will be below 1,617.3 (i.e.,1,617); a 90% probability that it will be in the range of 1,617 – 1,681.6 (i.e., 1,682); and a 5% probability that it will be above 1,682.

Figure 7. Average amount shipped distribution

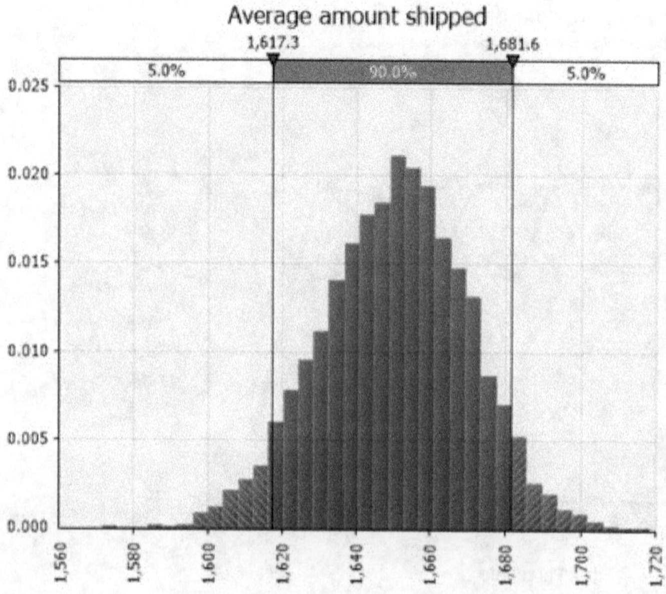

Statistics	Average amount sh...
Cell	Model!C5
Minimum	1,571.48
Maximum	1,718.26
Mean	1,650.34
90% CI	± 0.456
Mode	1,654.90
Median	1,650.88
Std Dev	19.58
Skewness	-0.1160
Kurtosis	2.9271
Values	5000
Errors	0
Filtered	0
Left X	1,617.3
Left P	5.0%
Right X	1,681.6
Right P	95.0%
Dif. X	64.23
Dif. P	90.0%

Sensitivity Analysis

Sensitivity analysis provides for identifying and quantifying the main contributors to variability and risk based on the probability distribution.

The Inputs Ranked by Effect on Output Mean are given in Figure 8.

The graph illustrates that the effect of the variable 21-Mar / Days of severe weather, on the Average amount shipped is a change in the range of 1,636.83 (i.e.,1,637) to 1,659.62 (i.e., 1,660), respectively left and right from the Baseline of 1,650.336 (i.e., 1,650), which is marked on the graph. The other outputs are less influential.

Figure 8. Average amount shipped inputs ranked by effect on output mean

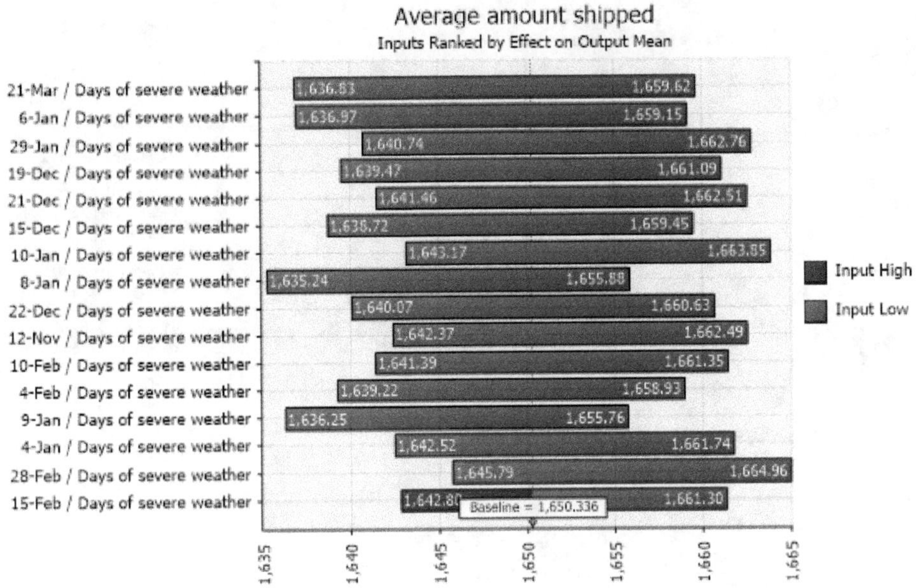

The Change in Output Mean Across the Range of Input Values graph is presented in Figure 9.

Figure 9. Average amount shipped chart

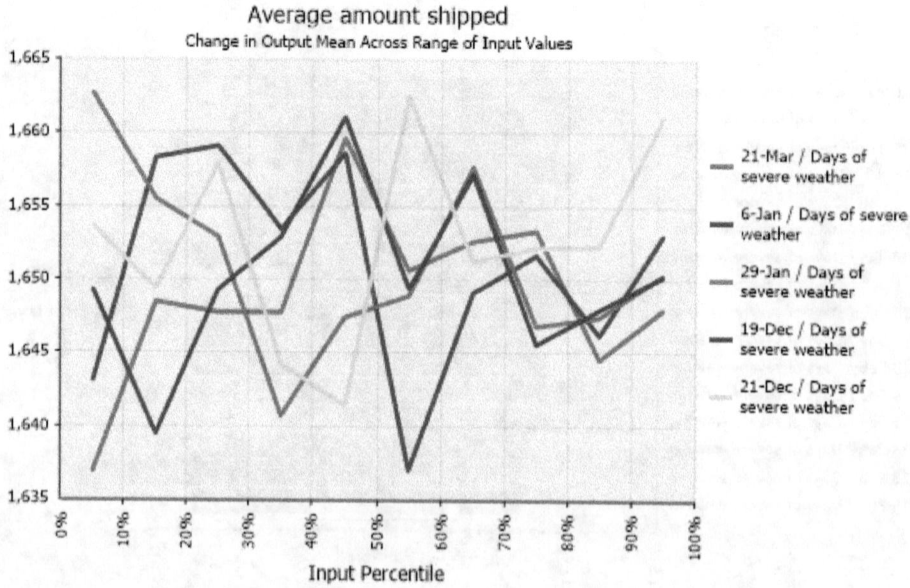

Figure 9 illustrates that the top variable 24-Feb / Days of severe weather (in Red), has a contribution of change increase from 1,637 to 1,660 respectively left and right from the Baseline of 1,650 to the variance of Average amount shipped. Other variables are less influential as the contribution to variance is smaller.

Average through Pipeline Analysis

Figure 10 displays the Average through pipeline distribution.

The Average thru-pipeline *Mean* is 608.750 (i.e., 609) and the *Standard Deviation* is 3.582 (i.e., 4). There is a 5% probability that the Average thru pipeline will be below 602.77 (i.e., 603); a 90% probability that it will be in the range of 603 – 602.77 (i.e., 603); and a 5% probability that it will be above 614.71 (i.e., 615).

Figure 10. Days' output-constrained distribution

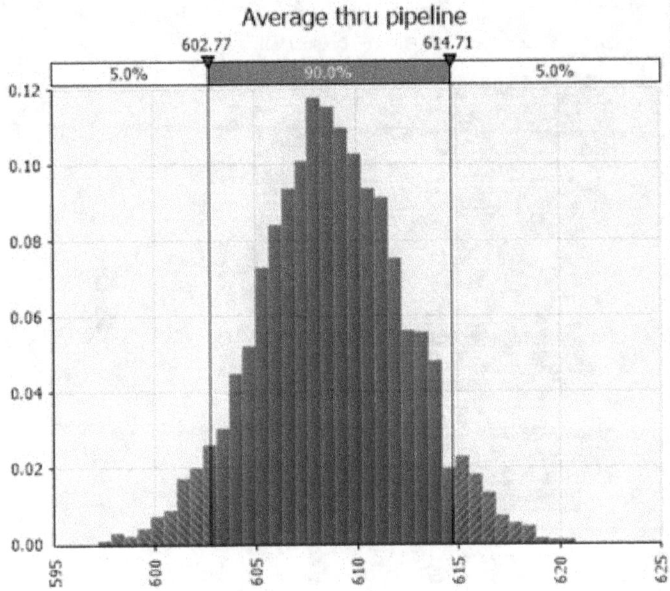

Statistics	Average thru pipeline
Cell	Model!C6
Minimum	597.121
Maximum	620.744
Mean	608.750
90% CI	± 0.0833
Mode	609.849
Median	608.710
Std Dev	3.582
Skewness	-0.0114
Kurtosis	2.9712
Values	5000
Errors	0
Filtered	0
Left X	602.77
Left P	5.0%
Right X	614.71
Right P	95.0%
Dif. X	11.943
Dif. P	90.0%

Sensitivity Analysis

Sensitivity analysis provides for identifying and quantifying the main contributors to variability and risk based on the probability distribution.

The Inputs Ranked by Effect on Output Mean are given in Figure 11.

The graph illustrates the effect of the variable 8-Oct / Amount thru pipeline, on the Average thru pipeline in the range of 608.07 (i.e.,608) to 609.34 (i.e., 609), respectively left and right from the Baseline of 608.7498 (609), which is marked on the graph. The other outputs are less influential.

Figure 11. Average thru pipeline inputs ranked by effect on output mean

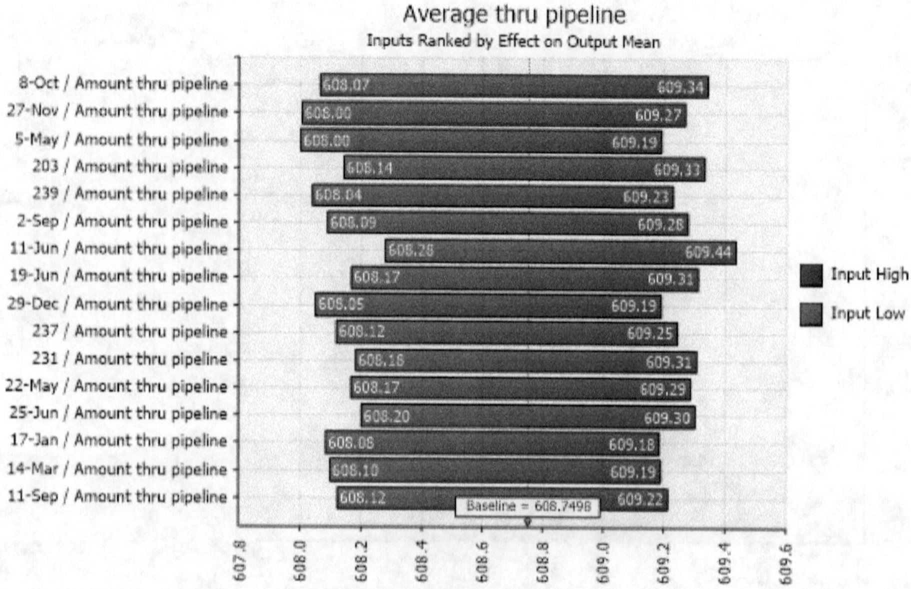

The Change in Output Mean Across the Range of Input Values graph presented in Figure 12 illustrates that the top variable 8-Oct / Amount thru pipeline (in Red), has a contribution of change increase from 608.07 (i.e.,608) to 609.34 (i.e., 609), respectively left and right from the Baseline of 608.7498 (609), to the variance of Average thru pipeline. Other variables are less influential as the contribution to variance is smaller.

Figure 12. Average through pipeline chart

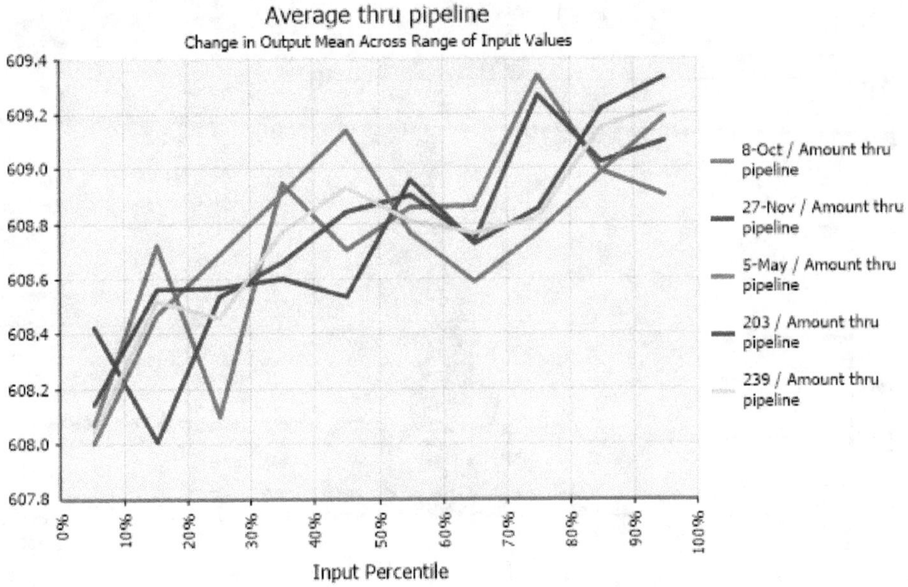

Average Final Inventory Analysis

Figure 13 displays the Average final inventory distribution.

The Average final inventory *Mean* is 38,529.71 (i.e., 38,530) and the *Standard Deviation* is 3.832 (i.e., 4). There is a 5% probability that the Average final inventory will be below 37,910; a 90% probability that it will be in the range of 37,910 – 38,972; and a 5% probability that it will be above 38,972.

Figure 13. Average final inventory distribution

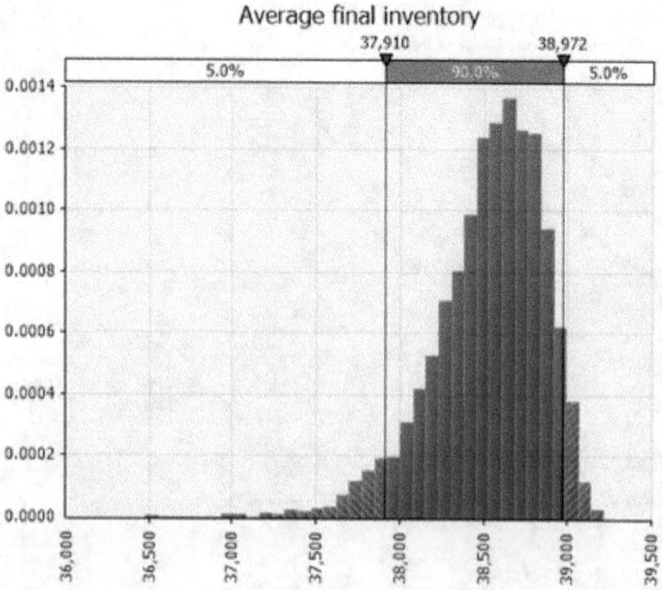

Statistics	Average final inven...
Cell	Model!C7
Minimum	36,479.50
Maximum	39,218.64
Mean	38,529.71
90% CI	± 7.56
Mode	38,677.27
Median	38,577.56
Std Dev	324.84
Skewness	-0.9281
Kurtosis	4.4061
Values	5000
Errors	0
Filtered	0
Left X	37,910
Left P	5.0%
Right X	38,972
Right P	95.0%
Dif. X	1,062.17
Dif. P	90.0%

Sensitivity Analysis

Sensitivity analysis provides for identifying and quantifying the main contributors to variability and risk based on the probability distribution.

The Inputs Ranked by Effect on Output Mean are given in Figure 14. The graph illustrates that the effect of the variable 3-Jan / Days of severe weather, on the Average final inventory is a change in the range of 38,448.94 (i.e., 38,449) to 38,917.20 (i.e., 38,917), respectively left and right from the Baseline of 38,529.71 (i.e., 38,530), which is marked on the graph. The other outputs are less influential.

Figure 14. Average final inventory inputs ranked by effect on output mean

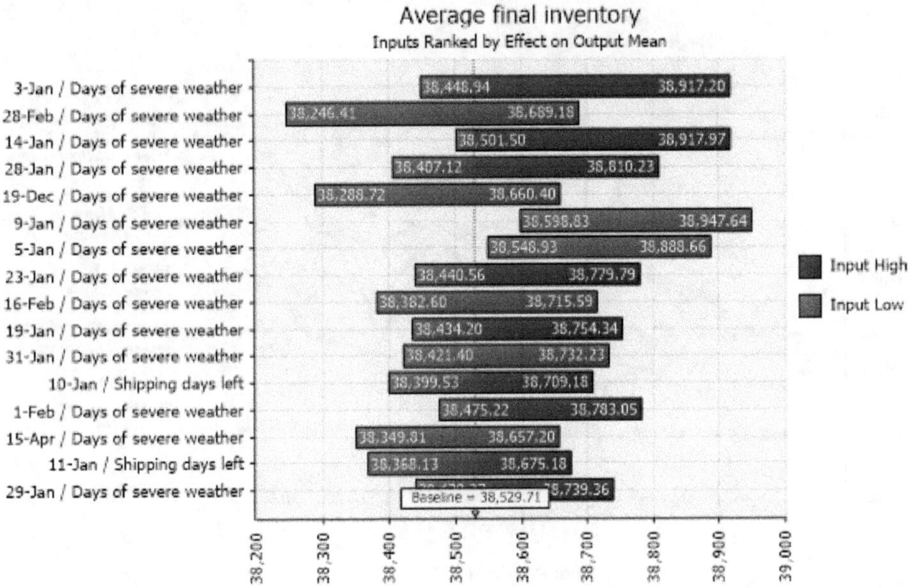

The Change in Output Mean Across the Range of Input Values graph is presented in Figure 15.

Figure 15. Ship loading days chart

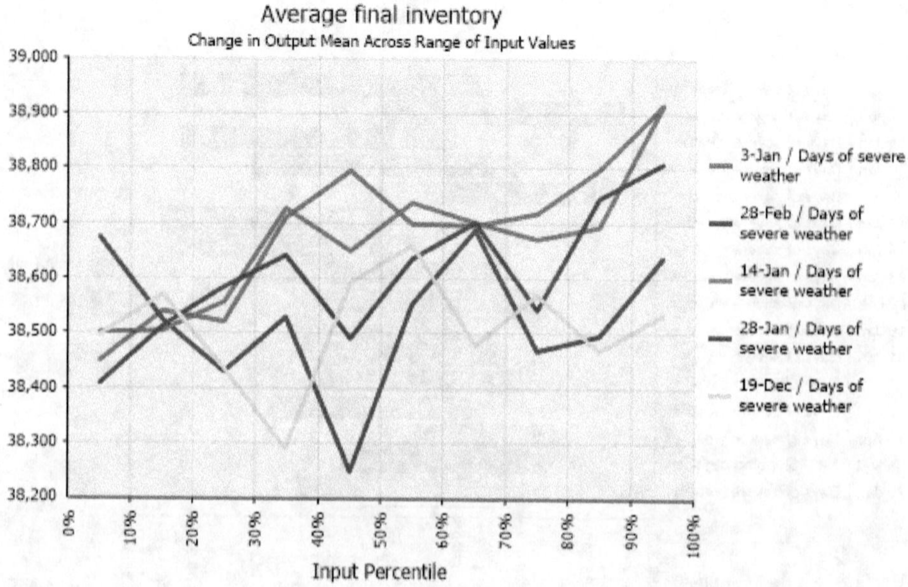

Figure 15 illustrates that the top variable 24-Feb / Days of severe weather (in Red), has a contribution of change increase from 38,448.94 (i.e., 38,449) to 38,917.20 (i.e., 38,917), respectively left and right from the Baseline of 38,529.71 (i.e., 38,530), to the variance of Average final inventory. Other variables are less influential as the contribution to variance is smaller.

Severe Weather Events Analysis

Figure 16 displays the Severe Weather Events distribution. The Severe Weather Events *Mean* is 26.961 (i.e., 27) and the *Standard Deviation* is 4.885 (i.e., 5). There is a 5% probability that the Severe Weather Event will be below 19.00; a 90% probability that it will be in the range of 19.00 – 35.00; and a 5% probability that it will be above 35.00.

Figure 16. Average amount shipped distribution

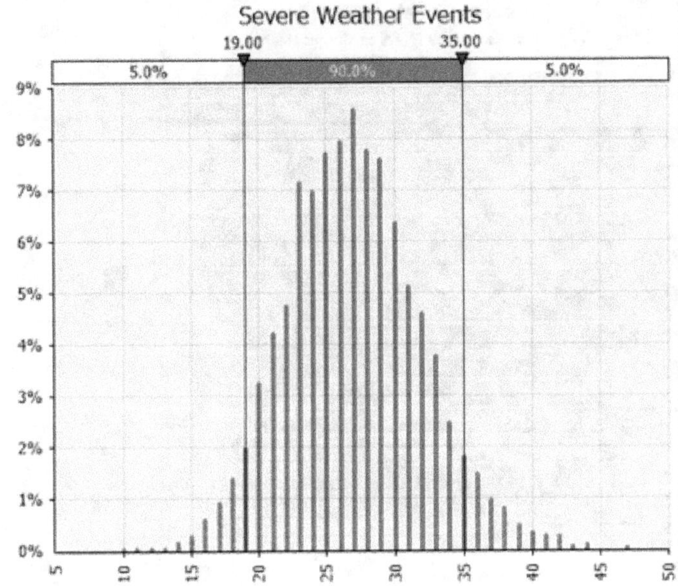

Statistics	Severe Weather Ev...
Cell	Model!F3
Minimum	10
Maximum	47
Mean	26.961
90% CI	±0.114
Mode	27
Median	27
Std Dev	4.885
Skewness	0.2446
Kurtosis	3.1691
Values	5000
Errors	0
Filtered	0
Left X	19.00
Left P	5.0%
Right X	35.00
Right P	95.0%
Dif. X	16
Dif. P	90.0%

Sensitivity Analysis

Sensitivity analysis provides for identifying and quantifying the main contributors to variability and risk based on the probability distribution.

The Inputs Ranked by Effect on Output Mean are given in Figure 17.

The graph illustrates that the effect of the variable 30-Jul / Days of severe weather, on the Severe Weather Events is a change in the range of 26.797 (i.e.,27) to 28.380 (i.e., 28), respectively left and right from the Baseline of 26.9606 (i.e., 27), which is marked on the graph. The other outputs are less influential.

Figure 17. Severe weather events inputs ranked by effect on output mean

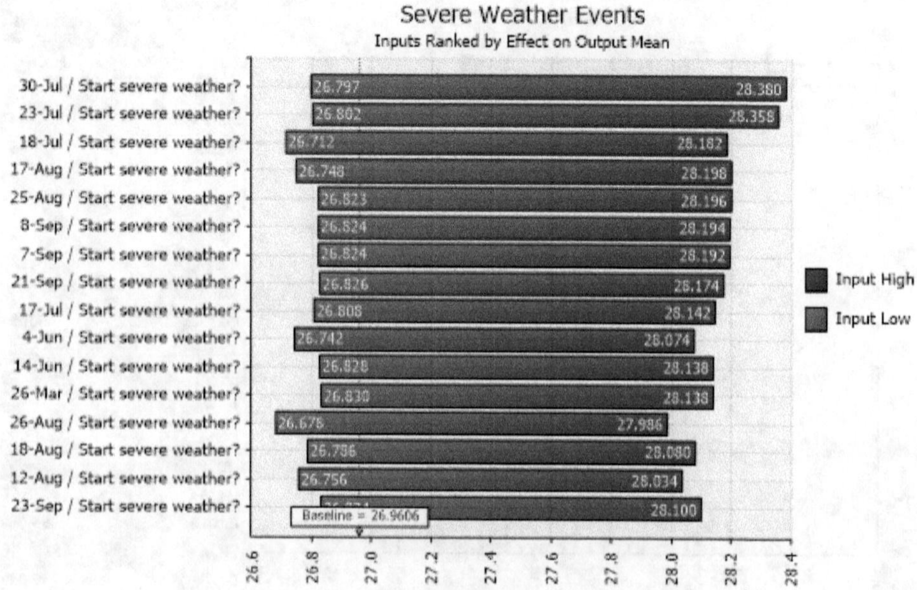

The Change in Output Mean Across the Range of Input Values graph presented in Figure 18 illustrates that the top variable 24-Feb / Days of severe weather (in Red), has a contribution of change increase from 26.797 (i.e.,27) to 28.380 (i.e., 28), respectively left and right from the Baseline of 26.9606 (i.e., 27), to the variance of Severe Weather Events. Other variables are less influential as the contribution to variance is smaller.

Figure 18. Severe weather events chart

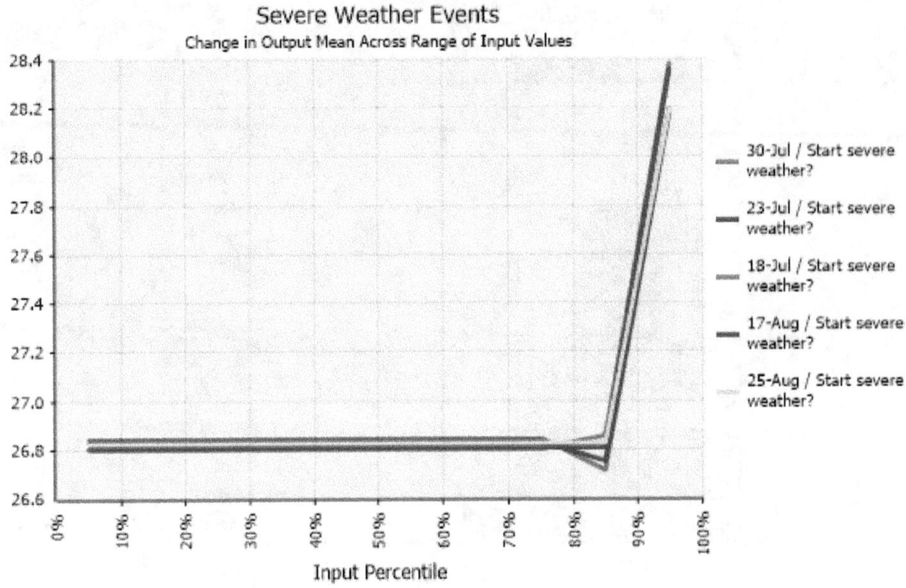

Severe Weather Days Analysis

Figure 19 displays the Severe Weather Days distribution. The Severe Weather Days *Mean* is 58.780 (i.e., 59) and the *Standard Deviation* is 11.576 (i.e., 12). There is a 5% probability that the Severe Weather Days will be below 41.00; a 90% probability that it will be in the range of 41.00 – 78.00; and a 5% probability that it will be above 78.00.

Figure 19. Severe weather days distribution

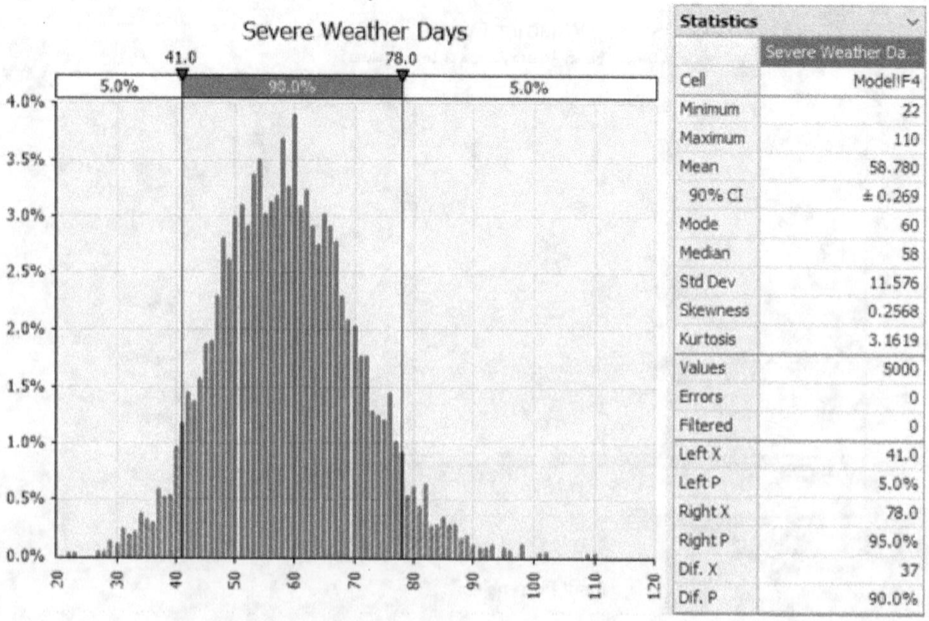

Sensitivity Analysis

Sensitivity analysis provides for identifying and quantifying the main contributors to variability and risk based on the probability distribution.

The Inputs Ranked by Effect on Output Mean are given in Figure 20.

The graph illustrates that the effect of the variable 22-Feb / Days of severe weather, on the Severe Weather Days is a change in the range of 53.947 (i.e., 54) to 71.842 (i.e., 72), respectively left and right from the Baseline of 58.780 (i.e., 59), which is marked on the graph. The other outputs are less influential.

Figure 20. Severe weather days inputs ranked by effect on output mean

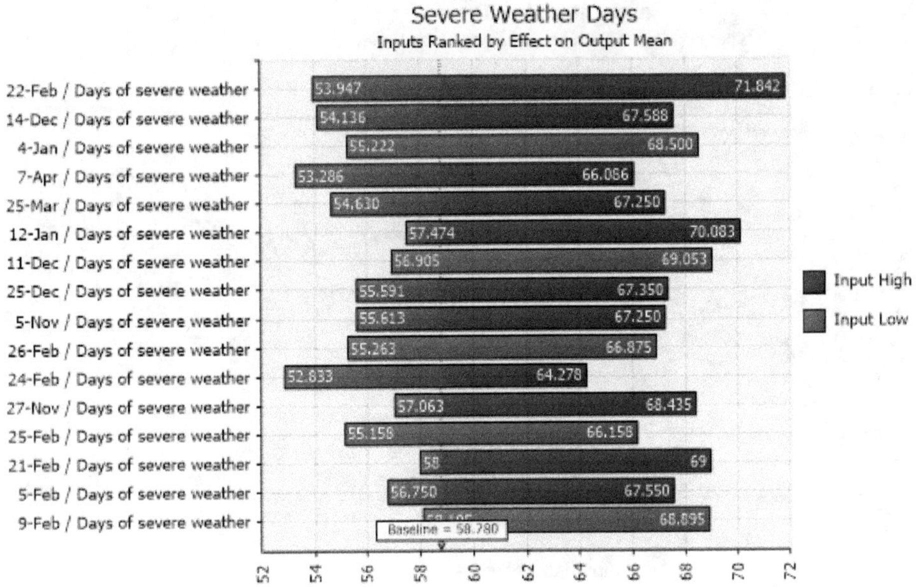

The Change in Output Mean Across the Range of Input Values graph is presented in Figure 18.

Figure 21. Severe weather days chart

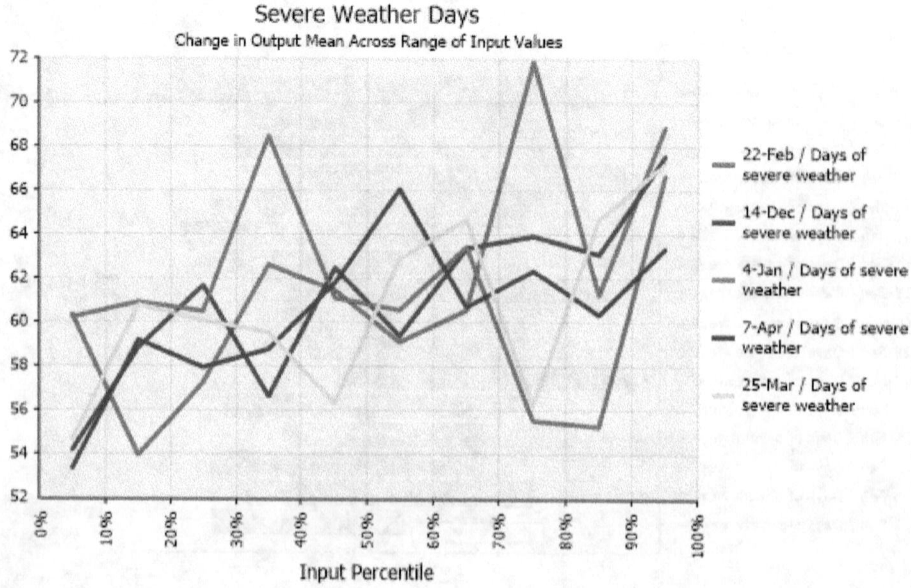

Figure 18 illustrates that the top variable 24-Feb / Days of severe weather (in Red), has a contribution of change increase from 53.947 (i.e., 54) to 71.842 (i.e., 72), respectively left and right from the Baseline of 58.780 (i.e., 59), to the variance of Severe Weather Events. Other variables are less influential as the contribution to variance is smaller.

CONCLUSION

Oil Transportation With Weather Disruptions

This model is based on an actual Palisade consulting experience. An oil rig in the middle of the Gulf of Mexico serves as an inventory stocking point for several other platforms. Crude oil is generated daily. Some of it is shipped to the coast, some is sent through a pipeline, and the rest is stored at the rig. The potential crude output generated daily is Pert distributed. However, this output is constrained because of storage capacity. Specifically, if the inventory after shipping and pipeline amounts are greater than the storage capacity, the crude output is decreased so that the final inventory that day is equal to the storage capacity. This logic is implemented in the Inventory Calculations section of the Model sheet.

There is always the potential for severe weather. There are two sources of uncertainty: whether severe weather starts on any given day, and if so, how long it lasts. The random weather behavior is implemented in the Weather Calculations section of the Model sheet. These use the parameters in the Weather Parameters sheet, which are based on historical data. In particular, the probability of severe weather varies by month. Conditional formatting is used to color the font of days with severe weather red. Pay particular attention to the logic in columns H-J. Note that with this logic, two or more severe weather events can overlap, but this causes no problems.

Severe weather interrupts shipments. For example, if a shipment normally take 5 days, but severe weather occurs on 2 of these days, the actual shipment time is increased to 7 days. Also, ship loading is possible only on days when there is no severe weather. This logic is implemented in columns M and N of the Model sheet.

The @RISK outputs are listed in red cells at the top of the Model sheet.

REFERENCES

Akaky, T. (2005). The Transportation of Oil by Sea. iUniverse.

Frittelli, J. (2014). *U.S. Rail Transportation of Crude Oil: Background and Issues for Congress*. Congressional Research Service.

Saxton, P. (2023). Helicopters and North Sea Oil: A Story of Service, Danger and Survival. Pen and Sword History.

United States Government Accountability Office (Author). (2014). Oil and Gas Transportation: Department of Transportation Is Taking Actions to Address Rail Safety, but Additional Actions Are Needed to Improve Pipeline Safety. United States Government Accountability Office.

Chapter 9
Projecting Oil Prices

ABSTRACT

This model projects oil prices in the presence of "nonrandom" market mechanisms. Historical daily oil prices are listed. The absolute price changes fit a nonnegative distribution, and the best-fitting distribution is the exponential distribution to simulate future absolute price changes. Each of these price changes can be positive or negative, and two rules are used to determine (randomly) the direction of each price change, which are: First if the current price is near prescribed minimum and maximum limits, the direction of the next price change tends to be away from the relevant limit. Second, for prices not too near the limits, there is a tendency to have a positive price change if the average of the most recent 50 days is greater than the average of the most recent 200 days, and there is a tendency to have a negative price change otherwise.

INTRODUCTION

Projecting Oil Prices

Crude oil holds a prominent position in the global commodities market because oil price changes affect the global economy. Thus, those countries or groups that produce crude oil also impact economies worldwide.

Oil prices are largely dependent on two factors: geopolitical developments and economic events. These two variables can lead to changes in oil demand and supply levels, which drive oil price fluctuations from one day

DOI: 10.4018/979-8-3373-0959-0.ch009

to the next. For instance, the 1973 Arab oil embargo, the 1980 Iran-Iraq war, the 1990 Gulf War, the Asian financial crisis of 1997, and the global financial crisis of 2007 to 2008 are some of the historical geopolitical developments that have significantly affected oil prices.

- Oil prices are driven by many factors including supply and demand.
- Member countries of the Organization of the Petroleum Exporting Countries (OPEC) produce about 40% of the world's crude oil.
- OPEC's oil exports represent about 60% of the total petroleum traded internationally.
- OPEC (especially Saudi Arabia) has the upper hand in determining the direction of oil prices, but Russia has also become a key player.
- Evidence is inconclusive as to whether non-OPEC countries are influential in determining crude oil prices.

Organisation of the Petroleum Exporting Countries (OPEC) is an organization that sets production targets among its members to manage oil production. OPEC member countries produce about 40% of the world's crude oil. Additionally, OPEC's oil exports represent about 60% of the total petroleum traded internationally, according to the United States Energy Information Administration.

Because of this market share, OPEC's actions have a huge influence on international oil prices. In particular, OPEC's largest producer of crude oil, Saudi Arabia, has the most frequent effect on oil prices. Historically, crude oil prices have seen increases in times when OPEC production targets are reduced.

Countries involved in global oil production are either members of OPEC, OPEC+, or non-OPEC nations. OPEC has 13 members: Algeria, Angola, Congo, Equatorial Guinea, Gabon, Iran, Iraq, Kuwait, Libya, Nigeria, Saudi Arabia, the United Arab Emirates, and Venezuela.

Ten non-OPEC nations joined OPEC to form OPEC+ in late 2016 to have more control over the global crude oil market. These countries were: Azerbaijan, Bahrain, Brunei, Kazakhstan, Malaysia, Mexico, Oman, Russia, South Sudan, and Sudan. Not surprisingly, OPEC+ has a level of influence over the world economy that is even larger than OPEC's.

Responding to the highly dynamic economic and geopolitical developments, these groups make changes to their oil production capacities, which affect the oil supply levels and result in oil price volatility.

OPEC's oil exports account for roughly 60% of the total petroleum traded worldwide. The Energy Information Agency also reports that more than 80% of the world's proven crude oil reserves lie within the boundaries of the OPEC countries. Of that, roughly two-thirds lay within the Middle Eastern region in 2021.

Additionally, all OPEC member nations have been continuously improving technology and enhancing explorations leading to further enhancements to their oil production capacities at reduced operational costs.

Within the OPEC group, Saudi Arabia is the largest crude oil producer in the world and remains the most dominant member of OPEC. It is also the leading exporter of crude oil globally. Each time there is a cut in Saudi oil production, there is a sharp rise in oil prices, and an increase in Saudi oil production stimulates a drop in oil prices.

Since the 1973 Arab oil embargo, Saudi Arabia has managed to call the shots as far as oil prices are concerned, by controlling supply. All major oil price fluctuations in recent history can be attributed to changing production levels in Saudi Arabia, along with other OPEC nations. Source: World's Top Exports (Exporters) and U.S. Energy Information Administration (Producers)

OPEC+ controls over 50% of global oil supplies, according to Tamas Varga, senior analyst at PVM Oil Associates and quoted by CNBC. OPEC+ remains influential due to three primary factors:

1. An absence of alternative sources equivalent to its dominant position.
2. A lack of economically feasible alternatives to crude oil in the energy sector.
3. The comparatively low-cost price advantage against the relatively high-cost non-OPEC production.

In short, OPEC+ has the economic capability to disrupt or enhance the supply of oil to substantial levels at any time, severely affecting oil prices. For example, the 1973 Arab oil embargo by OPEC saw prices quadruple from \$3 to \$12 per barrel, and more recently, the sudden ramp-up in production by Saudi Arabia in March 2020 led to a sharp decline in the price of oil. On April 20, 2020, following the temporary lack of coordination between Russia and Saudi Arabia added to the lockdown, the front-month May 2020 West Texas Intermediate (WTI) crude contract dropped 306%, or \$55.90, for the session, to settle at *negative* \$37.63 a barrel on the New York Mercantile Exchange. This suggests that holders of oil had to pay to get takers to their production.

Non-OPEC oil producers are crude oil-producing nations outside of the OPEC group and Shale Oil producers. Interestingly, some of the top oil-producing countries are non-OPEC nations. This includes the United States of America, which is the number one producer, as well as Canada and China.

Most non-OPEC countries have high consumption levels and, thus, limited capacity to export. Many are net oil importers despite being high producers, which means they have minimal influence on oil prices. However, with the discovery of shale oil and shale gas, non-OPEC oil producers, particularly the United States, have enjoyed increased production and greater market share in recent times. While this has been a game-changer of sorts, shale oil technology requires substantial upfront investments, which acts as a deterrent to shale oil producers.

So far, the jury is out as to whether non-OPEC producers can have a material impact on the price of crude oil. High production levels from non-OPEC members from 2002 to 2004 and in 2010 did not result in price declines and instead brought higher oil prices. This is probably because non-OPEC members did not have sufficient market share to affect the market price of oil. High production from 2014 to 2015, however, did cause prices to decline. Market pundits have opined that the decline in prices was probably due to an increase in supply from OPEC producers to counter the threat posed to their hegemony by non-OPEC producers.

Oil prices are also affected by geopolitical developments and economic interests. Additionally, "black swan" events, or unexpected events, greatly affect the supply/demand paradigm.

One such event occurred in January 2020 when the global economy was roiled by the pandemic. The plummeting global demand for oil led to a fracturing of OPEC+, specifically between Saudi Arabia and Russia, the two largest oil exporters. In response, Saudi Arabia ratcheted up production. This overt attempt to capture market share led to a precipitous decline that saw the price of WTI breach $20/barrel.

An "extraordinary" meeting between OPEC and non-OPEC (read: Saudi Arabia and Russia) led to an agreement to cut production by about 10 million barrels per day (B/D). In what was a classic buy-the-rumour-sell-the-fact trade, oil prices rose and then cratered as the market was not impressed by a global supply cut of 10 million B/D while global demand was projected to decline by 30 million B/D.

Organisation of the Petroleum Exporting Countries (OPEC) refers to a group of 13 major oil-exporting nations. Founded in 1960, OPEC aims to manage the supply of oil to set market prices, working to avoid fluctuations that might affect the economies of oil-producing and oil-purchasing countries. The member countries of OPEC are Iran, Iraq, Kuwait, Saudi Arabia, and Venezuela (the five founders), plus Algeria, Angola, Congo, Equatorial Guinea, Gabon, Libya, Nigeria, and the United Arab Emirates. In late 2016, 10 non-OPEC nations formed OPEC+, establishing a broader coalition with even more control over the global crude oil market.

The price of crude oil can fluctuate significantly in reaction to many variables. Supply and demand prospects along with the perceived risk of market disruptions are a big part of the picture. Periods of economic growth tend to increase oil demand and drive-up prices, whereas economic slowdowns may send oil demand and prices downward. OPEC and OPEC+ also affect oil prices by influencing global supply through the negotiation of production quotas.

There are many ways that you can make an investment based on your expectations of the direction of crude oil prices. You can speculate on the price of crude by trading oil futures and options, related exchange-traded funds (ETFs) and exchange-traded notes (ETNs), and individual energy stocks.

The dynamics of the oil economy are complex, and oil prices depend on more than the rules of demand and supply, although at its most primal level, the market is the final arbiter of the price of oil. Under normal global market conditions, OPEC+ will continue to maintain its dominance in oil price determination. Despite challenges such as fracking technology and oil discovery in non-OPEC regions, OPEC's share of the global market allows the organization to manipulate production quotas and continue to be a central player in oil price determination.

LITERATURE

U.S. Department of the Interior (2015): The purpose of this study is to analyse the dynamic interaction between changes in crude oil prices, oil and gas industry activity in the OCS (measured in terms of petroleum production), and selected indicators of the Gulf Coast economies. The scope of the study is expanded to include E&P activity in the Deepwater. A vector auto-regression (VAR) model framework showing the interaction between crude petroleum price, oil, and gas production, the U.S. interest rates, the U.S. gross domestic product, and selected indicators of the state of the Gulf Coast economy—personal income, unemployment rate and revenue—was developed and estimated. The model framework enables us to establish the direction, symmetry, causation, duration, responsiveness, and correlation between industry activity and state economic activity indicators and oil price changes over time.

Carollo (2011): It's a fair bet that most of what you think you know about oil prices is wrong. Despite the massive price fluctuations of the past decade, the received wisdom on the subject has remained fundamentally unchanged since the 1970s. When asked, most people – including politicians, financial analysts, and pundits – will respond with a tired litany of reasons ranging from increased Chinese and Indian competition for diminishing resources and tensions in the Middle East to manipulation by OPEC and exorbitant petrol taxes in the EU. Yet the facts belie these explanations. For instance, what happened in late 2008 when, in just a few weeks, oil prices plummeted from $144 to $37 a barrel? Did Chinese and Indian demand suddenly dry up? Did Middle East conflicts magically resolve themselves? Did OPEC flood the market with crude? In each case, the answer is a definitive no – quite the opposite. Industry expert Salvatore Carollo explains that the truth behind today's increasingly volatile oil market is that over the past two decades, oil prices have come untethered from all classical notions of supply and demand and have transcended any countries, consortiums, cartels, or corporate entity's powers to control them. At play is a subtler, more complex game than most analysts realise (or are unwilling to admit to), a very dangerous game involving runaway financial speculation, self-defeating government policymaking, and a concerted disinvestment in refinery capacity among the oil majors. In Understanding Oil Prices Carollo identifies the key players in this dangerous game, exploring their competing interests and motivations, their moves, and countermoves. Beginning with the 1976 oil embargo and moving through the 1986 Chornobyl incident, the implementation of the US Clean Air Act Amendments of 1990, and the precipitous expansion of the oil futures market since the turn of the century, he traces the vast structural changes which have occurred within the oil industry over the past four decades, identifying their economic, social and geopolitical drivers, and analysing their fallout in the global economy. He explores the oil industry's decision to scale down refining capacity in the face of increasing demand and the effects of global shortages of petrol, diesel, jet fuel, fuel oil, chemical feedstocks, lubricants, and other essential finished products, and describes how beginning in the year 2000, the oil futures market detached itself almost completely from the crude market, leading to the assets of oil, and the crippling impact reckless speculation in oil futures has had on the global economy. Finally, he proposes new, more sophisticated models that economists and financial analysts can use to make sense of today's oil market while offering industry leaders and government policymakers prescriptions for stabilising the market to ensure a relatively steady flow of affordable oil. A concise, authoritative guide to understanding the complex, oft-misunderstood oil markets, Understanding Oil Prices is an important resource for energy market participants, commodity traders, and investors, as well as business journalists and government policymakers alike.

Rauscher (1989): Oil price fluctuations and their impact on economic performance Drastic oil price fluctuations have been a major characteristic of the world petroleum market since the beginning of the seventies. The oil crises of 1973n4 and 1979/80 were followed by a dramatic drop in the oil price during the first two quarters of 1986. Starting from a level of less than 2 $ per barrel in 1972, the spot market price of Arabian Light crude oil increased to some 35 $ in 1980, then slowly decreased, and finally fell to 13 $ in 1986 (annual averages). If monthly data are considered, the peaks of the oil price movement look even more dramatic. In December 1980 Arabian crude was traded for more than 40 $ a barrel, and in August 1986 the price was down to 8 $. The spot market price of Saudi Arabian Light crude oil! Data are taken from the Petroleum Economist and the OPEC Bulletin, on various issues. After the Second World War petroleum has become the most important energy resource. During the fifties and sixties, its price was relatively low compared to other energy sources like coal and firewood and it tended to drive them out of the market.

ELABORATION

Projecting Oil Prices (Define)

The Historical Data, from Jan 03, 2005, to Apr 24, 2012, are known. Only partial data is shown in Table 1. The first ten are from Jan 03, 2005, to Jan 12, 2005. The last ten are from Apr 11, 2012, to from Apr 24, 2012.

Table 1. Oil prices, Jan 03 to Jan 14 and from Apr 11 to Apr 24

Date	$/Bbl	Abs Change
Jan 03, 2005	$42.16	
Jan 04, 2005	$43.96	$1.80
Jan 05, 2005	$43.41	$0.55
Jan 06, 2005	$45.51	$2.10
Jan 07, 2005	$45.32	$0.19
Jan 10, 2005	$45.31	$0.01

continued on following page

Table 1. Continued

Date	$/Bbl	Abs Change
Jan 11, 2005	$45.66	$0.35
Jan 12, 2005	$46.46	$0.80
Jan 13, 2005	$48.11	$1.65
Jan 14, 2005	$48.41	$0.30
Apr 11, 2012	102.66	$1.54
Apr 12, 2012	103.69	$1.03
Apr 13, 2012	102.84	$0.85
Apr 16, 2012	102.92	$0.08
Apr 17, 2012	104.23	$1.31
Apr 18, 2012	102.65	$1.58
Apr 19, 2012	102.38	$0.27
Apr 20, 2012	103.58	$1.20
Apr 23, 2012	102.68	$0.90
Apr 24, 2012	103.1	$0.42

The Distribution of absolute price changes is given in Table 2:

Table 2. Distribution of absolute price changes

Distribution of absolute price changes
=@RiskExpon(1.3366,RiskName("Abs Price Changes"))

Fit Comparison for Abs Price Changes: @RISK was used to fit the absolute changes, using a fixed lower limit of 0. The Exponential Distribution shown below provides the best fit and is used in this model.

Figure 1. Fit comparison for abs price changes

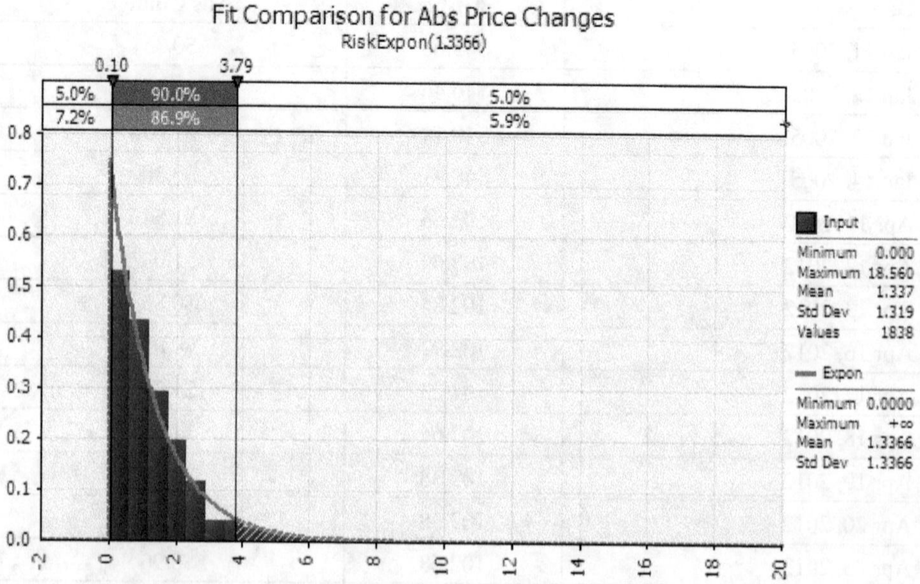

The Limits on prices are given in Table 3:

Table 3. Limits on prices

Minimum	$40
Maximum	$150

The Parameters affecting the probability of a daily price increase are in Table 4:

Table 4. Parameters affecting probability

Extreme low prices			**Uniform parameters**	
Within	5%	of min	0.8	1
Within	10%	of min	0.6	0.8
Extreme high prices				

continued on following page

Table 4. Continued

Within	5%	of max	0	0.2
Within	10%	of max	0.2	0.4
Not extreme and MA50 > MA200			0.5	0.6
Not extreme and MA50 < MA200			0.4	0.5

The rules above imply that if the price is close to the minimum limit of \$40, the probability of a price increase is high. Specifically, if the price is within 5% of the minimum limit, the probability of a price increase is uniformly distributed between 0.8 and 1. Otherwise, if the price is within 10% of the minimum limit, the probability of a price increase is uniformly distributed between 0.6 and 0.8. Similar statements in the opposite direction hold if the price is near the maximum limit of \$150.

In the first 200 days (before a 200-day moving average, or MA, can be calculated), if none of these conditions hold, the probability of a price increase is 0.5. However, beyond 200 days, not only are the extreme price rules above checked, but there is also a check on whether the average for the most recent 50 days is greater than, or less than, the average for the most recent 200 days. In the first case, the probability of a price increase is relatively high, uniform between 0.5 and 0.6 (a "buy bias"). In the second case, the probability of a price increase is relatively low, uniform between 0.4 and 0.5 (a "sell bias").

The Monthly Average prices are for 120 Months. Table 5 will present the first five and the last five to show the concept:

Table 5. Monthly average prices, i.e., the first five and the last five

Month	Average Price
1	=@RiskOutput(,”Monthly Average”,1)+AVERAGEIF(\$I\$205:\$I\$2724,Q4,\$M\$205:\$M\$2724)
2	=@RiskOutput(,”Monthly Average”,2)+AVERAGEIF(\$I\$205:\$I\$2724,Q5,\$M\$205:\$M\$2724)
3	=@RiskOutput(,”Monthly Average”,3)+AVERAGEIF(\$I\$205:\$I\$2724,Q6,\$M\$205:\$M\$2724)
4	=@RiskOutput(,”Monthly Average”,4)+AVERAGEIF(\$I\$205:\$I\$2724,Q7,\$M\$205:\$M\$2724)
5	=@RiskOutput(,”Monthly Average”,5)+AVERAGEIF(\$I\$205:\$I\$2724,Q8,\$M\$205:\$M\$2724)

continued on following page

Table 5. Continued

Month	Average Price
116	=@RiskOutput(,"Monthly Average",116)+AVERAGEIF($I$205:$I$2724,Q119,$M$205:$M$2724)
117	=@RiskOutput(,"Monthly Average",117)+AVERAGEIF($I$205:$I$2724,Q120,$M$205:$M$2724)
118	=@RiskOutput(,"Monthly Average",118)+AVERAGEIF($I$205:$I$2724,Q121,$M$205:$M$2724)
119	=@RiskOutput(,"Monthly Average",119)+AVERAGEIF($I$205:$I$2724,Q122,$M$205:$M$2724)
120	=@RiskOutput(,"Monthly Average",120)+AVERAGEIF($I$205:$I$2724,Q123,$M$205:$M$2724)

The Yearly Average prices are for 10 Years given in Table 6:

Table 6. Yearly average prices for 10 years

Year	Average Price
1	=@RiskOutput(,"Yearly Average",1)+AVERAGEIF($J$205:$J$2724,T4,$M$205:$M$2724)
2	=@RiskOutput(,"Yearly Average",2)+AVERAGEIF($J$205:$J$2724,T5,$M$205:$M$2724)
3	=@RiskOutput(,"Yearly Average",3)+AVERAGEIF($J$205:$J$2724,T6,$M$205:$M$2724)
4	=@RiskOutput(,"Yearly Average",4)+AVERAGEIF($J$205:$J$2724,T7,$M$205:$M$2724)
5	=@RiskOutput(,"Yearly Average",5)+AVERAGEIF($J$205:$J$2724,T8,$M$205:$M$2724)
6	=@RiskOutput(,"Yearly Average",6)+AVERAGEIF($J$205:$J$2724,T9,$M$205:$M$2724)
7	=@RiskOutput(,"Yearly Average",7)+AVERAGEIF($J$205:$J$2724,T10,$M$205:$M$2724)
8	=@RiskOutput(,"Yearly Average",8)+AVERAGEIF($J$205:$J$2724,T11,$M$205:$M$2724)
9	=@RiskOutput(,"Yearly Average",9)+AVERAGEIF($J$205:$J$2724,T12,$M$205:$M$2724)
10	=@RiskOutput(,"Yearly Average",10)+AVERAGEIF($J$205:$J$2724,T13,$M$205:$M$2724)

Simulation: Projecting Oil Prices (Analysis)

Monthly Average Price Analysis

Figure 2 displays the Month 1 Average Price distribution. The Month 1 Average Price *Mean* is $98.949, and the *Standard Deviation* is $24.393. There is a 5% probability that the Month 1 Average Price will be below $56.97; a 90% probability that it will be in the range of $56.97 – $133.51; and a 5% probability that it will be above $133.51.

Figure 2. Month 1 average price distribution

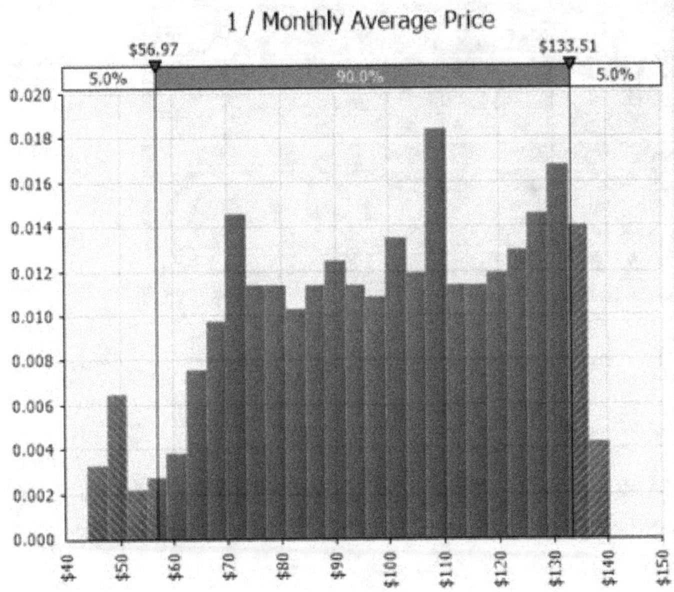

Statistics	1 / Monthly Averag...
Cell	Model!R4
Minimum	$43.801
Maximum	$140.120
Mean	$98.948
90% CI	± $1.798
Mode	$124.840
Median	$100.438
Std Dev	$24.393
Skewness	-0.2583
Kurtosis	2.0686
Values	500
Errors	0
Filtered	0
Left X	$56.97
Left P	5.0%
Right X	$133.51
Right P	95.0%
Dif. X	$76.544
Dif. P	90.0%

Sensitivity Analysis

Sensitivity analysis provides for identifying and quantifying the main contributors to variability and risk based on the probability distribution.

The Inputs Ranked by Effect on Output Mean are given in Figure 3.

The graph illustrates that the effect of the variable 1869 / Prob Increase, on the Month 1 Average Price is a change in the range of $43.801 to $128.40 respectively left and right from the Baseline of $98.948, which is marked on the graph. The other outputs are very close and similarly influential.

Figure 3. Month 1 average price inputs ranked by effect on output mean

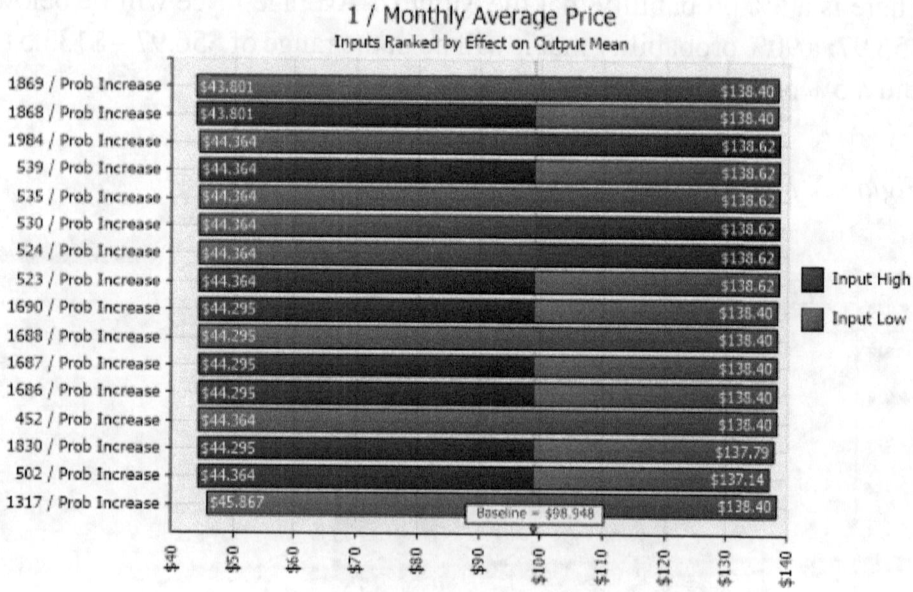

The Change in Output Mean Across the Range of Input Values graph is presented in Figure 4.

Figure 4. Month 1 average price chart

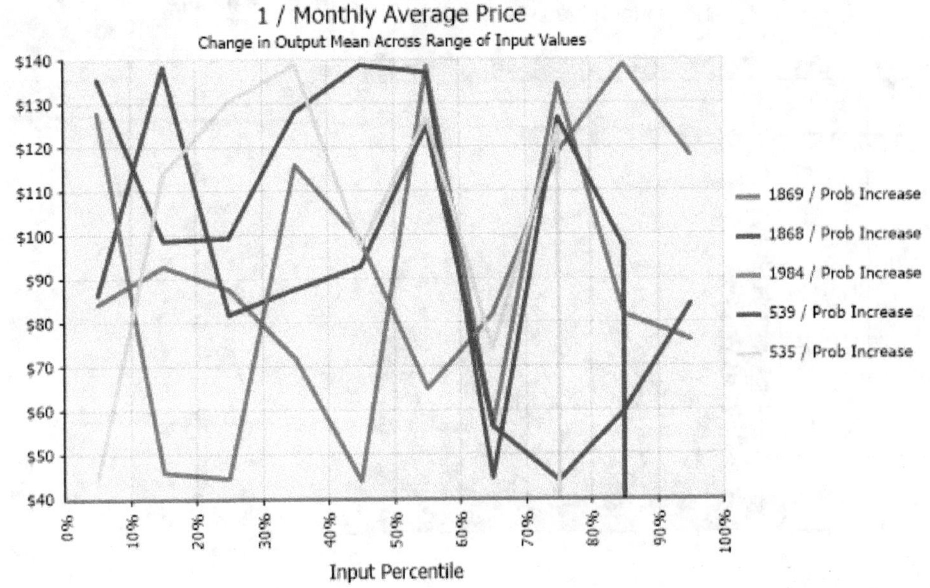

3. Figure 4 illustrates that the top variable 1869 / Prob Increase (in Red), has a contribution of change increase from $43.801 to $128.40, respectively left and right from the Baseline of $98.948, to the variance of Month 1 Average Price. Other variables are similar as the contributions to variance are very close.

Figure 5 displays the Month 120 Average Price distribution.

Figure 5. Month 120 average price distribution

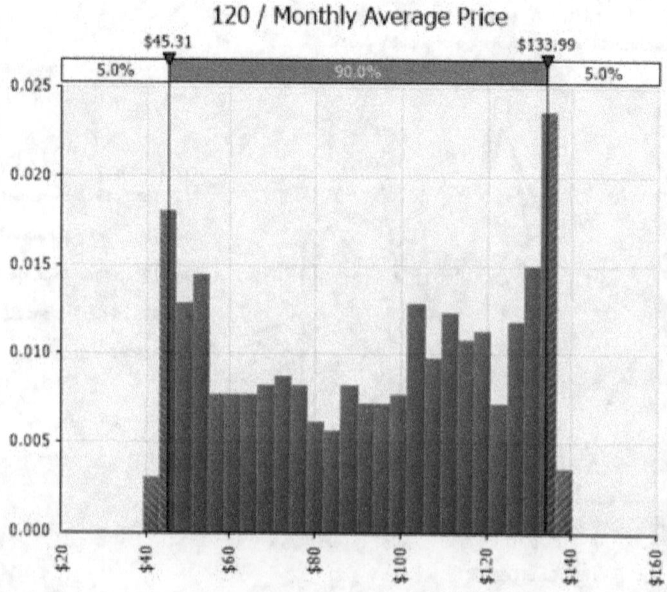

Statistics	120 / Monthly Aver...
Cell	Model!R123
Minimum	$39.39
Maximum	$140.41
Mean	$92.25
90% CI	± $2.273
Mode	$44.33
Median	$95.49
Std Dev	$30.84
Skewness	-0.1421
Kurtosis	1.6138
Values	500
Errors	0
Filtered	0
Left X	$45.31
Left P	5.0%
Right X	$133.99
Right P	95.0%
Dif. X	$88.68
Dif. P	90.0%

The Month 120 Average Price *Mean* is $92.25, and the *Standard Deviation* is $30.84. There is a 5% probability that the Month 120 Average Price will be below $45.31; a 90% probability that it will be in the range of $45.31 – $133.99; and a 5% probability that it will be above $133.99.

Sensitivity Analysis

Sensitivity analysis provides for identifying and quantifying the main contributors to variability and risk based on the probability distribution.

The <u>Inputs Ranked by Effect on Output Mean</u> are given in Figure 6.

Figure 6. Month 120 average price inputs ranked by effect on output mean

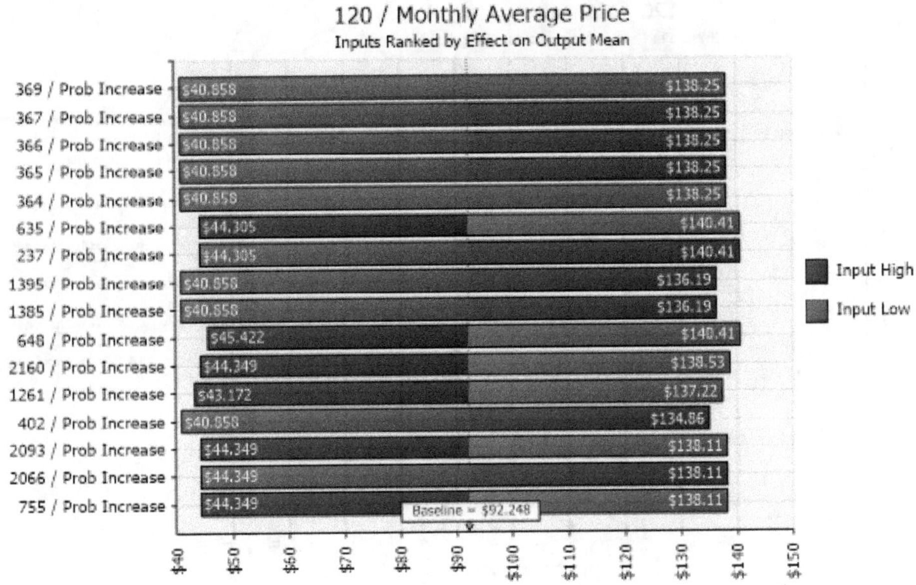

The graph illustrates that the effect of the variable 369 / Prob Increase, on the Month 120 Average Price is a change in the range of $40.858 to $138.25 respectively left and right from the Baseline of $92.248, which is marked on the graph. The other outputs are very close and similarly influential.

The Change in Output Mean Across the Range of Input Values graph presented in Figure 4 illustrates that the top variable 1869 / Prob Increase (in Red), has a contribution of change increase from $40.858 to $138.25 respectively left and right from the Baseline of $92.248, to the variance of Month 120 Average Price. Other variables are similar as the contributions to variance are very close.

Figure 7. Month 120 average price chart

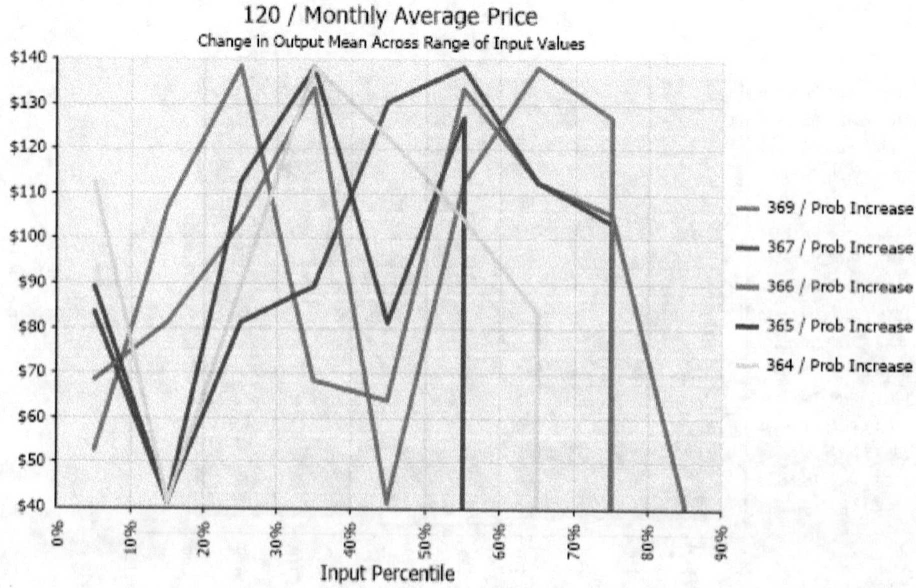

Yearly Average Price Analysis

Figure 8 displays the Year 1 Average Price distribution.

Figure 8. Year 1 average price distribution

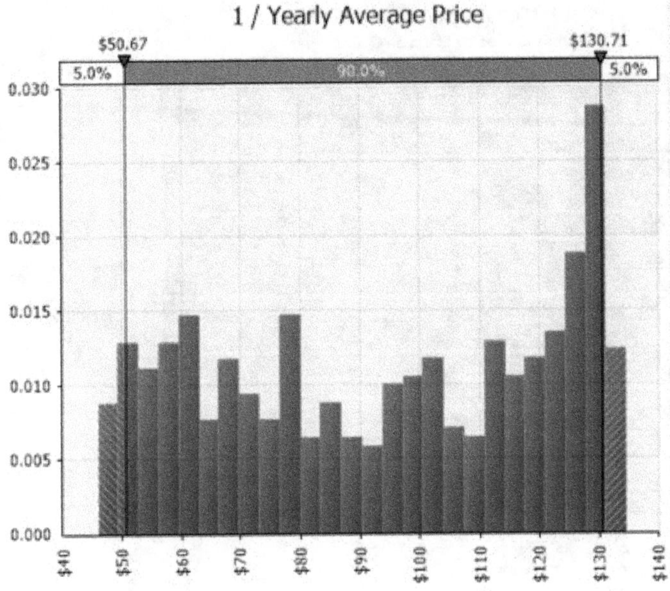

Statistics	1 / Yearly Average ...
Cell	Model!U4
Minimum	$45.862
Maximum	$134.616
Mean	$93.789
90% CI	± $2.047
Mode	$79.813
Median	$96.595
Std Dev	$27.782
Skewness	-0.1277
Kurtosis	1.5887
Values	500
Errors	0
Filtered	0
Left X	$50.67
Left P	5.0%
Right X	$130.71
Right P	95.0%
Dif. X	$80.041
Dif. P	90.0%

The Year 1 Average Price *Mean* is $93.789, and the *Standard Deviation* is $27.782. There is a 5% probability that the Year 1 Average Price will be below $50.67; a 90% probability that it will be in the range of $50.67 – $130.71; and a 5% probability that it will be above $130.71.

Sensitivity Analysis

Sensitivity analysis provides for identifying and quantifying the main contributors to variability and risk based on the probability distribution.

The Inputs Ranked by Effect on Output Mean are given in Figure 9.

Figure 9. Year 1 average price inputs ranked by effect on output mean

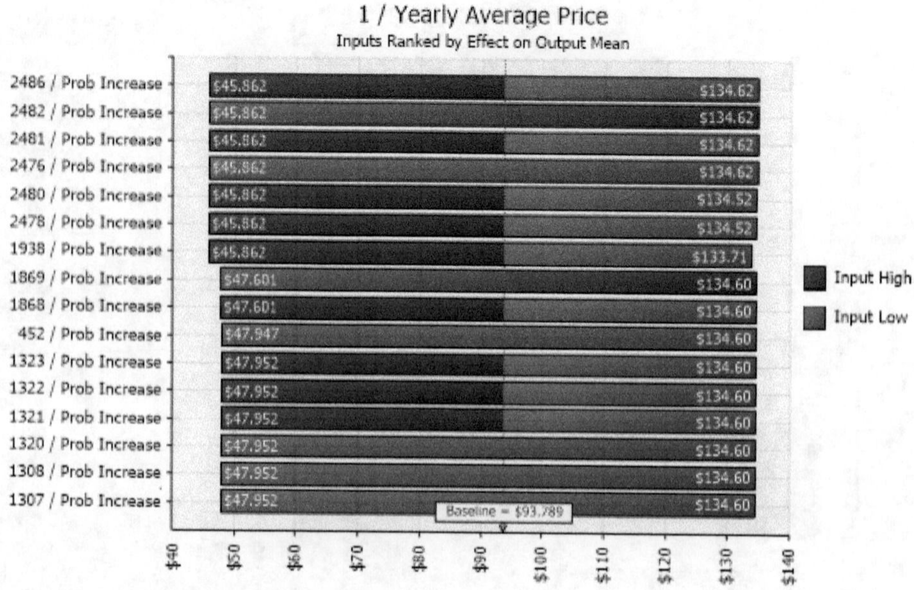

The graph illustrates that the effect of the variable 2486 / Prob Increase, on the Year 1 Average Price is a change in the range of $45.862 to $134.62 respectively left and right from the Baseline of $93.789, which is marked on the graph. The other outputs are very close and similarly influential.

The Change in Output Mean Across the Range of Input Values graph is presented in Figure 10.

Figure 10. Year 1 average price chart

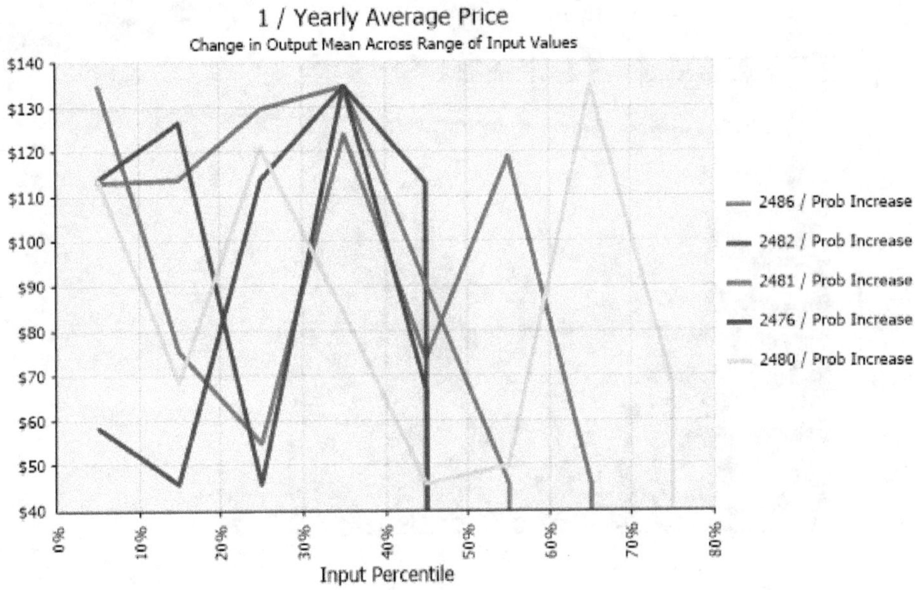

Figure 10 illustrates that the top variable 2486 / Prob Increase (in Red), has a contribution of change increase from $45.862 to $134.62 respectively left and right from the Baseline of $93.789, to the variance of Year 1 Average Price. Other variables are similar as the contributions to variance are very close.

Figure 11 displays the Year 10 Average Price distribution. The Year 10 Average Price *Mean* is $90.463 and the *Standard Deviation* is $28.116. There is a 5% probability that the Year 10 Average Price will be below $48.16; a 90% probability that it will be in the range of $48.16 – $130.77; and a 5% probability that it will be above $130.77.

Figure 11. Year 10 average price distribution

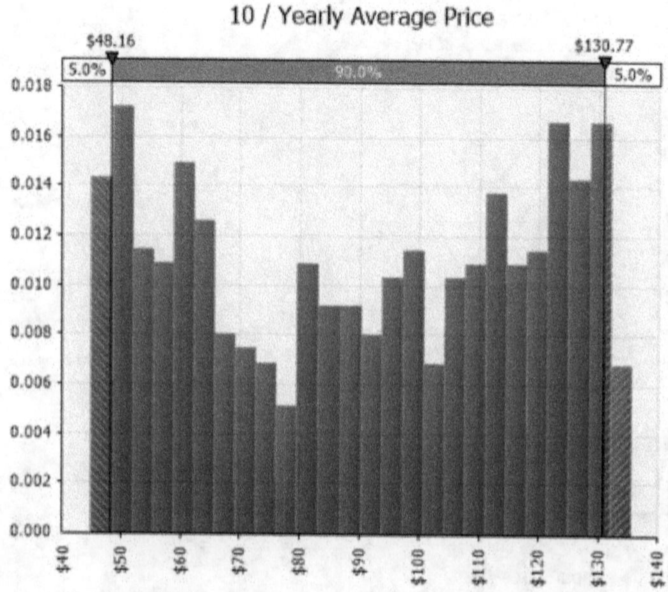

Statistics	10 / Yearly Averag...
Cell	Model!U13
Minimum	$44.825
Maximum	$135.485
Mean	$90.463
90% CI	± $2.072
Mode	$123.220
Median	$91.878
Std Dev	$28.116
Skewness	-0.0790
Kurtosis	1.6079
Values	500
Errors	0
Filtered	0
Left X	$48.16
Left P	5.0%
Right X	$130.77
Right P	95.0%
Dif. X	$82.615
Dif. P	90.0%

Sensitivity Analysis

Sensitivity analysis provides for identifying and quantifying the main contributors to variability and risk based on the probability distribution.

The Inputs Ranked by Effect on Output Mean are given in Figure 12.

The graph illustrates that the effect of the variable 1816 / Prob Increase, on the Year 10 Average Price is a change in the range of $45.275 to $135.49 respectively left and right from the Baseline of $90.463, which is marked on the graph. The other outputs are very close and similarly influential.

Figure 12. Year 10 average price inputs ranked by effect on output mean

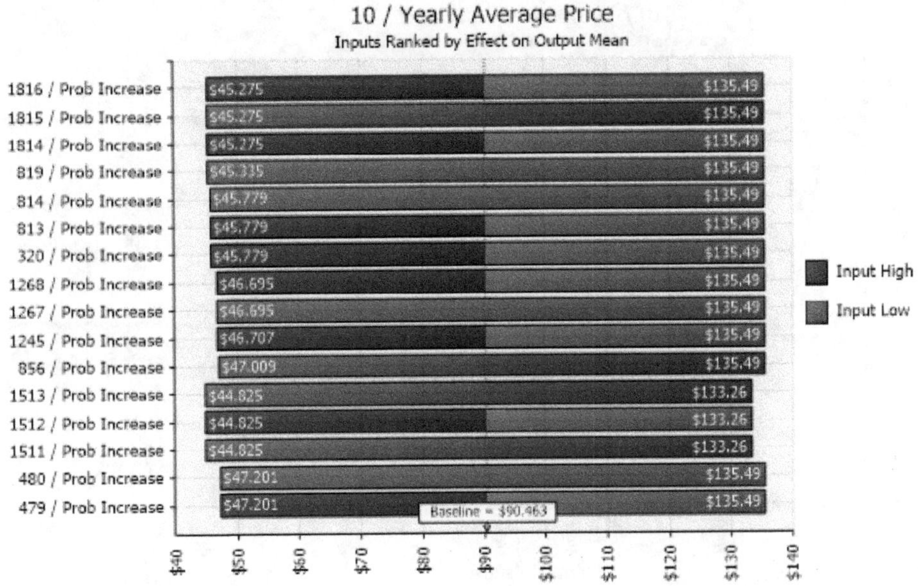

The Change in Output Mean Across the Range of Input Values graph is presented in Figure 13.

Figure 13. Year 10 average price chart

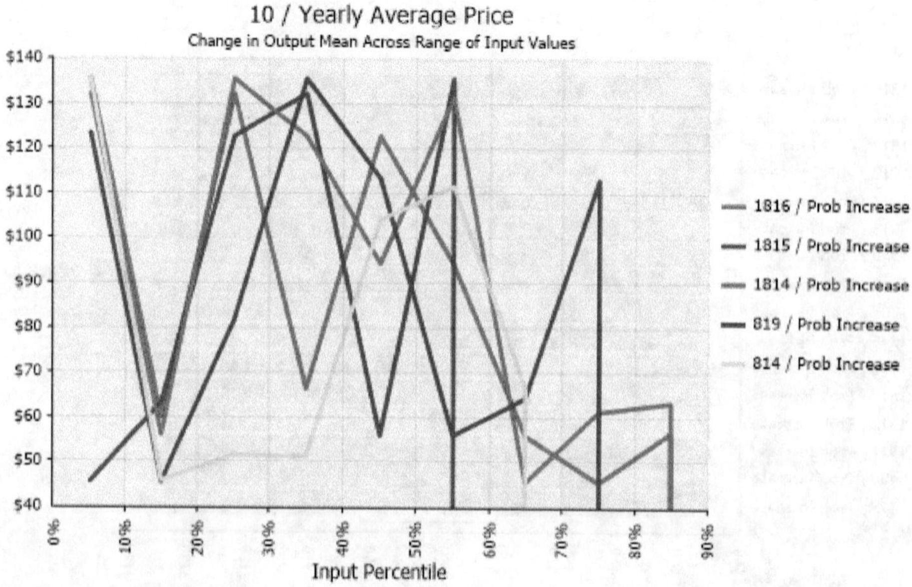

Figure 13 illustrates that the top variable 1816 / Prob Increase (in Red), has a contribution of change increase from $45.275 to $135.49 respectively left and right from the Baseline of $90.463, to the variance of Year 10 Average Price. Other variables are similar as the contributions to variance are very close.

Monthly Averages and Yearly Averages Price Values and Graphs

The 120 Months Monthly Average prices are given approximately in Figure 14.

Figure 14. Monthly averages approximately

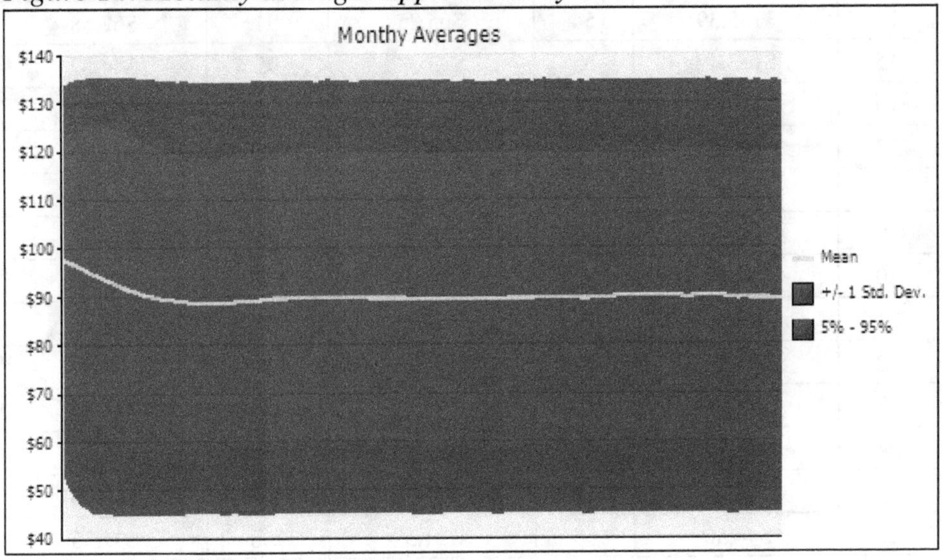

The Monthly Averages start at $44,56 in Month 1, to $49.08 in Month 120. The Monthly Average prices are for 120 Months given in Table 7:

Table 7. Monthly average prices from month 1 to month 120

1	$44.56	41	$122.72	81	$109.36
2	$44.63	42	$94.65	82	$132.84
3	$61.24	43	$66.58	83	$135.45
4	$89.31	44	$45.64	84	$135.39
5	$117.38	45	$44.56	85	$135.45
6	$135.13	46	$44.50	86	$135.39
7	$135.45	47	$44.56	87	$135.45
8	$135.39	48	$44.50	88	$135.39
9	$135.45	49	$44.56	89	$135.45
10	$135.39	50	$44.50	90	$135.39
11	$135.45	51	$44.56	91	$135.32
12	$135.39	52	$44.50	92	$118.71
13	$135.45	53	$45.33	93	$90.64

continued on following page

Table 7. Continued

14	$135.39	54	$65.25	94	$62.58
15	$133.42	55	$93.32	95	$44.82
16	$110.69	56	$121.39	96	$44.50
17	$82.62	57	$135.45	97	$44.56
18	$54.81	58	$135.39	98	$44.50
19	$44.56	59	$135.45	99	$44.56
20	$44.50	60	$135.39	100	$44.50
21	$44.56	61	$135.45	101	$44.56
22	$44.50	62	$135.39	102	$44.50
23	$44.56	63	$135.45	103	$44.56
24	$44.50	64	$135.39	104	$46.54
25	$44.56	65	$135.45	105	$69.26
26	$44.50	66	$131.57	106	$97.33
27	$44.56	67	$106.68	107	$125.14
28	$50.74	68	$78.61	108	$135.39
29	$77.28	69	$51.69	109	$135.45
30	$105.35	70	$44.50	110	$135.39
31	$130.87	71	$44.56	111	$135.45
32	$135.39	72	$44.50	112	$135.39
33	$135.45	73	$44.56	113	$135.45
34	$135.39	74	$44.50	114	$135.39
35	$135.45	75	$44.56	115	$135.45
36	$135.39	76	$44.50	116	$135.39
37	$135.45	77	$44.56	117	$129.21
38	$135.39	78	$44.50	118	$102.67
39	$135.45	79	$53.73	119	$74.60
40	$135.39	80	$81.29	120	$49.08

The Yearly Average prices are for 10 Years given approximately in Figure 15:

Figure 15. Yearly average prices approximately for 10 years

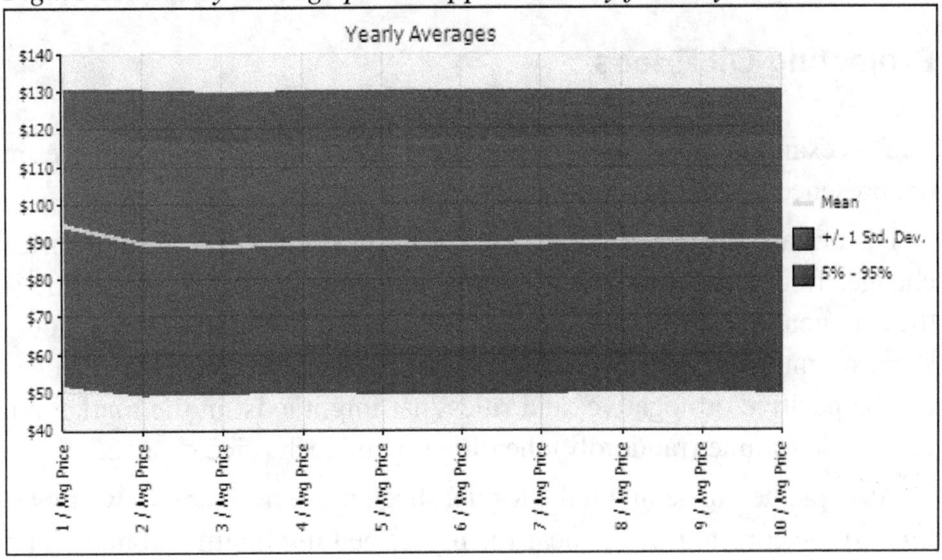

The Yearly Average prices start at $108.73 in Year 1 and end at $119.91. The Yearly Average prices are for 10 Years given in Table 8:

Table 8. Yearly average prices from year 1 to year 10

1	$108.73
2	$76.63
3	$97.91
4	$87.45
5	$87.09
6	$98.27
7	$76.27
8	$109.09
9	$65.45
10	$119.91

CONCLUSION

Projecting Oil Prices

This example illustrates one possible model for projecting oil prices in the presence of "nonrandom" market mechanisms.

Historical daily oil prices are listed on the next sheet. The absolute price changes fit a nonnegative distribution, and the best-fitting distribution is the exponential distribution shown. This distribution is used on the Model sheet to simulate future absolute price changes. Each of these price changes can be positive or negative, and rules that might exist in the market are used to determine (randomly) the direction of each price change.

As explained in detail on the Model sheet, these rules are of two types. First, if the current price is near the prescribed minimum and maximum limits, the direction of the next price change tends to be *away* from the relevant limit. Second, for prices not too near the limits, there is a tendency to have a positive price change if the average of the most recent 50 days is greater than the average of the most recent 200 days, and there is a tendency to have a negative price change otherwise. These latter rules might mimic the manipulation of the market by algorithms slavishly reacting to such moving averages.

The graphs on the last sheet, based on a simulation with 10,000 iterations, show clearly that over time, the distribution of average price is u-shaped between the extremes. It is not uniform or normal.

REFERENCES

Carollo, S. (2011). *Understanding Oil Prices: A Guide to What Drives the Price of Oil in Today's Markets (The Wiley Finance Series)*. Wiley.

Rauscher, M. (1989). *OPEC and the Price of Petroleum: Theoretical Considerations and Empirical Evidence (Studies in International Economics & Institutions)*. Springer-Verlag Berlin and Heidelberg GmbH & Co.

U.S. Department of the Interior. (2015). *Economic Effects of Petroleum Prices and Production in the Gulf of Mexico OCS on the U.S. Gulf Coast Economy*. U.S. Department of the Interior.

Chapter 10
Waterflood Project With Production Scenarios

ABSTRACT

A waterflood project analyses where recoverable oil must be estimated, and one of four production schedules is used to generate a revenue stream. The model combines volumetric estimates, prices, costs, and production scheduling. The overall objective is to estimate the NPV and IRR for the project over an 18-year horizon, given information about initial costs, operating costs, reservoir description, production schedules, prices, working interest, and taxes. The volumetric analysis calculates the total reserves STB. The initial startup costs are considered fixed, but the annual electricity, labor, and overhead costs, as well as the price of oil, are modeled as random walks, using the parameters shown. The key aspect of the model is the production schedule: the percentage of total reserves extracted each year. Four possible production schedules are listed. On each iteration, one of these schedules is chosen randomly. Outputs from the simulation are averages over the possible schedules.

DOI: 10.4018/979-8-3373-0959-0.ch010

INTRODUCTION

Oil Production Scenarios

Peak oil refers to the hypothetical point at which global crude oil production will hit its maximum rate, after which production will start to decline. This concept is derived from geophysicist Marion King Hubbert's "peak theory," which states that oil production follows a bell-shaped curve.

In the traditional vision of peak oil, the production decline accelerates as the cost of extracting new reserves grows. This would put pressure on existing reserves that are drawing down over time. If new reserves are not brought online more rapidly than the existing reserves drawdown, then peak oil has been reached. Peak oil has been declared several times, but each deceleration has proved premature because of new extraction technologies like hydraulic fracturing and better surveying techniques.

- Peak oil is a hypothetical scenario where oil production hits a maximum rate and begins to decline.
- When peak oil is reached, the discovery of new reserves cannot keep pace with the decline in existing reserves.
- Although declared several times, peak oil has not happened thanks to new technology that helped sustain oil production, keeping global supplies flowing.
- Peak oil might also happen due to declining demand, which would result from more efficient technologies and alternative energy sources.
- Studies of climate change suggest that a decline in oil consumption in favour of alternative energy sources will be necessary to avert catastrophic climate change.

Because oil is a non-replenishing resource, there is a limit to how much the world can extract and refine. However, the scenario of total depletion is just one version of peak oil. In theory, peak oil can be brought on by the production squeeze—the drawdown as new reserves get more expensive to extract. It can also be caused by a production decline when oil alternatives become more cost-effective, pricing oil out of the market and making it unprofitable to explore new reserves.

The Organization of Petroleum Exporting Countries (OPEC) brought peak oil to the forefront in 1973 when it orchestrated an oil embargo that exposed the United States' vulnerability to a drop in oil supplies. Since then, peak oil on the supply side, either from total drawdown or difficulty of extraction, has been a major concern for energy-dependent nations. But this same fear spurred investment in exploration and technology, which has continually pushed peak oil's projected date into the future.

Every time prices increase based on peak oil forecasts; the higher prices incentivize new investments in technology that postpone the peak. Of course, there is still a ceiling to oil extraction, but that may not be reached due to peak oil demand.

Peak oil demand refers to a scenario in which production falls due to lower consumption, rather than scarcity of resources. This is especially likely if green technology and alternative energy become more cost-effective than extracting oil. In 2016, OPEC (the one-time bogeyman of peak oil supply) started to discuss peak oil demand as a possibility within a decade.

One possible indication of peak oil occurred in 2020 when U.S. crude oil production fell by more than 8%, the largest recorded year-on-year drop. The drop was largely attributed to low oil prices, due to reduced consumption during the COVID-19 pandemic. So peak oil is once again appearing on the horizon—just not for the reasons expected in the 1970s.

There have been many predictions about when and if the world's oil production would peak. In 1962, Hubbert predicted that global oil production would peak near the year 2000 at a rate of 12.5 billion barrels per year. Twelve years later, he estimated that the world would hit peak oil if the current trends continued. Both his theories proved incorrect.

Some analysts and industry officials have predicted peak oil before 2030, but making these forecasts isn't always because of the difficulty in estimating the actual size of the world's unexplored oil reserves.

Some of the most obvious consequences of hitting peak oil supply are directly related to the economy. A sudden drop in oil supplies will lead to a sharp spike in prices, with a ripple effect in oil-dependent industries. Major sectors like agriculture could see a steep decline, due to the scarcity of oil-based fertilizers and fuel. The ripple effect could continue to shipping, transportation, and even the food and manufacturing industries. In a worst-case scenario, large areas of the world could experience famine because of higher food prices.

Peak oil would also have a sizeable effect on the climate, by reducing the carbon footprints of oil-dependent industries. Fossil fuels such as oil, coal, and natural gas are major sources of atmospheric carbon dioxide and a leading factor in anthropogenic climate change. A 2021 report by the Intergovernmental Panel on Climate Change (IPCC) warned that global temperatures have already risen by around 1.07 degrees Celsius due to human activity. Without "deep reductions" in carbon dioxide and other greenhouse gas emissions, global temperatures will likely increase by over 2 degrees Celsius before 2100.

LITERATURE

Riva (2019): The authors of this book assess the prospects to produce oil and gas from U.S. domestic reserves and resources to the year 2000, using different scenarios with varying assumptions about numbers of discoveries, size of fields, and rates of recovery. Oil production, claim the authors, will decline by at least 17 percent by the end of the century. Borg (2017): The book contents are: i) The Key Features of Contractual Arrangements - Between the Oil Company the Primary Contractors, Sub-contractors and Vendors; ii) Measures to be included in the License to Meet Governmental Objectives of Rapid Development, Local Content, and Environmental Protection; iii) Negotiation of PSA Main Components to Reduce Risks to Host Country Revenues; iv) Effect of Variations in Production, CAPEX and OPEX in O&G Project to IOC's and the Governmental Revenues; v) Technical Risk Management on the Design, Construction, and Operation Phases of an Offshore O&G Project; and vi) Measures to be Taken by Developing Country to Avoid "Curse of Oil".

Raymond & Leffler (2018): This nontechnical treatment of oil and gas production is an excellent introduction for anyone from petroleum engineers and geologists new to their careers to financial, marketing, legal, and other professionals and their staffs interested in the industry. E&P

service company personnel will find it particularly beneficial to understand the roles played by their clients. Not only does it cover production fundamentals, but it backs up to give the necessary upstream background—geology, origins of oil and gas, and ownership and land rights—as well as surface operations and even production company strategy development. Key Features: i) A comprehensive view of the entire E&P function; ii) Geology and the origins of petroleum; iii) Reservoir characteristics and behaviour; iii) Expanded coverage of drilling and hydraulic fracturing; iv) Conventional and not-so-conventional (oil sands plus shale oil and gas) producing operations; v) Production problems and solutions; and vi) The different types of companies and jobs in the oil patch and how they interact.

ELABORATION

Inputs (Define)

The Oil Reservoir Inputs are shown in Table 1:

Table 1. The oil reservoir inputs

Area	**500**	**acres**
Net pay	=@RiskTriang(F4,G4,H4)	feet
Porosity	=@RiskTriang(F5,G5,H5)	fraction
Recovery factor	=@RiskTriang(F6,G6,H6)	STB/bbl.
Total reserves	=@RiskOutput("STB")+7758*C3*C4*C5*C6	STB

The Parameters of Triangular Distributions are given in Table 2:

Table 2. Parameters of triangular distributions

Net pay	**10**	**15**	**20**
Porosity	12%	17%	22%
Recovery factor	0.2	0.3	0.4

The Monetary Inputs are shown in Table 3:

Table 3. Monetary inputs

Initial start-up cost	**$11,500,000**	
Initial annual electricity cost	$100,000	
Initial annual labour cost	$175,000	
Initial annual overhead cost	$25,000	
The initial price of crude	$90.00	per STB
Working interest	87.50%	
State tax	5%	on gross sales
Discount factor	15%	

The *Mean*, Standard Deviation of annual percentage changes are shown in Table 4:

Table 4. Mean and standard deviation of annual percentage changes

1.00%	0.25%
2.00%	0.50%
1.00%	0.25%
0.0%	3.0%

The Possible production schedules are shown in Table 5:

Table 5. Possible production schedules

Year	Schedule1	Schedule2	Schedule3	Schedule4
1	0%	0%	0%	0%
2	0%	0%	0%	0%
3	0%	0%	0%	0%
4	4%	4%	3%	3%
5	13%	9%	9%	7%
6	18%	11%	10%	9%

continued on following page

Table 5. Continued

Year	Schedule1	Schedule2	Schedule3	Schedule4
7	21%	18%	13%	10%
8	17%	18%	15%	13%
9	12%	13%	12%	11%
10	9%	11%	11%	11%
11	5%	7%	9%	9%
12	1%	5%	7%	9%
13	0%	3%	5%	5%
14	0%	1%	3%	5%
15	0%	0%	2%	3%
16	0%	0%	1%	3%
17	0%	0%	0%	1%
18	0%	0%	0%	1%
Check	100%	100%	100%	100%

Outputs (Define)

The Outputs from the simulation are shown in Table 6:

Table 6. Outputs from the simulation

NPV	=@RiskOutput("NPV")+SUM(I28:I46)
IRR	=@RiskOutput("IRR")+IRR(I28:I46,0.15)

The Simulations from revenues are shown in Table 7 and Table 8.

Table 7. Production schedule

Production schedule	=@RiskDiscrete({1,2,3,4},{0.25,0.25,0.25,0.25})

The Simulation formulas concept in Table 8, and Table 9 presents Years 0, 1, 2, 17, and 18. The concepts are easy to understand without other years.

Table 8. The simulation part 1 (Year 0 to 3 & Year 17 to 18)

Year	Oil price	Revenue	Electricity
0	=C15		
1	=C28*(1+@ RiskNormal($F$15,$G$15))	=C29*VLOOKUP(B29,$J$4:$N$21,$C$25+1, TRUE)*$C$8	=C12*(1+@ RiskNormal(F12,G12))
2	=C29*(1+@ RiskNormal($F$15,$G$15))	=C30*VLOOKUP(B30,$J$4:$N$21,$C$25+1, TRUE)*$C$8	=E29*(1+@ RiskNormal($F$12,$G$12))
3	=C30*(1+@ RiskNormal($F$15,$G$15))	=C31*VLOOKUP(B31,$J$4:$N$21,$C$25+1, TRUE)*$C$8	=E30*(1+@ RiskNormal($F$12,$G$12))
17	=C44*(1+@ RiskNormal($F$15,$G$15))	=C45*VLOOKUP(B45,$J$4:$N$21,$C$25+1, TRUE)*$C$8	=E44*(1+@ RiskNormal($F$12,$G$12))
18	=C45*(1+@ RiskNormal($F$15,$G$15))	=C46*VLOOKUP(B46,$J$4:$N$21,$C$25+1, TRUE)*$C$8	=E45*(1+@ RiskNormal($F$12,$G$12))

Table 9. The simulation part 2 (year 0 to 3 & year 17 to 18)

Year	Labour	Overhead	Total expense	DCF
0			=C11	=-H28
1	=C13*(1+@ RiskNormal(F13,G13))	=C14*(1+@ RiskNormal(F14,G14))	=VLOOKUP(B29,$J$4: $N$21,$C$25+1,TRUE) *SUM(E29:G29)	=MAX($C$16*(D29*(1-$C$17)-H29)/ (1+$C$18)^B29,0)
2	=F29*(1+@ RiskNormal($F$13,$G$13))	=G29*(1+@ RiskNormal($F$14,$G$14))	=VLOOKUP(B30,$J$4: $N$21,$C$25+1,TRUE) *SUM(E30:G30)	=MAX($C$16*(D30*(1-$C$17)-H30)/ (1+$C$18)^B30,0)
3	=F30*(1+@ RiskNormal($F$13,$G$13))	=G30*(1+@ RiskNormal($F$14,$G$14))	=VLOOKUP(B31,$J$4: $N$21,$C$25+1,TRUE) *SUM(E31:G31)	=MAX($C$16*(D31*(1-$C$17)-H31)/ (1+$C$18)^B31,0)
17	=F44*(1+@ RiskNormal($F$13,$G$13))	=G44*(1+@ RiskNormal($F$13,$G$13))	=VLOOKUP(B45,$J$4: $N$21,$C$25+1,TRUE) *SUM(E45:G45)	=MAX($C$16*(D45*(1-$C$17)-H45)/ (1+$C$18)^B45,0)
18	=F45*(1+@ RiskNormal($F$13,$G$13))	=G45*(1+@ RiskNormal($F$13,$G$13))	=VLOOKUP(B46,$J$4: $N$21,$C$25+1,TRUE) *SUM(E46:G46)	=MAX($C$16*(D46*(1-$C$17)-H46)/ (1+$C$18)^B46,0)

Simulation: Waterflood Project with Production Scenarios (Analysis)

Total Reserves Stock Tank Barrels (STB) Analysis

Figure 1 displays the Total Reserves STB distribution. The Total Reserves STB *Mean* is 2,969,009.41 STB and the *Standard Deviation* is 688,132.28 STB. There is a 5% probability that the Total Reserves STB will be below 1.954 MM STB; a 90% probability that it will be in the range of 1.954 MM STB – 4.180 MM STB; and a 5% probability that it will be above 4.180 MM STB.

Figure 1. Total reserves STB distribution

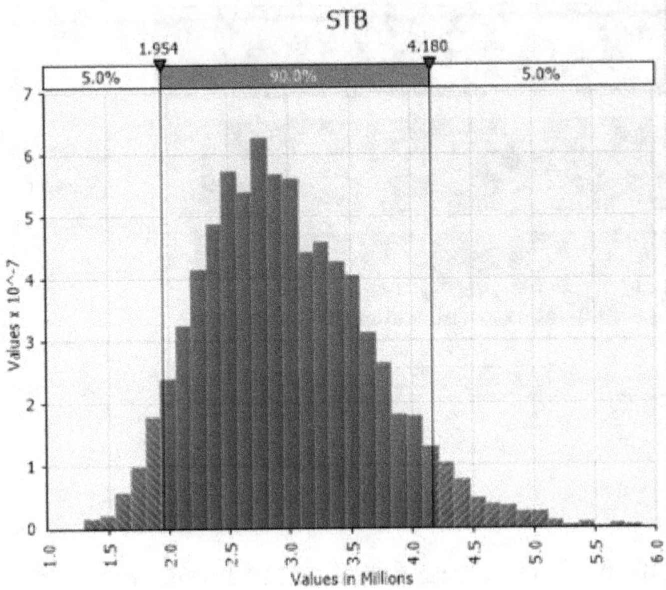

Statistics	STB
Cell	C8
Minimum	1,294,594.73
Maximum	5,872,930.13
Mean	2,969,009.41
90% CI	± 16,010.12
Mode	2,808,522.44
Median	2,899,496.84
Std Dev	688,132.28
Skewness	0.5025
Kurtosis	3.2171
Values	5000
Errors	0
Filtered	0
Left X	1,953,739.42
Left P	5.0%
Right X	4,180,345.93
Right P	95.0%
Dif. X	2,226,606.51
Dif. P	90.0%

Sensitivity Analysis

Sensitivity analysis provides for identifying and quantifying the main contributors to variability and risk based on the probability distribution.

The Inputs Ranked by Effect on Output Mean are given in Figure 2.

The graph illustrates that the effect of the variable Net pay, on the Total Reserves STB is a change in the range of 2,257,464.50 STB to 3,726,424.96 STB respectively left and right from the Baseline of 2,969,009.41 STB, which is marked on the graph. The other outputs Recovery factor and Porosity are very close and similarly influential.

Figure 2. Total reserves STB inputs ranked by effect on output mean

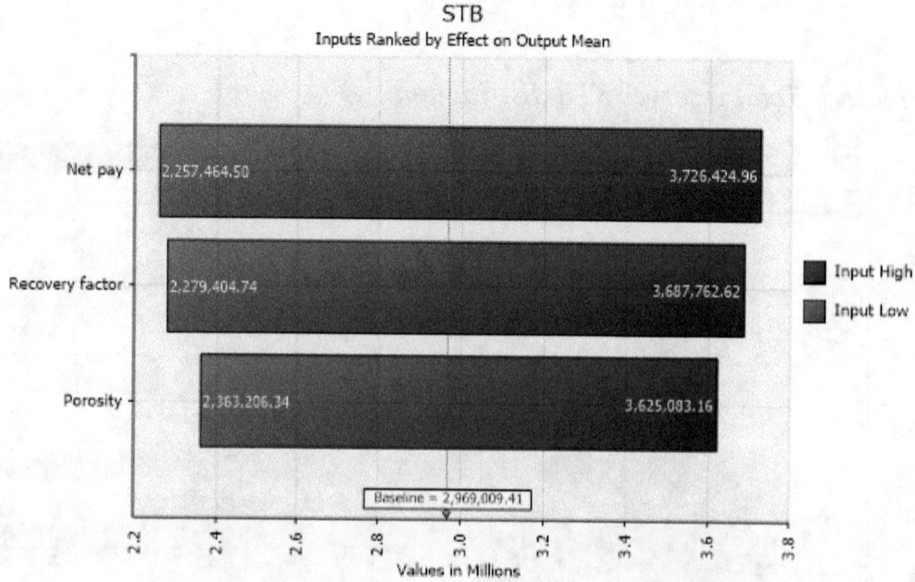

The Change in Output Mean Across the Range of Input Values graph is presented in Figure 3.

Figure 3. Total reserves STB spider chart

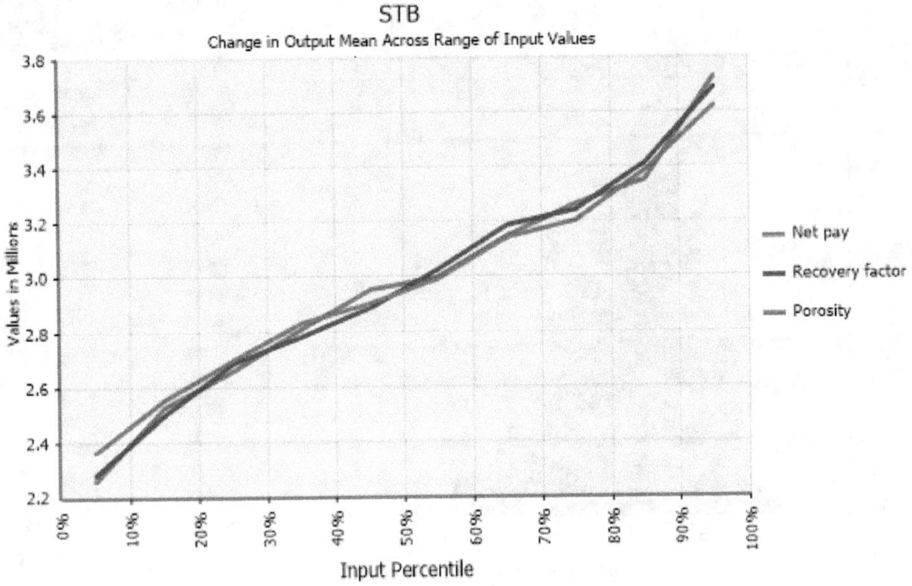

Figure 3 illustrates that the top variable 1869 / Prob Increase (in Red), has a contribution of change increase from $2,257,464.50 STB to 3,726,424.96 STB respectively left and right from the Baseline of 2,969,009.41 STB, to the variance of Total Reserves STB. Other variables Recovery factor and Porosity are similar as the contributions to variance are very close.

Net Present Value (NPV) Analysis

Figure 4 displays the NPV distribution. The NPV *Mean* is $60,960,730.17 and the *Standard Deviation* is $30.84. There is a 5% probability that the NPV will be below $33.86 MM; a 90% probability that it will be in the range of $33.86 MM – $94.85 MM; and a 5% probability that it will be above $94.85 MM.

Figure 4. NPV distribution

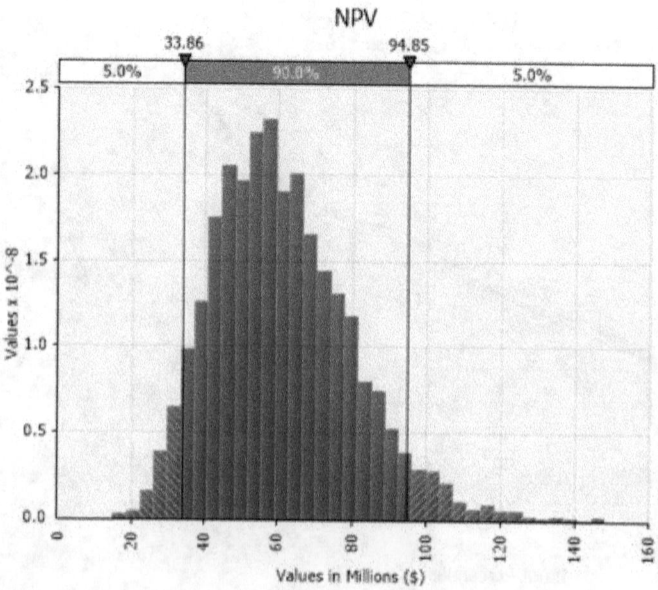

Statistics	NPV
Cell	C21
Minimum	$14,866,225.77
Maximum	$148,138,951.37
Mean	$60,960,730.17
90% CI	± $437,446.88
Mode	$58,984,653.33
Median	$58,813,421.85
Std Dev	$18,801,937.21
Skewness	0.6440
Kurtosis	3.5736
Values	5000
Errors	0
Filtered	0
Left X	$33,855,988.25
Left P	5.0%
Right X	$94,849,877.42
Right P	95.0%
Dif. X	$60,993,889.17
Dif. P	90.0%

Sensitivity Analysis

Sensitivity analysis provides for identifying and quantifying the main contributors to variability and risk based on the probability distribution.

The Inputs Ranked by Effect on Output Mean are given in Figure 5.

The graph illustrates that the effect of the variable Net pay, on the NPV is a change in the range of $43,754,376 to $79,461,669 respectively left and right from the Baseline of $60,960,730.17, which is marked on the graph. The next three outputs Recovery factor, Porosity, and Production schedule are very close and similarly influential. The other outputs are less influential variables.

Figure 5. NPV inputs ranked by effect on output mean

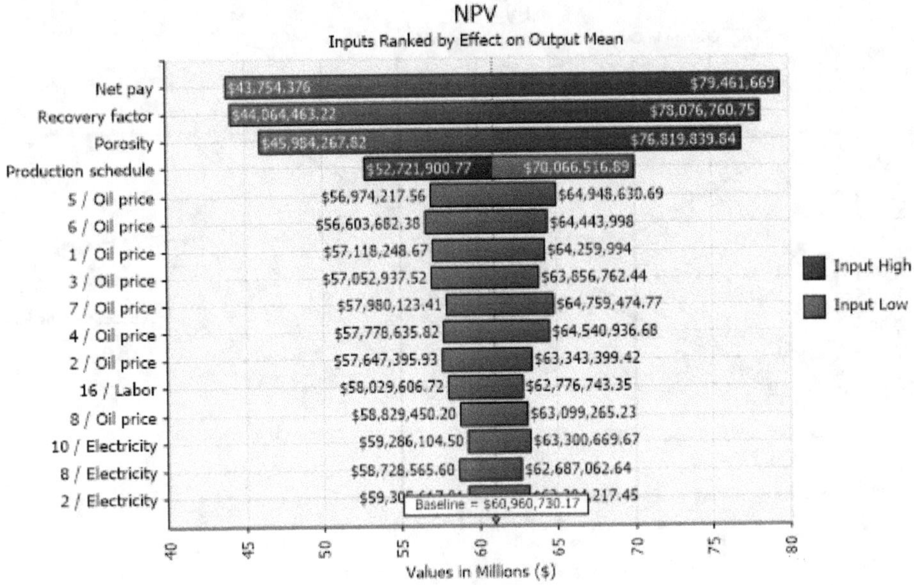

The Change in Output Mean Across the Range of Input Values graph presented in Figure 6 illustrates that the top variable Net pay (in Red), has a contribution of change increase from $43,754,376 to $79,461,669 respectively left and right from the Baseline of $60,960,730.17, to the variance of NPV. The next three outputs Recovery factor, Porosity, and Production schedule are very close and similarly influential. The other outputs are less influential variables

Figure 6. NPV spider chart

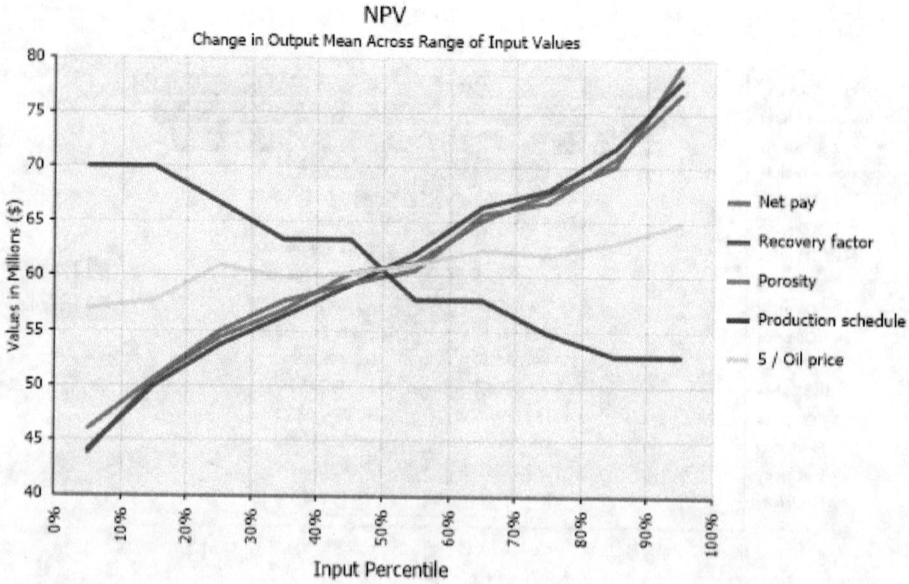

Internal Rate of Return (IRR) Analysis

Figure 7 displays the IRR distribution.

Figure 7. IRR distribution

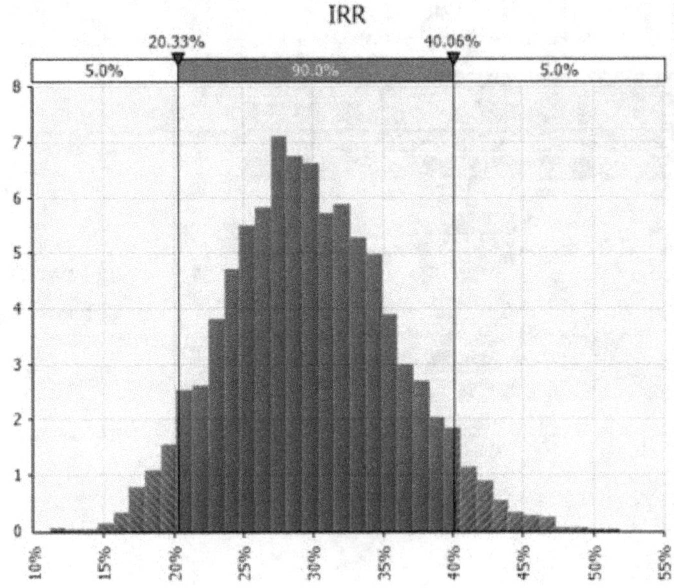

Statistics	IRR
Cell	C22
Minimum	11.128%
Maximum	51.861%
Mean	29.785%
90% CI	±0.138%
Mode	29.376%
Median	29.427%
Std Dev	5.941%
Skewness	0.2251
Kurtosis	2.9021
Values	5000
Errors	0
Filtered	0
Left X	20.33%
Left P	5.0%
Right X	40.06%
Right P	95.0%
Dif. X	19.735%
Dif. P	90.0%

The IRR *Mean* is 29.785% and the *Standard Deviation* is 5.941%. There is a 5% probability that the IRR will be below 20.33%; a 90% probability that it will be in the range of 20.33% – 40.06%; and a 5% probability that it will be above 40.06%.

Sensitivity Analysis

Sensitivity analysis provides for identifying and quantifying the main contributors to variability and risk based on the probability distribution.

The Inputs Ranked by Effect on Output Mean are given in Figure 8.

The graph illustrates that the effect of the variable Net pay, on the IRR is a change in the range of 24.649% to 34.685% respectively left and right from the Baseline of 27.785%, which is marked on the graph. The next three outputs Recovery factor, Production scheduling, and Porosity are very close and similarly influential. The other outputs are less influential variables.

Figure 8. IRR inputs ranked by effect on output mean

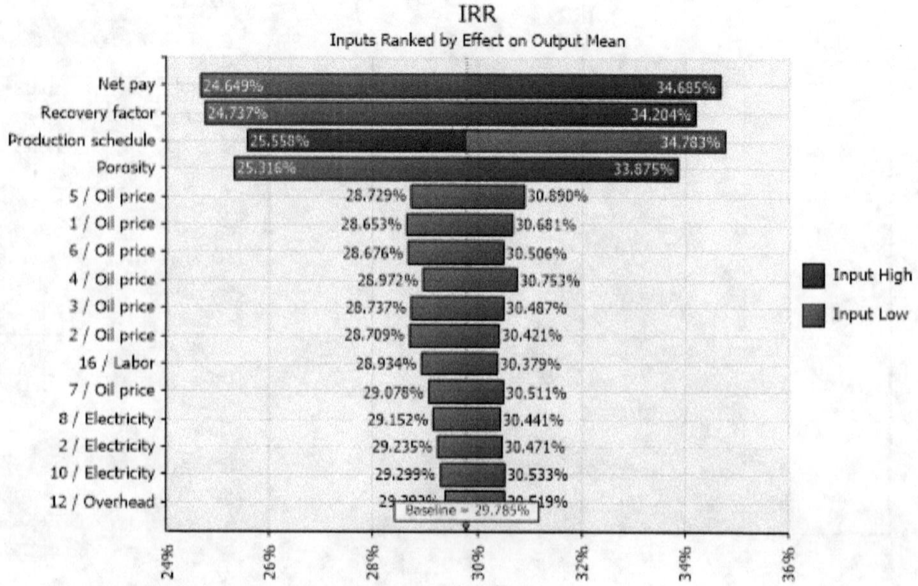

The Change in Output Mean Across the Range of Input Values graph is presented in Figure 9.

Figure 9. IRR spider chart

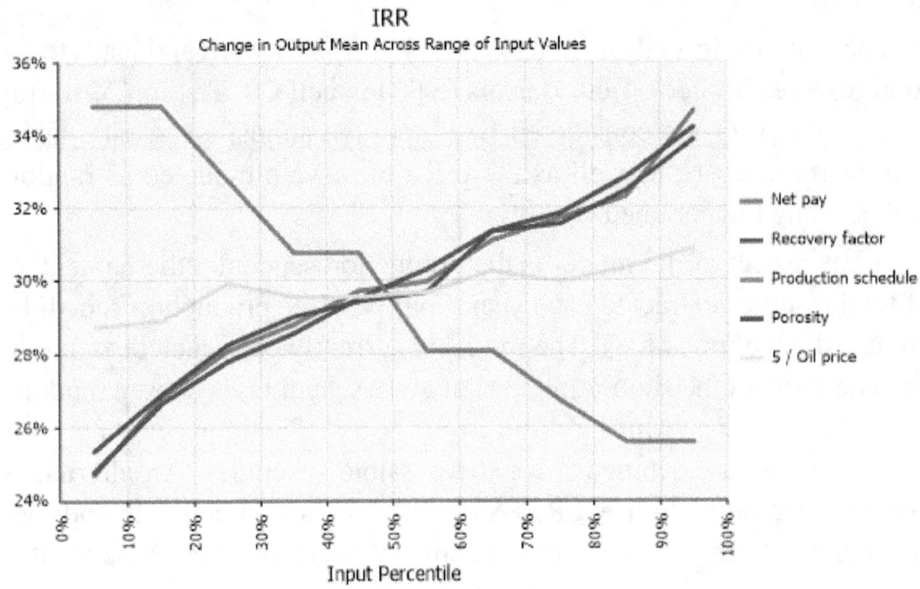

Figure 9 illustrates that the top variable Net pay (in Red), has a contribution of change increase from 24.649% to 34.685% respectively left and right from the Baseline of 27.785%, to the variance of IRR. The next three outputs Recovery factor, Production scheduling, and Porosity are very close and similarly influential. The other outputs are less influential variables.

CONCLUSION

Waterflood Project With Production Scenarios

This model analyses a waterflood project, where recoverable oil must be estimated and one of four production schedules is used to generate a revenue stream. The model combines volumetric estimates, prices, costs, and production scheduling. The overall objective is to estimate the Net Present Value (NPV) and Internal Rate of Return (IRR) for the project over an 18-year horizon, given information about initial costs, operating costs, reservoir description, production schedules, prices, working interest, and taxes.

The volumetric analysis in rows 3-8 is straightforward and leads to the total reserves in Stock Tank Barrels (STB) in cell C8. The initial startup costs in cell C11 are considered fixed, but the annual electricity, labor, and overhead costs, as well as the price of oil, are modeled as random walks, using the parameters shown.

A key aspect of the model is the production schedule: the percentage of total reserves extracted each year. Four possible production schedules are listed in columns K-N. The model is currently constructed so that on each iteration of the simulation, one of these schedules is chosen randomly. (This is the way Murtha did it in his book.) Therefore, outputs from the simulation are averages over the possible schedules. An alternative approach would be to use a RiskSimtable function in cell C25 and then run 4 simulations, one for each schedule. You can try this if you want to see how the distribution of IRR varies across production schedules.

The chart shows the histograms of STB, NPV, and IRR, from one run. This is an attractive project, at least with the current parameters.

REFERENCES

Borg, J. (2017). *Oil and Gas Management*. Routledge.

Raymond, M., & Leffler, W. (2018). Oil & Gas Production in Nontechnical Language. PennWell Corporation.

Riva, J. (2019). *U.S. Conventional Oil and Gas Production: Prospects to The Year 2000*. Routledge. DOI: 10.4324/9780429269639

Conclusion

Financial crises can expose underlying faults in the financial institution's systems and processes. The 2008 financial crisis exposed the failure of a prevalent laissez-faire economic and regulatory philosophy that financial institutions could and should manage their own risk with little outside interference. Now, many see the danger of fragile financial service networks bringing systemic risk to the real economy. So, financial organisations face increasing regulations such as Basel III for banks and businesses. To meet the requirements of the increased and rigorous regulation, financial organisations are striving to improve their formal risk assessment and management processes, which is their ultimate objective.

This book presented applications specifically to Business Risk Management offering improvements for financial institutions to achieve their ultimate objective and meet the regulators' requirements. In addition to conventional stochastic optimisation and Monte Carlo simulation, the book tactically applied Financial Risk Management. Financial Risk Management is generic, compatible, and complementary, so tactically merging them, resulted in a powerful synergetic tool.

The book elaborated on the following 10 chapters: i) Oil Drilling Schedule; ii) Oil Gas Forecast; iii) Correlation between Porosity and Water Saturation; iv) Exponential Decline; v) Forecasting Exponential Decline; vi) Oil Depletion Allowance; vii) Oil Pipeline Risk; viii) Oil Transportation with Weather Disruption; ix) Projecting Oil Prices; and x) Waterflood Project with Production Scenario.

Glossary

Asset and Liability Management (ALM): The administration of policies and procedures that address financial risks associated with changing interest rates, foreign exchange rates, and other factors that can affect a company's liquidity.

Basel: Financial Regulator for banks including Basel I, Basel II, Basel III, and Basel IV accords.

Beta: A measure of the volatility of an investment portfolio related to the financial market.

Cp – Process Capability: Six Sigma process capability metric, which is the measure of what the process can deliver.

Cpk – Process Capability Index: Six Sigma process capability metric, which is the measure of what the process can deliver.

Credit Risk: Credit risk is the risk of losses due to borrowers' default or deterioration of credit standing.

DMAIC (Define, Measure, Analyse, Improve, Control): Six Sigma methodology comprising five phases: Define; Measure; Analyse; Improve; and Control.

Efficient Frontier: A set of the optimal portfolios in the range of expected returns.

Foreign Exchange Risk: Foreign exchange risk is the risk of incurring losses due to fluctuations in exchange rates.

Interest Rate Risk: The interest rate risk is the risk of declines in net interest income, or interest revenues minus interest cost, due to the movements of interest rates.

Investment Management: Discipline that quantitatively and qualitatively studies the investments in financial markets.

Liquidity Risk: Liquidity risk is broadly defined as the risk of not being able to raise cash when needed.

LSL – Lower Specified Limit: Six Sigma process capability metric which specifies the lower limit of the target range.

Market Risk: Market risk is the risk of losses due to adverse market movements depressing the values of the positions held by market players.

Markov Chain: A Markov chain is a Markov process with discrete time and discrete state space. So, a Markov chain is a discrete sequence of states, each drawn from a discrete state space (finite or not), and that follows the Markov property. The Markov property expresses the fact that at a given time step and knowing the current state, we won't get any additional information about the future by gathering information about the past.

Markov Chain Monte Carlo: Markov Chain Monte Carlo (MCMC) methods comprise a class of algorithms for sampling from a probability distribution. By constructing a Markov Chain that has the desired distribution as its equilibrium distribution, one can obtain a sample of the desired distribution by recording states from the chain. The more steps are included, the more closely the distribution of the sample matches the actual desired distribution.

Monte Carlo Simulation: A simulation in which random data are generated from a specified distribution and used as input in a deterministic model (e.g., a formula for calculating a dependent variable (y) from the values of the independent variables).

Neural Networks: A neural network is a series of algorithms that endeavours to recognise underlying relationships in a set of data through a process that mimics the way the human brain operates. In this sense, neural networks refer to systems of neurons, either organic or artificial. Neural networks can adapt to changing input; so, the network generates the best possible result without needing to redesign the output criteria.

Operations Research (OR): Operations research (OR) is an analytical method of problem-solving and decision-making that is useful in the management of organisations. In operations research, problems are broken down into basic components and then solved in defined steps by mathematical analysis. Analytical methods used in OR include mathematical logic, simulation, optimisation, stochastic optimisation, network analysis, queuing theory, and game theory.

Optimisation: Method to find the optimal value, i.e., minimum or maximum, of a dependent variable from the values of many independent variables.

Portfolio Analysis: 1. Commerce: An analysis of elements of a company's product mix to determine the optimum allocation of its resources. The two most common measures used in a portfolio analysis are market growth rate and relative market share. 2. Securities: An analysis of an investment portfolio relative to an idealised balance of holdings, used as means of optimizing allocation.

Risk: 1. Finance: A possibility of financial loss that is inseparable from the opportunity for financial gain. 2. Pure Risk: The possibility of suffering some form of loss or damage where there is no corresponding opportunity for gain.

Risk Management: Risk management is the process of identifying, assessing, and controlling threats to an organisation's capital and earnings. These threats, or risks, could stem from a wide variety of sources, including financial uncertainty, legal liabilities, strategic management errors, accidents, and natural disasters.

Sensitivity Analysis: Sensitivity analysis determines how different values of an independent variable affect a particular dependent variable under a given set of assumptions. In other words, sensitivity analyses study how various sources of uncertainty in a mathematical model contribute to the model's overall uncertainty. This technique is used within specific boundaries that depend on one or more input variables.

Sharpe Ratio: A risk-adjusted measure of the performance of a portfolio related to the Risk-Free Rate.

Sigma Level: Six Sigma process capability metric is defined as the distance in terms of standard deviations between the mean of the actual performance of the process and the expected performance limits, which is the measure of process performance, i.e., the higher the Sigma Level, the better the performance.

Solvency: Financial Regulator for insurance companies including Solvency I, Solvency II, and Solvency III accords.

Solvency Risk: Solvency risk is the risk of being unable to absorb losses with the available capital.

Standard Deviation: A measure of the dispersion of statistical data. It is a square root of Variance. The standard deviation of the returns from an investment is used as a measure of risk.

Stochastic Optimisation: Method to find the optimal value, i.e., minimum or maximum, of a dependent variable from the probability distributions of the values of many independent variables.

Target Value: Six Sigma process capability metric which specifies the desired target value for the process.

USL – Upper Specified Limit: Six Sigma process capability metric which specifies the upper limit of the target range.

Value at Risk (VAR): a) The level of losses over a particular period that will only be exceeded in a small percentage of cases; b) A cut-off value for portfolio gains and losses (e.g., the bottom 1% of outcomes; VAR is then measured relative to that cut-off value.

Variance: Statistical measure of the dispersion of the distribution of outcomes. It is the square of Standard Distribution.

What-If Analysis: A what-if analysis is a technique that is used to determine how projected performance is affected by changes in the assumptions that projections are based upon. What-if analysis is used to compare different scenarios and their potential outcomes based on fluctuating conditions.

Compilation of References

Akaky, T. (2005). The Transportation of Oil by Sea. iUniverse.

Belyadi, H.2016). *Hydraulic Fracturing in Unconventional Reservoirs: Theories, Operations, and Economic Analysis*. Golf Professional Publishing.

Borg, J. (2017). *Oil and Gas Management*. Routledge.

Budhu, M. (2015). Soil Mechanics Fundamentals. Wiley-Blackwell.

Campbell, C. J. (2003). The Essence of Oil and Gas Depletion. Multi-Science Publishing Co.

Campbell, C. J. (2013). Campbell's Atlas of Oil and Gas Depletion. Springer. DOI: 10.1007/978-1-4614-3576-1

Carollo, S. (2011). *Understanding Oil Prices: A Guide to What Drives the Price of Oil in Today's Markets (The Wiley Finance Series)*. Wiley.

E, Y. (2021). *Day-to-day oil & gas trading and shipping delivery inside the oil & gas market (updated version)*. CreateSpace Independent Publisher.

Frittelli, J. (2014). *U.S. Rail Transportation of Crude Oil: Background and Issues for Congress*. Congressional Research Service.

Hawkins, R. (1978). Relationship between diagenesis, porosity reduction, and oil emplacement in late Carboniferous sandstone reservoirs, Bothamsall Oilfield, E Midlands. *Quartal Journal Geological Society, 135*(Part 1).

Heinberg, R. (2006). *The Oil Depletion Protocol: A Plan to Avert Oil Wars, Terrorism and Economic Collapse*. Clairview Books.

May, M. (2017). Investing in Oil and Gas *(Sixth Edition): A Handbook for Direct Investing in Oil and Gas Well Drilling Ventures*. CreateSpace Independent Publishing Platform.

Miesner, T. O., & Leffler, W. L. (2021). *Oil & Gas Pipelines in Nontechnical Language*. PennWell.

Patterson, M. C. (2019). The Oil Rig Guide: Lists of Offshore Drilling Employment Companies and Agencies: Offshore Job, Oil and Gas, Oil Platform, Offshore Career, Manage address book. Independent Publisher.

Patterson, M. C. (2022). The *Oil Rig Guide: A Comprehensive Guide on The Fundamentals of Oil Rig and How to Get a Job in Oil Rig*. Independent Publisher.

Piersol. (2021). Porosity, Total Liquid Saturation, and Permeability of Illinois Oil Sands; Report of Investigations No. 67. Hassell Street Press.

Poston, S., & Poe, B. D. (2020). Analysis of Production Decline Curves, Society of Petroleum Engineers. Society of Petroleum Engineers.

Rauscher, M. (1989). *OPEC and the Price of Petroleum: Theoretical Considerations and Empirical Evidence (Studies in International Economics & Institutions)*. Springer-Verlag Berlin and Heidelberg GmbH & Co.

Raymond, M., & Leffler, W. (2018). Oil & Gas Production in Nontechnical Language. PennWell Corporation.

Riva, J. (2019). *U.S. Conventional Oil and Gas Production: Prospects to The Year 2000*. Routledge. DOI: 10.4324/9780429269639

Saxton, P. (2023). Helicopters and North Sea Oil: A Story of Service, Danger and Survival. Pen and Sword History.

Selley, R. (1978). *Porosity gradients in North Sea oil-bearing sandstones. Quartal Journal Geological Society, 135*(Part 1). DOI: 10.1144/gsjgs.135.1.0119

Sun, H. (2015). *Advanced Production Decline Analysis and Application*. Golf Professional Publishing.

Timashev, S., & Bushinskaya, A. (2016). Oil & Gas Pipelines in Non-technical Language. Springer.

U.S. Department of the Interior. (2015). *Economic Effects of Petroleum Prices and Production in the Gulf of Mexico OCS on the U.S. Gulf Coast Economy*. U.S. Department of the Interior.

United States Government Accountability Office (Author). (2014). Oil and Gas Transportation: Department of Transportation Is Taking Actions to Address Rail Safety, but Additional Actions Are Needed to Improve Pipeline Safety. United States Government Accountability Office.

About the Author

Vojo Bubevski comes from Berovo, Macedonia where he completed his primary and secondary education. He has a Degree in Computer Science and Informatics from the University of Zagreb, Croatia in 1977. He started his professional career in 1978 as an Analyst Programmer at Alkaloid Pharmaceuticals in Skopje, Macedonia. At Alkaloid, he worked on applying Operations Research methods to solve commercial and technological pharmaceutical problems from 1982 to 1986. For these applications, he developed his software for optimisation including Linear and Non-Linear Programming, Dual Algorithms, and Integer Programming. In this period, he was a part-time lecturer at the "Koco Racin" Open University in Skopje, for which he, as a co-author, published a couple of textbooks. In 1987 Vojo immigrated to Australia. He worked for IBM™ Australia from 1988 to 1997. For the first five years, he worked in the IBM™ Australia Programming Centre developing systems software. The rest of his IBM™ career was spent working in the IBM™ Core Banking Solution Centre. In 1997, he immigrated to the United Kingdom where his IT consulting career started. As an IT consultant, Vojo worked for Lloyds Bank in London, Svenska Handelsbanken in Stockholm, and Legal & General Insurance in London. In June 2008, he was engaged as a Senior Consultant by TATA Consultancy Services Ltd. He is a specialist in Business Systems Analysis & Design (Banking & Insurance) and has delivered major business solutions across several organisations. He retired in May 2018. Vojo has a very strong background in Mathematics, Operations Research, Modelling and Simulation, Risk and Decision Analysis, Six Sigma, and Software Engineering, and a proven track record of delivering solutions applying these methodologies in practice. He has received several formal awards. Since 2007, he has been doing practical research in applications of Stochastic Risk & Decision Analysis. His work evolved and resulted in a novel stochastic Six Sigma DMAIC method for Risk Management. Vojo published many written works in eminent international conferences and journals and was featured as a guest speaker at several prominent conferences internationally. He published 12 papers on Risk Management in eminent international conferences and journals, and one chapter in an editor's book. He also published 80 books (Ref. ORCID: 0000-0002-7181-4445) including 22 books in English, which were printed in multiple languages, i.e., eight in French, Italian, Portuguese, Russian, and Spanish; seven in German; five in Dutch and Polish; and one in Macedonian. Also, he created his website "Bubevski Consulting™", which is available on the Internet (Link: https://bubevski-consulting.website/). Vojo's recognised books "Six Sigma Improvements for Basel III and Solvency II in Financial Risk Management" (2019) ranked with 4.09 stars, and "Six Sigma DMAIC and Markov Chain Monte Carlo Applications to Financial Risk Management" (2024) ranked with 4.21 stars in "The Best Financial Risk Management Books of All Time" by the BookAuthority (Ref. https://bookauthority.org/author/Vojo-Bubevski). This significant recognition confirmed that the applied methods for Risk Management are approved and acknowledged by the Book-Authority. Bernstein stated, "The risk will always be there, so we must explore many interesting tools that can help us to control risks we cannot avoid taking" (Bernstein & Damodaran 1998). The author's two recognised books are such tools.

Index

V

W

www.ingramcontent.com/pod-product-compliance
Lightning Source LLC
LaVergne TN
LVHW061541290926
849162LV00004B/869